Naqada and Ballas. 1895

CORRECTIONS.

In the five years since *Naqada* was published the evidence has accumulated, showing that the people there described are predynastic, and constituted the oldest civilized people of the land, about 7000—5000 B C   The conclusive proofs of this are that their later objects are similar to those of the early dynasties, and that in the VIIth—IXth dynasties at Dendereh the Egyptian civilization is continuous

As the facts were stated in *Naqada* with as little theory as possible, this makes no change in the arrangement or descriptions of the book, except in the following passages, which should be corrected

p 4 —The pottery supposed to belong to the Old Kingdom extends much earlier to before the close of the prehistoric time

pp 17, 18 —The stone vases here referred to the New Race were the same forms carried on into early dynasties

p 60, sect 95, D —These burials belong to the close of the prehistoric time , and the objects attributed to the Old Kingdom are really earlier.

p 61 —This conclusion from Mr Quibell s tombs having been corrected, this page should be cancelled

p 64 —*for* 3200 B C , *read* 7000—5000 B C
     for VIIth and IXth dynasties, *read* predynastic times

p. 66 —*for* VIIIth dynasty, *read* Predynastic

Pls XVII and LVIII —*for* VIIth—IXth Dyn , *read* Predynastic.

NAQADA AND BALLAS.

1895.

BY

W. M. FLINDERS PETRIE, D.C.L., LL.D.,

EDWARDS PROFESSOR OF EGYPTOLOGY IN UNIVERSITY COLLEGE, LONDON,
VICE-PRESIDENT OF THE ROYAL ARCHÆOLOGICAL INSTITUTE, LONDON,
MEMBER OF THE IMPERIAL GERMAN ARCHÆOLOGICAL INSTITUTE ;
MEMBER OF THE SOCIETY OF NORTHERN ANTIQUARIES,

AND

J E. QUIBELL, B.A.

WITH CHAPTER BY

F   C. J. SPURRELL

LONDON

BERNARD QUARITCH, 15, PICCADILLY, W

1896.

LONDON
PRINTED BY WILLIAM CLOWES AND SONS, LIMITED,
STAMFORD STREET AND CHARING CROSS

CONTENTS.

LIST OF PLATES.

NOTE ON PLATES

THE notation of the plates in this work has been specially arranged for the facility of denoting discoveries in future, by means of the letters and numbers here used As a very full variety of forms of pottery, &c , has been here drawn, these plates will serve for the registration of most of the pottery of the New Race that may be found in future researches Each class of vases is therefore designated by a letter, which is put at the head of the plate, and given in the list of plates here (II, S, B, P, F, C, N, W, D, R, and L) Each general type is numbered, and the numbers up to 99 are dispersed over the whole class , so as to leave unused numbers where wide differences exist in forms, that fresh types discovered in future may be numbered in the series Then sub-varieties are lettered, in case any one wishes for very exact description of a form , but in general, for rough use, the lettered sub-varieties can be ignored This system enables a number to be used without implying too rigorous a similarity to the drawing, or having to express a form by saying that it is equally like several different numbers Thus, in noting the contents of graves, in future it will suffice to mark a vase down as being H 33 or P 17 to define the type , while letters can be added, if further desired, as P 17 d. This system will give the full advantage of the use of such a corpus of forms as is here published.

For a general view of the subjects noticed in this volume the reader is requested to turn to the full index at the end

INTRODUCTION.

1. THE work described in this volume was conducted partly by myself, and partly by Mr Quibell, but the whole of it lay within a few miles along the edge of the desert, between Ballas and Naqada This district is about thirty miles north of Thebes, and on the western side of the Nile The work of Mr Quibell was in the northern part near Ballas, mine lay in the southern part around the ancient town of Nubt—the centre of Set worship—and southward near Naqada We were greatly assisted at both sites by the help of students who came to stay with us, Mr Hugh Price, who had worked for some time in Central America with Mr Maudslay, was most energetic in the excavating, and I had, for lack of time, to ask him to do the plans of the temple of Nubt, the south town, and neighbourhood Mi Grenfell also did a good deal of excavating between his Greek studies, and Mr Duncan, though only there for six weeks, rapidly developed into an active and precise observer, making excellent notes of the graves But for the diligence of these friends we could not possibly have recorded the plans and contents of nearly three thousand graves, and two towns, as we did in the four or five months of work That it was absolutely needful to work out all that we could, was amply proved by the result So soon as we left, a native dealer—without any delays about permissions, or any tribute to the Government Museum—went to work with a gang of men, and continued for many weeks to turn over the outskirts of our work Whatever we left behind was absolutely lost to all record Such destruction continually goes on all over the country, the native administration favouring the plunderers whenever they are accused by European officials, and it is only by pushing on the scientific excavations and record as quickly as may be, that we can save such results as are here recorded from being hopelessly destroyed

The arrangement of this volume is determined by the occurrence in Mr Quibell's ground of the most decisive evidence as to the date of the foreign remains of a hitherto unsuspected invasion, as this forms the ground-work of our historical view of the results, it comes first in this volume, in chapters I to V After his description of the produce of his work in the purely Egyptian remains (ch I, II), and next in those of the new race of foreigners (ch III-V), there follows the account of the results of my own work on this same New Race (ch. VI-IX), Mr Spurrell's account of the flints (ch X), the historical conclusions (ch XI), and lastly, the description of the temple of Nubt (ch XII), the centre of the worship of Set.

The presence of a body of invaders in Upper Egypt, which was as yet unknown, required us to coin some phrase to distinguish them in brief use, until their position and connection may be established, so that they may be really named descriptively As the favourite German phrase of nescience, x, is rather confusing if too generally applied, when every imaginable thing gets $x$ed, we have used as a tentative denomination, the "New Race" When they acquire a fixed standing, and may have a specific title, this temporary phrase may fall away Meanwhile "New Race," or N R remains, mean those which belong exclusively to certain invaders of Egypt of the type here described, which is entirely different to any known among native Egyptians

2. The workmen we employed were mainly those whom we had tried and proved the year before at Koptos I cleared a space along the north wall of the temple of Set, and built a row of huts, one for each of our English party, and two large ones for our men There we lived as a community all the time, with the most complete sense of security in our good friends from Koptos, many of whom we heartily liked and esteemed Mr Quibell built huts for himself and his sister, Miss Quibell, at his work at Ballas to the north, and had likewise a colony of picked men to live beside him We also had a few

of my still earlier workers from the Fayum, whom we brought up the country with us, and who were especially valuable as being entirely in our interest without any local ties In researches such as are described in this volume, the exactness of the information is the very essence of its value, and as the manual work of excavating was mainly performed by Egyptians, who have ordinarily no idea of exactness, it is needful to give a full account of the mode of securing the information and the way of working Some credentials are certainly needed before asking any person to take on credit the details of minute arrangements of bones or of vases in tombs excavated by the *fellahin*

In the first place, strict discipline was maintained among the men, and new comers were carefully allotted with old hands, so as to be educated Carelessness in breaking up skeletons was punished, sometimes severely At one part of the work, where a friend of mine was not accustomed to the men, the skeletons came often to grief So I announced that the next man who broke bones would be dismissed, and closely worked every grave myself A rather good man was the unlucky one, and when I found two fresh fractures, he was paid up at once, and sent off Every lad trembled in his hole after that, and was terrified if I came on even a snapped rib In another case, where a lad tried to recompose a skeleton which he had broken up, he turned some vertebræ upside down, he was never allowed tomb-digging afterwards, and was set to the dullest and most unproductive of big holes in the town

The constant rule enforced on the diggers was that any bones once disturbed must never be put back in place unless the cast of them remained in the earth If the place could not be proved, they must be set aside as shifted From the ordinary workman nothing was taken on credit, but every object must have the undisturbed bed of it left in the earth, whether it was accidentally moved or no, the final clearing of every grave being reserved for our own hands

The rule enjoined on all my friends who worked with me, was to observe how everything lay before disturbing it in the least, to make absolutely certain of any point of importance on the spot, and to remember that a single fact, well-considered and proved, which had no shadow of doubt attaching to it, was worth a bookful of dubious notes Nothing with a query should be recorded But as no man can feel so certain of what he hears as of what he sees

and observes for himself, I have only in very few and very clear cases quoted the observations of others, and every conclusion stated by me is mainly drawn from what I have observed myself

Every workman was carefully educated by myself or our older hands. I brought with me my best lad, Ali Suefi, who has been kindly rescued from conscription by the Sirdar, for the interests of archæology, and I also had two or three other old hands from Illahun The bulk of the men were the picked workers from Koptos, selected from the year before. Many of them were excellent fellows for their integrity and good work, and some of the boys were charming helpers to us in clearing the tombs, from their quickness, thoughtful observation, and handiness. Down in a narrow hole it is impossible to have a man to help in moving stuff, but the smallest and lightest of the boys used to wait at the edge, and be lifted down, and set to clear a place like a little digging machine, in a space where a grown man could not reach, and then lifted out of the way again when he had done.

III In the best part of the cemetery, which I had most continuously in my own hands, and where the work was most completely organised, the system of a compound gang was as follows The whole party consisted of two pairs of boys, two inferior pairs of man and boy, two pairs of superior men, Ali, and myself First a pair of boys were set to try for a grave, and if the ground was soft they were to clear around up to the edges of the filling, but not to go more than a couple of feet down At that point they were turned out to try for another, and an inferior man and boy came in to clear the earth until they touched pottery or bones in more than one place They then turned out to follow where the boys were working, and the pair of superior men came in to dig, or to scrape out with potsherds, the earth between the jars While they were at work Ali was in the hole with them, finishing the scraping out with a potsherd, or with his hands, his orders being to remove every scrap of loose earth that he could without shifting or disturbing any objects. When he had a favourable place his clearing was a triumph, every jar would be left standing, still bedded to the side of the grave, while all the earth was raked out between one jar and another, the skeleton would be left with every bone in its articulation, lying as if just placed on the ground, the cage of ribs emptied, and the only supports being little lumps of earth left at the joints. The flint knives or other valuables would be each covered with a potsherd, to keep it from being shifted, and a pebble laid on that, to denote that it marked an object Any group of beads was cleared round as closely as possible without shifting them in the soil But in every case enough evidence of exact position was left to satisfy my inspection If some jars were found at a higher level, so that the lower part could not be cleared without letting them shift, the work was stopped until I could come and record them before going further Lastly, when I came up to the party I found several graves thus prepared After drawing a plan of the position of everything that could be seen, I inquired of Ali what important things there were, and what parts of the tomb floor could be safely stepped on without breaking bones or small objects Then I jumped into the grave, from three to eight feet in depth, and if it were a crowded one, there was often barely room to place the feet safely Beginning at the clearest part, I began to lift out the pottery, having each jar emptied by a boy on the surface, and noting the contents in my plan, whether ashes, burnt sand, clean sand, brown organic matter, gravel, etc The labour of lifting and tossing up dozens of jars of about 30 lbs weight each was considerable. Where any amount of earth had to be moved, so soon as some object had been taken away, I lifted down a boy and set him to fill baskets, which I lifted out to another on the top When about half or a third of a large grave was done, we then turned all the earth and the pottery which was not required to be kept, over on to the cleared part, and the boy generally worked at scraping over all the loose earth with his hands while I was lifting things out and recording.

When the grave was finished the last matter was to mark the number of the grave on every jar that was kept, the bones were generally put into a large jar to go to the huts, and there every pot and every large bone was numbered with black varnish

At noon and in the evening all the workers assembled at our huts, standing in a row along the outside of the dwarf wall of the courtyard, some seventy feet long Each placed on the wall before him his baskets of pottery and bones, each lot was looked at, and the bakhshish assessed which I should give them, sometimes a halfpenny or a penny, sometimes a dollar or a pound, and duly entered against their names in the wages-book. Then came the long work of the permanent marking of everything, and putting it away The pottery increased so that

we soon had to turn it out of the courtyard, excepting the rarest and finest vases, and a field of stacked pottery occupied all the space far out in front of the premises The bones were stacked up in the courtyard until we could scarcely get out of our huts, and inside my hut the more perishable and valuable things filled all the spare space—under my bed, on shelves, and in heaps

Of course, many tombs did not require such careful and complete treatment A small and plundered tomb often had only a few shifted bones and two or three broken pots in it, and such were entirely cleared by Ali, so long as he did not find anything to leave in position Owing to the plundering, shifted objects were often found in the earth filling, and such were moved out by the workers, if they had no connection with anything around or below them But nothing was recorded as exact in position unless I saw it unmoved, or with the cast of its bed in the earth, if any important conclusion was to be drawn from it Where no particular result followed, and there was sufficient reason for an object or two having been moved accidentally in clearing, I accepted the statements of Ali, or of the best men, as to its general position But any shifting more than might be reasonably due to the accidents of careful work was strictly objected to, and it was well known that a bad case would result in a man being dismissed or kept to surface clearance

These details will, I hope, give sufficient confidence in the general accuracy of the results noted No doubt errors might creep in, but probably more from misunderstanding the evidence than from inaccuracies of detail. To clear out some dozen or two of large burials every day, it was absolutely needful to employ native labour, as far as could be safely done, so as to cover as much as might be of the most important work with one's own hands. The first week is the most trying, the skin gets worn through, cracking and bleeding from excessive scraping in the sand and grit, but after a proper horn has been grown, a large amount of clearing can be done with the hands Yet, if many hours are given to it each day, that allows but twenty or thirty minutes for a grave, so that only the most important parts can be done by the recorder The above gradation of the skilled labour enabled, probably, the maximum of results to be obtained For important as skilled record is (and often I spent a couple of hours on a single tomb, if it were complex), yet as only one tomb in twenty gave any

b

result of value in either objects or information, we needed to open as many as possible, in order to get a sufficient number of valuable ones examined. Hence the work could not be allowed to drag, or go on with too much refinement or detail Whatever we left was sure to be lost for ever, as any cemetery known to the natives is completely grubbed out very soon The hundreds—thousands—of open tomb-pits all along the desert, rifled and re-rifled in recent years, shew this only too plainly I tried dozens of places by the known cemeteries, without finding a single fresh tomb, not cleared by recent dealers And it was only because they had not been attracted to the foreign cemetery that we found anything to work on Whatever we left unworked was therefore irrevocably to be destroyed, after we had once shewn the way

In recording the skeletons distinctive outlines were used for each of the limb bones, marking the two ends differently The vertebræ that were connected were usually counted, and sometimes they were measured as they lay, in order to ascertain the length of a certain number in life, before the decay of the cartilages The position of the skull, and its direction, were always noted

Where any beads were noticed the workmen always left them for me to clear out myself If the find was important the boy was generally sent over to look for me, and shew me the sample of what had been already disturbed Then I used to lie down with my eyes close to the ground and begin searching for the undisturbed part of the beads in the dust By blowing gently it was often possible to uncover half a dozen or a dozen at once, and so to note the pattern and arrangement of them An anklet of very small beads occupied about two hours to pick out and secure

Thus it will be seen that, so far as our time and skilled oversight could extend we have endeavoured to secure the maximum amount of results, without losing that accuracy and certainty which is essential to render them of any value

iv In the management of the great mass of material brought to England Mr Quibell and myself have had the most hearty assistance from many fellow-workers To deal with over three hundred cases of objects, exhibit and distribute them, to draw over eighty plates, which are here given, and to work out to even a preliminary extent the many questions involved, needed the labours of many helpers in the short time available My most constant friends, Mr Spurrell and Dr Walker, have done much in different parts of the business, in the drawings we have been assisted by Miss Mabel Holland, Miss Whidborne, Miss Murray, Miss Gladstone, Mr. Bowman, and Mr Mathieson, and in the measurement of the skulls and bones, Mr Herbert Thompson, Mr. Warren, and Mr Spain, as well as Dr Walker, have made a tolerably complete examination My best thanks are due also to Mr Frank Haes, for photographing many of the objects both from Naqada and from Koptos, and allowing me to publish his plates

The cost of Mr Quibell's work has been met by the Egyptian Research Account in which so many have cordially joined to extend scientific exploration The expenses of my own excavations have been met, as in past years, by my constant friends, Mr Jesse Haworth and Mr Martyn Kennard Without their liberal co-operation my visits to Egypt would have borne but little of the fruit which has enriched our knowledge in the past years After supplying the Ghizeh Museum, we agreed to jointly present the most complete series of the New Race remains to the Ashmolean Museum, Oxford, which will be, for the future, the essential place for the study of this period Other museums in England, Germany, and America, have also received considerable selections, and a large part of the Research Account results were sent to the principal contributor, the University of Pennsylvania In the matter of the transport and packing of the skulls and skeletons, Mr Pearson-Gee generously contributed the cost, and the contents of over seventy cases are now lying at University College, and being gradually studied by Mr Warren

In every direction it will be seen that this work is a voluntary labour in the interests of archæology Without so free a contribution of both time and money from so many private sources, it would be impossible to obtain any such results, as there is no item of official help or assistance in the very smallest degree

CHAPTER I

THE CEMETERIES OF BALLAS.

1 The excavations made during the winter of 1894–5 for the Egyptian Research Account were at two sites, Deir and Ballas Deir is a village about two hours south of Qeneh, at the point where the river, bending to the west, comes close to the high desert cliffs We engaged workmen, built huts, and turned over a considerable part of the ruins But the whole had been thoroughly plundered, worked by a dealer at Qeneh as well as others Some interesting points were discovered in long desert walks undertaken in search of crocodile mummies, of which there were reports The desert cliffs which one sees from the river are not, as they appear, foothills to further ranges, but are the edge of a plateau which stretches on one high level to the west, and is scored only at this edge by ravines and beds of old waterfalls On the slopes of these cliffs, and on the high plateau as well, were found several groups of stone circles, each circle about 6 feet across, and formed of large nodules of flint (1 foot thick) placed close together , the northern part of the wall being often one row higher than the rest In some, but not all, there were remains of late Roman pottery These circles may have been huts of hermits I also observed just north of Deir a long wall made of piled desert nodules , starting from near the cultivation, it leads to the top of the plateau, and is flanked in its upper part by a roughly made path To one looking down upon the valley from the high desert, this wall appears as a black serpentine line It may have been part of the nome boundary between Ombos and Tentyra.

2 An ancient settlement near Deir, the scanty remains of which seemed to be quite un-Egyptian and to belong rather to some foreign immigrants, we called the North Town, and after working that a

move was made to the point where the Ballas embankment across the cultivation joins the desert , here another house was built For this we adopted the local method of building with water-jars, instead of bricks. The large conical jars with broad base (*Ballas*, pl. *Ballalis*) used throughout Egypt, are made at Ballas , and those spoilt in the kiln supply a cheap building material To make a wall a row of the pots is placed mouth downwards, the broad bases just in contact, and the mouths embedded in a mixture of mud and chopped straw The triangular spaces between the pots are filled in with brickbats and more mud A dab of mud is then laid on the base of each pot, another row is built on the top, and the spaces blocked as before Two courses can be laid in a day , after one day's drying two more courses may be built, and these are sufficient for the height of a room

Around this house we then examined the mastaba burials, the staircase tombs, and the cemetery of foreigners, on which most of our time was spent During the last three weeks I had great help from Mr Duncan, who came over daily from Mr. Petrie's house at Nubt, and caused the number of tombs examined to rise to nearly nine hundred Nor must I omit to recognise the help of my sister, through whose care the comfort of life in the desert was so greatly increased, and whose help lightened much of its drudgery With the packing of the finds my work for the Research Account ended, and on the 16th of March we moved to Mr Petrie's house, to continue his excavations and pack all the finds from the great cemetery near Naqada The description of this part of the work is given by Mr Petrie in the volume on that site

In what follows I describe solely the work done for the Research Account, but it is impossible to avoid some cross-reference, for at both Ballas and Naqada were cemeteries of one race and period , and week by week, as the work progressed, evidence obtained at

one end would solve some difficulty at the other
The non-Egyptian remains of an invading people we
here term the foreigners, or the New Race, in order
to avoid complications with theories before stating
the facts

3 *The North Town*—This site had attracted our
attention in the previous year, for an axe-head of
green stone was picked up there, and a large number
of flint flakes, it was believed also that some small
knives sold by one of the Qeneh dealers had been
found in the same place The layer of ruins was
extremely thin, varying from half an inch to two feet,
in most places not more than one foot This layer
consisted of clay dust, ashes and potsherds No bricks
(except from intrusive burials) were found, to indicate
the material of the dwellings, it is therefore possible
that they were of wattle and daub Very few objects
appeared in scraping over this site but the fragments
of pottery which were thickly strewn on the ground
were exactly similar in material, shape and decoration, to the types obtained from the neighbouring
cemetery of non-Egyptian character, which proves
that the site had been used by the same people A
large adze was found, made of slate identical with
that used for the paint-palettes of the foreigners
Two fine alabaster vases (of types H 47 and 52), lay
six inches below the surface the mouth of the
smaller inside the larger one A fragment of blue
glazed quartz, a bead of the same material, and two
bodkins (for leather-work ?) made from the leg bones
of a deer, were all similar to objects found afterwards
in graves Certain bars of a coarse red pottery, about
15 inches in length and 4 inches in width, of semi-
circular section, with the ends roughly shaped by the
impress of a hand, were not of obvious use They
were found in three places, in one they were scattered, in the second several were laid side by side, as
if for a pavement, in the third they stood on end,
surrounding and slanting outwards from the fragments of a large coarse pot, pieces of charcoal lay
below This position suggests that they were used
as fire-bars, but an empty grave found later in the
cemetery was lined with these same bars, this time
used like bricks No trace of the foundations of
buildings could be seen, but at one point there was a
strange system of trenches, consisting of a long groove
(12 feet long, 3 inches wide, and 3 inches deep) from
which branched at right angles three other trenches,
alternately at one side and the other Charcoal was
found in several places, in one it was mixed with
sheep's dung This material was found afterwards

under an inverted bowl (red and black) and was
doubtless used as fuel Several small holes, 6 inches
deep, cut in the native soil, served as receptacles for
hammer-stones or weights, and for grinding-stones.
Besides the querns for corn-grinding, other stones,
used evidently for some kind of polishing, were
discovered They are of basalt, hemispherical, and
well polished on the flat side, weighing about six or
eight pounds They fit in pairs, the smaller of the
two being rounded on the top, and the larger flattened
below They may have been used for beating out
and polishing leather Among other objects belonging to the foreigners were a number of limestone
spindle-whorls of two patterns, conical and barrel-
shaped, also one of the lozenge-shaped slate paint-
palettes which were common in the graves There
were a few objects of later date, such as a group of
ostraca found together, a bead of Arab times, and a
cache of grain (very modern indeed) stolen by the
neighbouring Arabs from the fields

4. But besides these few objects in the surface-layer
of earth there were in this ground burials of two
classes —

(1) Burials of children The body was in a contracted position, lying in a hole just large enough to
contain it, along with two or three cups and bowls of
the red and black pottery These were similar to
the burials of foreigners, afterwards found in large
numbers The children had apparently been buried
inside the houses, like the Egyptian babies of the
Middle Kingdom at Kahun

(2) Intrusive burials of adults These were of a
different people and period They consisted of long
graves sunk about 3 feet in the débris of the town,
walled and barrel-vaulted with brick The side walls
were continued before the mouth of the arch and
formed an entrance-well, as in modern Muslim graves
Inside the tomb the skeleton was laid at full length,
but not mummified Round the head, and sometimes
at the feet, were grouped cups and vases of a good
wheel-made pottery, chiefly drab-yellow in colour,
with a few pieces of a dull red ware The cups were
semi-circular in section, the mouth either plain or
pinched (E 27, 26, PL XLVI) The vases were
"drop-shaped" (E 34 PL XLVI), and this first led
to the suspicion that these burials were of the
XIIth dynasty Bead necklaces occurred in several
cases, made of separate uniform strings—white discs
of ostrich shell, black glaze, small disc beads of blue
glaze, and rough discs of carnelian In one case a
button, perhaps to fasten a cape, lay upon a man's

jaw One scarab only was found, and this had no name In two tombs there was a worn alabaster kohl pot, the shape is known both in the XIIth and early XVIIIth dynasty (XVII, 195) These tombs were clearly of a period posterior to that of the foreign race, and it became of great importance to determine their date This was achieved when a detached burial of the same class was found in the ravine near the dyke (PL I, A)

5 A quarter of a mile south of the dyke was a group of mastabas Of these two were well-marked mounds 20 feet in height The others were almost entirely denuded, patches only of the brickwork being discernible, while several had been wholly removed, only the wells remaining to mark their site. The largest, called locally Kom es Shair, had obviously been opened, for there was a depression in the centre of its rounded top The well was soon found, the upper part of it had been bricked round, and we attempted to reach the sepulchral chamber After sinking 30 feet we got into water, and though the well was left for two months and then tried again when the Nile had sunk almost to its lowest point, it was impossible to finish the clearance The mastaba was constructed of loose pebbles enclosed by a brick wall, the upper part of the well was enclosed in the same way, but no Serdab chamber was discovered, though a careful search was made The bricks had been eaten through and through by white ants—creatures not now seen in this part of Egypt The other mastaba wells were also cleared, but all except two had been robbed Fragments of Old Kingdom pottery were however found, which sufficed to prove their date One undisturbed burial remained at the bottom of a shallow (12 feet) well The chamber was to the north of the pit, and was bricked up by a wall 10 inches thick When this was opened the body was seen lying full length, with head N and face E but there was no funeral furniture whatever In the second case we found in a deep well another bricked-up chamber (PL III, 1) Inside was a skeleton, excellently preserved, but extremely fragile The rise of the water-level had flooded the tomb-chamber for some part of the year, the air in it was very moist and hot, and all the tomb furniture and the skeleton very frail The body lay on its left side, the head to the N, face E, and the legs slightly flexed Before it was a large circular table, and on this a bowl, both were of good alabaster, but damaged by water, and the bowl was broken in two Over the whole floor of the tomb, in the bowl, and everywhere except under the alabaster table and the pottery, was a layer of wet sand that had fallen gradually from the rough-hewn roof It was under this weight doubtless that the bowl had broken The skeleton was not disturbed, except that a stone of thirty pounds' weight, which had probably fallen from the roof, lay upon the legs Four coarse hand-made pots of the usual conical, Old Empire shape (PL XLI, 72), stood upright in the tomb It is strange that so little should be found in the burial chamber, as the well was 30 feet deep, and cut through hard gravel, it is possible that the original interment was robbed, and that this is a second use of the tomb, but no direct evidence of this was observed In no other well in this part of the cemetery was an undisturbed body found, but two late extended burials were found in the brickwork of the large mastaba, and half way down another well was found pottery of the XVIIIth dynasty

6 Another small class of burials, found among the stair tombs, recalled the contracted burials found by Dr Petrie at Medum Wells, 7 to 10 feet deep, opened below on the W side into small bricked-up chambers, in which the body lay, drawn up, with head N and face E, the thighs being not so much bent as is the case in New Race burials Fragments of IVth dynasty pottery were found in the filling (Tombs 235, 277), or a single pot of that period at the skeleton's head (143, 466)

7 *Stairway Tombs*—The most interesting parts of the cemetery, where the evidence for the date of the invaders was obtained, were the groups of stairway tombs These had originally been mastabas, built of brick and sometimes plastered, but most of the brickwork had been carried away or denuded In one case a wall three bricks high (but all covered by earth) ran the whole circuit of the mastaba, in other cases only patches, a couple of feet in length, enabled the outer walls to be measured, but more often every trace of the brickwork had disappeared and only the shaft of the tomb remained The shaft was of a new form, instead of being a simple well, it had one side cut away to form a staircase The entrance was usually to the N. and the deep part to the S, on the average the graves were 12 feet long, 2 feet wide at the top of the staircase, and 3 to 4 feet wide at the deep end The steps were roughly hewn and about 6 inches high (PL IV), and at the bottom were one, two or three small chambers to the S or S, E and W In the smaller examples these chambers were not found Of all the graves of this type not one was unrifled, and all conclusions had to be drawn from

B 2

confused successive burials Besides this type there
were in this group small vertical wells with chambers,
and also contracted burials of the foreign type In
two of the staircase tombs cists of red pottery
(PL XLIV, 2, 3) were found in the side chambers,
the cist fitting the chamber, and therefore probably of
the same date as the tomb In one of the cists a
contracted burial was found Such cists were occasionally found outside this group of tombs, in the
ordinary foreign graves, but never at the Naqada
cemetery, which was purely foreign The fact that
they were found only in that part of the cemetery
where the burials were mixed leads to the conjecture
that they were of Egyptian origin Bodies were also
found in another kind of receptacle—a large round
pot of a coarse red ware, 2 feet in diameter These
burials occurred both inside and outside the staircase
tombs, and the mouth of the pot was sometimes
upwards, sometimes down No grave was found
certainly undisturbed, but some Old Kingdom pottery
was found in each of them, and it is probable the
original mastabas (staircase tombs) were of the Old
Kingdom, and also the circular pots All the clay
coffins are perhaps of the same period, those which
were found in the foreign cemetery having been
robbed from the neighbouring Old Kingdom tombs.

The most important result of the examination of
this cemetery was the proof given of the date of the
foreign contracted burials In two of these tombs
there was a mixture of Egyptian and foreign objects,
and in the upper part of one of them was found a
burial in contracted position, with the head S and
face W With it were pots containing ashes These
must have been deposited after the ruin of the Old
Empire tombs

In several of the other tombs as well there was a
mixture of objects of Egyptian and foreign origin

CHAPTER II

SELECTED EGYPTIAN TOMBS

8 We now turn to describe in detail some of the
more important Egyptian tombs Tomb 353 (PL IV,
15) was a very long tomb of the staircase type It
was made for a IVth dynasty burial, as fragments of
Old Kingdom pottery and of a round alabaster table
were found at the lowest level. Half way up the
stairway of the tomb were five burials in circular
pots In four cases the pots were placed mouth up,

in one mouth down. At the top of the stair, and at
the narrow end of it, was an extended burial, with
head to the north This had been in a coffin of wood
1½ inches thick, and 14 inches wide inside, only
some vertebræ and ribs remained but scattered
among the bones were the beads of a necklace of
carnelian, amethyst, and blue glaze, all of the spherical XIIth dynasty type This proves the circular
pots to be subsequent to the staircase tombs, and
both types to be not later than the XIIth dynasty

Tomb 179 was a large stairway tomb entered from
the S, it had a groove for a portcullis before the
chamber At a high level over the stairway (50
inches from top) was a burial in the contracted
foreign position. Six coarse hand-made vases (L, 72)
were to the W of the figure, with two coarse flat
dishes 6 inches across About 20 inches above the
body were some ivory rings (bracelet) The whole
grave was filled with heavy mud This must have
come from the washed-in brickwork of the original
mastaba

The chamber below was large (15 feet square), but
almost empty A hemispherical bowl, pebble-polished
inside, in the later foreign style, and two coarse hand-
made vases (L, 72) were alone found. Here then
were two burials of the foreigners, without any trace
of the original Egyptian interment

Tomb 524 (PL III, fig. 3) must have been robbed
in recent times The grave had been dug into and
left open, and the top of the chamber mouth could be
seen The small boy who had been doubtless sent
in as soon as a hole big enough for him had been
made, found the chamber filled with earth, and no
large object to be seen, and so left the bottom of the
grave untouched In the E chamber was an empty
pottery cist, another of the same kind, taken apparently from the S chamber, stood on end in the
staircase A contracted burial, incomplete and disturbed, was in the S chamber—the head of this
was to the N, while just outside the chamber was
another skeleton, complete, and in the regular position
of the New Race bodies. One hand was under the
head, the legs were sharply bent In one corner
of the S. chamber were two pots of coarse hand-made
Old Kingdom work and a fragment of an alabaster
table. Here the Old Kingdom burial being ruined
while the New Race skeleton lay undisturbed, points
to the invaders being the later of the two Having
noted these most conclusive instances, we now turn
to the other tombs in order of their numbers

Tomb 71 had two chambers, E. and W. In each

was a contracted burial, but the body in the W chamber faced W, with head S, while that in the E. chamber faced W, head to the N In the staircase between the two chambers was a pottery cist containing a skeleton lying in the same position as that in the W chamber

Tomb 107 was a staircase tomb, with one chamber S and another E The S chamber, which was about 100 inches square, contained a burial in the New Race position, and with it several fragments of alabaster and a flint of Old Kingdom type (LXXV, 97) Another contracted burial, lying with head W and face S, was found in the well close to the chamber mouth. In the filling were fragments of the sharp-edged Old Kingdom bowls of fine red ware, and two of the coarse pots of the same period (XLI, 78 and 76) Here again we have an undoubted case of New Race position and an Egyptian tomb

Tomb 161 A staircase tomb, with the usual N entrance, and small chambers, 36 inches high, E. and W There were remains of a brick wall, 10 inches thick, which had blocked up the W chamber The sides of the tomb were covered with a white plaster in the rough upper part, which was cut in the gravel, while the lower part was cut in the limestone. Two pots of the IVth–VIth dynasty ware and fragments of a large circular pot were found, also a shell with green stains The last may be later in date.

Tomb 162 had small chambers to E and W At the N end, at a high level, were some scattered bones and coarse pots (XLI, 78), and a small stone vase (XI, 26) Four skulls and some broken bones were in the E chamber At the lowest level were three coarse hand-made vases (like XLI, 72, but with collar) Just outside this grave, on the W side, and close under the surface, was the far later limestone stela of Set and Hathor (XLIII) The heads are covered with gold leaf, put on carelessly, and spreading irregularly ¼ inch beyond the outline

Tomb 201 (PL IV, 16) had a staircase entering from the N, and one small chamber, this contained only a fragment of a round table of alabaster, a rough vertical alabaster jar, and a sharp-edged red pottery bowl, all of the Old Kingdom shapes that are shewn in the paintings of the Medum tombs With these was a coarse vase made with a strainer in the mouth, this is known from the purely foreign or New Race tombs.

No 212 (PL. III, fig 10) was a stairway with a small chamber at the S end—a poor example of the staircase tomb The chamber contained six skulls,

but no other bones. In the stairway, lying aslant across its axis, lay a cist containing a body (head W) A piece of the broken lid of the cist was fixed between the cist and the side of the grave. The cist was perhaps once in the chamber, and was moved out in order to bury the skulls.

No 265 was entered from the E., the chamber was larger than usual, and may have contained two or three burials Its entrance had been bricked up, but the tomb had been rifled in ancient times, and only the lower courses of the stopping-wall remained The upper part of the chamber was empty, but as the staircase filled up the earth had poured over the broken wall, and on this sloping surface of earth lay a very small alabaster table, and the bones of a child The table was of the regular IVth–VIth dynasty shape At the E end, and 4 feet from the surface, lay a cist of unbaked clay enclosing a burial in the usual New Race position The box had no bottom, it had probably been inverted over the burial Three bowls were inverted over the skeleton, they were encased in mud, and seem to have been used to strengthen the base of the cist. These were of the regular Old Kingdom shape, but of poor quality and colour, and were perhaps foreign imitations of that ware

Below this burial and to the E of it was another of a child in a small clay cist of good pottery, the body lay upon its back, head to the S A shell lay by the left side. Beside and below this burial were scattered a number of bowls (XLI, 78 c) The shape of the tomb and the character of the lowest remains point to this being originally an Old Kingdom burial

Tomb 358 The chamber was in this case bricked up. Inside were two burials, one had been in a wooden box, so decayed that it fell to pieces as soon as the grave was opened The wood was 1½ inches thick, and had been painted in red, with two broad horizontal stripes The box was placed E and W, the body lay with its head W, the legs were flexed but the arms extended.

To the W of the box, and pressed between it and the wall, lay a youthful skeleton, extended on its back, but with the hands crossed on the breast.

No objects were placed with the bodies, but four scraps of pottery had been left—one was black polished inside—of the New Race kind

Outside the chamber, in the stairway, were two coarse hand-made pots (XLI, 72) and two small flat dishes (XLI, 28)

Tomb 365 contained a burial in a large circular pot (XLIV, 1), and close by, a coarse hand-made pot of Old Kingdom type (XLI, 76)

Tomb 522 This was another instance of a mixture of Egyptian and New Race objects The tomb had probably been plundered in both ancient and modern times, for it was partially cleared, and the top of the chamber was visible No bones were found, but there were four flints of regular IVth–VIth dynasty type, a small vertical alabaster vase (2 inches high), which might be either foreign or Egyptian, some chips of malachite, three shells, two of them with green stains, and two stone vases, one with horizontally pierced handles These are all exactly similar to those found in New Race graves

Tomb 526 was a much simplified form of the staircase type Two or three steps led into the grave, which had no chambers, and was indeed two shallow for them to be constructed In the filling were found one vertical alabaster jar, broken (PL X, 4a), fragments of two more, three coarse flat saucers of pottery, a hand-made Old Kingdom pot (XLI, 72), a fragment of a diorite bowl (XIV, 136), and a fragment of a pink marble flat dish All these objects except the saucers are known to be of the Old Kingdom

Tomb 530, a stairway tomb, entirely ruined In the filling were found fragments of the sharp-edged IVth dynasty bowls (XLI, 78c), a small coarse saucer, shewing wheel-marks below (XLI, 29a), and sherds of the coarse hand-made pottery of the same period, together with pieces of a large circular pot of the kind frequently found in these graves This is evidence, so far as it goes, that the grave was made in the Old Kingdom and that the large circular pot is not earlier in date

Tomb 686 was small In the narrow N end of the staircase was a burial in a pottery box In the chamber was a burial in a circular pot, and also a third body, without any covering, which lay in the contracted position, with head to the S

Tomb 764 had a long, steep and narrow staircase, and one chamber In the chamber were a table (broken but complete), a cup (XV, 157), a small vertical jar, and fragments of bowls (XIII, 104), all of alabaster In the filling of this staircase were a vertical red and black pot, and a smooth red bowl, both of common New Race forms This is another proof that the New Race are later than the staircase tombs

Tomb 836 contained eight large blue glazed globular beads (XIIth dynasty), a vertical alabaster jar, and a small pot with strainer mouth

Tomb 850 could not be entirely cleared out, owing to water But the two common types of coarse Old Kingdom pottery (XLI, 72 and 76), and the sharp-edged bowls of good ware, lay on the steps, and lower down a small vase (XXXVII, 69) and a fragment of a ledge-handled pot These two last are New Race

Tomb 865 had a staircase and one chamber to the E In this was a pottery cist with lid, containing a complete burial The arms were sharply doubled, and the legs bent over the body, with the knees above the chest There were remains of much cloth under the body, but all black and falling to dust The bones were exceptionally clean and strong The head was to the south, the body on its back This cist must have been made in imitation of a panelled wooden one (PL XLIV, 2)

Counting over all the stairway tombs we find that sixteen out of twenty-nine contain pottery of known Old Kingdom types, while of later date only one contains an XVIIIth dynasty object, and only two have beads or pots of the Middle Kingdom We are therefore fairly safe in attributing these tombs to the Old Kingdom

9 Taking now the wells not entered by a staircase, we have in the same group —

Tomb 311 (PL II, fig 9) This was a mastaba with a well 7½ feet deep Opening from this to the north was a chamber. In the bottom of the well were three vertical alabaster jars and eight coarse hand-made pots of Old Kingdom shapes Of these two contained ashes and two mud In the chamber were seven more of these pots (five of them full of ashes), a fragment of a sharp-edged bowl (XLI, 78), and a body buried in the regular contracted position Here we have a body in the New Race position, with the New Race provision of ashes, but the pottery of distinctly Egyptian character It is probable that this last was left in the tomb from the first burial

Tomb 235 This was a shallow well (PL III, 2), 12 feet deep, situated not in the group of staircase tombs, but W of the Arab tomb (Map I) There was a small recess to the E, and a bricked-up chamber, 3 feet high, to the W In the latter was a burial, contracted like those of the New Race, but with head N instead of S, and face E instead of W, the position being that obtained by turning a New Race burial half way round in a horizontal plane There was no pottery with the body. This must be compared with the burials in this position and direction, without pottery, and in well-chambers, found at Medum by Mr Petrie.

Tomb 446 (PL III, fig 8) was another square well Ten inches below the surface was the body of a child, closely contracted, but with head W. and face N In front of it was a single coarse pot of Old Kingdom type. Another of these pots lay 10 inches lower down The grave, therefore, must have been made in the early Old Kingdom times, and anything found below this undisturbed burial is probably not later than IV–VIth dynasty. Two chambers opened into the well below In each of these was a body, head N, face E, lying in a contracted position In the E. chamber the body was as sharply drawn up as in the New Race burials In the W one, the legs had been bent at the knees, but the knees were not brought up before the face This again is the position of the Medum burials But there was a fourth burial in this well In the centre of the well, on the lowest level and between the two chambers, was a large circular pot, containing a body The bones were somewhat decayed, and their position could not be well seen, the head was broken, but the brain remained as red dust This affords good proof that the large circular pots used for burial were of the Old Kingdom Nothing has been found inconsistent with this hypothesis

Tomb 143 was another small well, ten feet deep, with four small chambers, only large enough for contracted burials. The N and E chambers were empty In the southern chamber were two pots (XLI, 72 and 76), in the western one a skeleton with legs slightly bent, and a coarse pot above the head This grave had been recently robbed

Tomb 180 In the group of staircase tombs there was one burial just below the surface of the ground, under another of these large circular pots The body had not completely decayed

Another group of these large tombs was opened south of the Arab tomb (vide map), but nothing of importance was found They had been thoroughly looted

10 A few burials in wooden boxes, large circular pots and cists, were found away from the group of staircase tombs.

No 314 (PL. III, fig 11) was in a box of wood (25 × 12 inches, the wood 1½ inches thick) The box was sunk in a narrow grave 4 feet deep, and in the space between the side of the box and the E side of the grave were four coarse hand-made pots The body lay in the contracted position, with head S

No 260 (PL. III, fig 13) was a burial in a pottery cist, also in the contracted position and with head S In the box were two alabaster vases of type XI, 26 This shape of alabaster vase was only found at the Ballas end of our site, where there was undoubtedly a mixture of foreign and Egyptian objects, and as not one was found among the large number of vases taken from the cemetery of Naqada, it is probable that the shape is Egyptian

No 275 was another burial in a cist, close to the surface It was in the largest group of mastabas. The body was in the contracted position, with head S. and face W., and no other object was in the cist itself, but close outside it, at the S end, was an alabaster vase of the same shape as the last mentioned

No. 300, another burial in a cist, was but a few inches below the surface The loose upper gravel was here not very deep, and a shallow (3-inch) cut had been made in the hard desert below, to receive the box Jammed between the end of the box and the side of this depression was a sharp-edged bow (PL XLI, 78 c) The skeleton was disturbed and incomplete, but two hip bones and the foot bones were in the N end of the box, and a tibia lay at that end, so the head had probably been to the S. This may then have been a New Race burial, the cist being obtained by robbing one of the Egyptian tombs which lay near The bowl was, perhaps, caught in its place accidentally Many such pots may have been lying near, turned out of tombs

No 178 was another cist, just under the ground The head was to the S, lying on its right side, with long hair undisturbed Some cloth, blackened with age and nearly broken to dust, covered the whole bottom of the cist, it was not, therefore, probably a mere waistcloth

No 62 was a child's burial, similarly placed, but the body lay upon its left side.

No 367 was a cist lying E and W., not like the rest, N and S The body lay on its left side, and the head was to the W This was in the middle of the New Race cemetery, and just below the ground surface.

No 103 (PL. III, fig 14) contained another

peculiar burial of two bodies One was in the contracted position, head S, but face E. At its feet
lay a cist containing another contracted body In
this case the head was E and face N Two coarse
bowls, and a copper fish-hook without a barb, were
the only other objects in the tomb

11 There had been an Egyptian cemetery at the
end of the embankment, shewn at the N of the
plan (PL. I) The shafts of the tombs lay open,
having been cleared out within the past two years
by dealers from Thebes On the S edge of a spur
of the desert were found some early tombs, which
had not been disturbed in modern times. The tombs
had been formed by making a cutting in the sloping
side of the gravel bed, and excavating a chamber
with its opening in the vertical face of the end of
the trench, thus forming the regular Egyptian façade
tomb The chamber was about 20 feet wide, and of
irregular shape, smaller side chambers being made in
the side, to receive some of the bodies The roofs of
the chambers had in all cases fallen, so that we had
to sink 12 feet through heavy gravel to reach the
untouched base, and here the condition of most of
the bodies shewed that the tombs had been robbed
before the roof fell in

The best preserved burial was in extended position in a wooden coffin The wood had entirely
disappeared, but a line of white paint remained,
which proved its former existence A necklace of
globular amethyst beads, small beads of blue glaze, a
vertical alabaster jar (XIII, 94), and a *kohl* pot at
the head, pointed to this being a burial of the
XIIth dynasty

From another burial remained the good scarab
(PL LVIII) of *An, son of Ab*, and with it part of a
slender torque of silver Beads of green felspar and
amethyst, in the shape of hawks and androsphinxes,
were also found From this same group of disturbed
tombs came the pots in shape of a monkey and a
goose (PL XLV, 21, 22), the model of a hut (XLIV, 4)
and the strange inverted shape (XLV 20) This
latter is formed from the type of an ordinary vase
by closing the mouth and using it for a base, and
opening a sort of window with grooves at the side,
in which a wooden lid might slide.

The hut shews the courtyard, the lower room, the
stairway to the upper room, the bed and table, the
row of water-jars, and the gate, and the ox-head
and the forequarter are arranged as in the table of
offerings shewn on the same plate (7).

The two other tables (5 and 6) are from the intrusive

burials in the N. town, presumably of the XIIth
dynasty.

The duck-pot (XLV, 22) is interesting as being
probably derived from similar shapes found in the
foreign cemetery

12 While we were working at Deir, a fellah brought
me a small block of limestone, which he had just
found while digging sebakh. It had been trimmed
down, and used for building, but was happily just
long enough to preserve both of the names of
Ra sekhem.men taui se.ra Tahuti (PL. XLIII)

The cutting was good, but not deep, and there was
a trace of green paint in the signs The name
Tahuti had been recognised as that of a king by
Prof Erman (Ae Z XXX, 47), but the throne-name
is new

The type of name is similar to that of two of the
Sebekhoteps (*Ra.sekhem khu.taui* and *Ra sekhem.
suas taui*) of the XIIIth dynasty, while the name
of a deity, being adopted by a king, recalls the case
of Hor, who belongs to the same dynasty Tahuti
may therefore, with great probability, belong to this
age

CHAPTER III

PRODUCTS OF THE NEW RACE.

13 Though a large number of Egyptian tombs of
the Old and Middle Kingdom were found, as we have
already described, yet the majority of the burials
about Ballas were in graves of a wholly un-Egyptian
type These were first brought to my notice by the
sebakh diggers, for these men were always en-
deavouring to make their labour profitable by sur-
reptitiously plundering tombs near my work, while
digging for the earth to spread on their fields One
of these men was thus found by me unearthing a
fish-shaped slate and some cylinder pots with lattice
pattern Pots and slate were alike well known, but
not attributed to any Egyptian period in history
About the same time Dr Petrie, two miles to the
south, had come on slight depressions in the soil,
under which were found burials of bodies laid in a
peculiar and new position The head was to the
S, the face W, the body lay upon its left
side, arms and legs were both sharply bent, the
hands were before the face, and the knees were
brought up in front of the chest The position of

the skeleton alone sufficed to indicate that the bodies were non-Egyptian Working into other graves, Dr Petrie found further burials in the same position, with pottery. Near the place where the sebakh digger got the fish-slate, I found other tombs, with new forms of pottery associated with the contracted position of the skeleton Grave after grave was turned out and recorded, so that 3000 were worked through at Ballas and Naqada during this year in all of these the same contracted position, and the new varieties of pottery, were found, and it was evident that we had excavated a large cemetery of a hitherto unknown race

14 The graves were of varying sizes, 5 feet by 3½ feet and 3½ feet deep was a very common size, but graves 10 feet by 8 feet by 6 to 8 feet deep, or even larger, were often found Many poor tombs barely afforded space for the contracted skeleton, others were like small rooms, and had as many as 80 pots ranged round their walls The usual axis of the graves was north to south, but the orientation was only rough, and every inclination—even to east and west—was occasionally found The position of a grave was not generally visible on the surface, but they were so close together that it was necessary to take great care lest the workmen should throw the earth from one tomb upon the top of another

A man and a boy, or two men, worked together, using turryeh and basket until bones or pottery were reached, then the turryeh was laid down, and the earth or gravel scraped away from the objects with a potsherd This work was left to the more skilled men The rounded sherds, which had originally been used in digging the tombs, were often found, and were convenient for our purpose A good workman would in this way clear a tomb so that every bone and scrap of pottery could be clearly seen, each lying bedded in its place, and shewing its cast in the earth when it was moved Then it was our work to measure the tomb, sketch in the position of each object, and, taking out bones and pots one by one, to mark each with the number of the grave The rest of the earth was then turned out, or at least raked over, to find any small objects which might remain Then into the tomb so left empty was thrown the earth from the next one

In the evening the baskets were carefully packed for the journey to the house, there each man took his place, with all his finds before him, and the backshish was assessed and entered to his account For average pots about a penny would be paid, for a fine

flint as much as a napoleon We have every reason to believe that this system worked so well that not a single object was stolen during the year By the time that all the backshish was written the last light had gone, but the day's work was not finished, for after dinner came the task of repeating on each object, in black paint, the pencilled marks made at the time of excavating Delicate objects had to be safely stowed away, broken vases to be built up to see if they were complete, and the skeletons had to be marked bone by bone, which was a tedious occupation

There was evidence that much of the robbery had taken place soon after the making of the graves For the plunderers had known of the position of the bodies, and had avoided working in the less profitable ends of the graves The ends of the graves, where stood great masses of pottery but no small objects of metal, were often found intact, while the centre of the grave was disturbed

15 The greater number of the tombs had been anciently robbed But among those in which the pottery, etc, shewed no sign of disturbance, many contained imperfect skeletons In some the head was missing or lay separated from the rest of the body, and at a slightly higher level, generally about six inches above Frequently some of the arm-bones were missing In many other graves the legs and a few vertebræ were all that could be found, and there were only two cases of the upper part of the body being found without the lower These disturbances would most readily be attributed to plunderers, but it is not easy to see why plunderers should attack such a grave as No 395 In this the body was found complete, with fingers and toes, but without a head, there was no pottery in the tomb, which was a very small one, and no search could have been made in it, or the bones would have been disarranged Much evidence of mutilation was obtained in the older and less disturbed graves of the cemetery of Naqada, and this is supported by the frequent absence or displacement of the head and upper part of the body in the cemetery of Ballas

16 The body was laid upon the floor of the grave, no sign of any cloth wrapping was seen Under the body was often found reed matting, occasionally a skin, and in good tombs fragments of wood These were probably from a bier or tray, on which the body was laid

A coffin was very rare, but in one case a pottery cist had been used for a foreign burial (99) In the

c

following details of the Ballas graves there are a few trifling divergences from the customs observed in the Naqada cemetery, so that this account does not fully apply to both —

Distribution—Graves of the same class were generally found together At one place, for instance, a group of a very wide and shallow type was found At another a shoal of light and easily-worked gravel had been seized on for a group of poor burials In these there were not more than three or four pots, and the graves were ill-shaped, and overlapped one another. Good tombs were found far up on the desert, and on the edges of the cemetery, they were not crowded together like the poor ones The large graves, though they had nearly always been robbed, still contained more objects of interest than the untouched poor ones A few small beads of gold and lapis lazuli were found in good tombs, and it was probably for such spoil that they had all been attacked

17 *Slates*—Before the face of the skeleton there was, in all but the poorest graves, a slate, in some cases more than one Often they were found stained with green malachite, as were the very smooth pebbles, one to four of which were placed by the side of the slate The forms of the slates were derived from fish, antelopes, tortoises, and a form surmounted by two birds' heads Lozenge-shaped slates, square pieces bordered with lines, and the shapeless lumps were the latest forms

Many of the slates were pierced for suspension, and some of the smaller ones (66, 67) were wrapped round at the top with leather The small slate figures of men were suspended head down in the same way, and inlaid eyes of shell were made to many of them, which in some cases remained

Besides the stains on the slates and pebbles, shells and little leather bags filled with ground malachite were frequently found, and chips of the unground material were very common, so, as the other objects near the head—hair-pins, beads, and combs—were undoubtedly for toilet purposes, it is probable that the slates were used as palettes for face paint, and that the foreigners, like the Egyptians in the earliest times, painted round the eyes with green

18. *Hair-pins* were occasionally found lying south of the head, sometimes with hair round them They were of bone and ivory, and either plain or carved in imitation of a thread binding, while the head sometimes represented a bird The ivory was, in some graves, very strong, in others too weak to be readily

moved, a difference that depended on the amount of water that filtered through

Combs were also found in the same position, which were clearly intended for ornament The teeth are too long and too weak to comb out such heavy shocks of hair as the Libyans often wore, and the tops, too, are carved into ornamental figures, oftenest birds and antelopes

Beads—The beads were extremely characteristic They were generally near the head, often under the hands, but in some cases they were also under the neck and behind it, and in one instance (100) beads were worn as an anklet

The stone forms were the oldest, and even when pottery was used the cylindrical shape shewed that stone beads were being imitated The most common materials used were clear and opaque carnelian, steatite, serpentine, and clay, but alabaster, limestone, garnet, agate, hæmatite, malachite, gold, lapis-lazuli, silver, ivory, green and blue paste were also employed. In shape they were very often un-Egyptian, and such forms as spears' heads, owls' faces, claws, and crescents were very typical Also there were numbers of unpolished pebbles, flakes of clear flint, or rough, dark carnelian, which were pierced and strung as beads, and a great variety of land and sea shells were threaded into necklaces

19 *Stone Vases*—A large series of stone vases was obtained, but these were the produce of many hundred graves, and it was very rare that any tomb afforded more than one, while many good tombs contained no stone vase at all

The horizontal piercing of the handles was the most distinctive feature of the New Race vases Other characteristics were a thin, flat foot (PL VIII, 28) and a small and useless foot (PL IX, 68)

The materials were breccia, syenite, and porphyry in the older and finer pots, while alabaster, steatite, and the coarse long shapes of basalt belong to the later period

Beside the handled vases, which were evidently for hanging, there were vertical forms and bowls, one of which, made of finely-grooved porphyry, is the earliest example of the working of that material It was found in a robbed grave along with a pottery bowl of Old Empire type, but was more probably of foreign origin, as two other grooved pots (PL XII, 64), undoubtedly foreign, were also discovered

In one tomb (867) were five basketfuls of alabaster and slate fragments lying in a heap, and out of these more than twenty bowls, of the shapes given in

PL XIV and XV, were rebuilt, together with five upright alabaster jars This tomb was of exceptional size, 20 feet long by 11 wide and 8 deep, but narrowed on the W and S by dwarf walls, while at the N end was a further hole 6 feet by 2½ and 4½ feet deep The alabaster heap was at the S E. corner The only other objects were a few potsherds of the later varieties of New Race pottery, and three of the "marbles" used for the game of skittles (PL VII) As these wide and thin alabaster bowls were not found in any other case in foreign graves, but were found repeatedly in the staircase tombs, it is possible that this great pile of fragments did not originally belong to the grave in which it was lying.

20 *Pottery* —Of this there were several well-marked classes, and all of these, except the few specimens of Old Kingdom type, were made by hand The wheel must have been well known to the Egyptians at this time, but it was not in use by the New Race, for although many of the pots (especially of the red polished variety) are so truly rounded and so well finished that it seems difficult to believe they were hand-made, yet no horizontal striations can be seen on them, and the elliptical dishes, which are just as truly made, cannot have been turned upon the wheel

The clay must have been moulded rather dry, for on many pots were a series of short parallel marks, these had been produced by the jumping of the scraper when trimming the surface of the damp clay with a piece of wood If the clay had been very wet the scraper would have travelled smoothly over it, but an over-dry surface would make the tool catch and move by jumps

21 *Marks* —Marks were occasionally found on the pots, but were much rarer at Ballas than at Naqada They were nearly all scratched on the pots after baking, probably by the owners The usual forms were a cross, a crescent, a palm-tree, a scorpion, a mark like a gallows, and two instances of a pentagram

These pots must have been highly valued, many were found that had been broken, and mended again in ancient times, by drilling holes near the edge of the broken sherds, and tying them together, most likely by leather thongs Very often they seemed never to have been used, but to have been made especially for the burials This was particularly noticeable in the case of some painted pots, the colour on which was perfectly fresh

22 *The rough pottery* —The pottery called rough (R) was of a porous, straw-marked, rough clay,

varying in colour from dull brown to pinky brown Conical pots of this class were generally used to contain ashes (PL. XXXVIII, 81–88, and XLI, 72) These and the small flasks (57–69) were by far the commonest forms Ashes were found in most of the graves of the earlier period, and the pots containing them (usually about eight to twelve in number) were ranged together at one end These ashes were probably the remains of a great funeral feast That they were not the ashes of the human bodies is shewn, not only by the great quantity of them, but also by the fact that a burnt or charred human bone was never found, whereas several times we came upon half-burnt dorsal spines of fishes (identified by Dr Fowler) In robbed graves the ash-jars had frequently been emptied, and in late times may have been searched for valuables, but there was evidence that many graves had been robbed not long after they were made, and if, as one of our workmen suggested, this was done by the "undertakers," perhaps the ashes might have been made to serve a second burial

23 *Wavy-handled vases* —(PLS XXXI, XXXII) The first examples found of these vases were filled with mud, the use of which was not clear, but in other tombs it was found to have a distinct scent, and afterwards vases were found filled with an aromatic fat The mud was doubtless used as a covering material, and then as a substitute

The fat was extremely light and porous, no doubt because of the gradual melting of its most fusible constituents, but it melted readily under an April sun

The scent was much like that of cocoa-nut, but the analysis of the fat (*v* Naqada volume) did not point to such an origin, and its nature remains undetermined

A chronological sequence can be traced in the series of vases. Those with well-formed shoulders and sharply waved handles, passed by gradual degradation of the handles and straightening of the curve of the pot (33–34), to a form (47) where the wavy handle has become a mere shapeless bar After this the handle is more carefully worked (51), but is merely ornamental, it runs nearly all round the pot, but not quite, thus shewing clearly its descent from the ledge handle In the next stage (53) the wavy pattern runs completely round, and later we have a form with a painted lattice pattern (62)

Probably all the earlier shapes were carried in basket-work frames, which were afterwards found unnecessary and were omitted, but the appearance of basket-work had still to be preserved. In the later vases this lattice pattern also disappears, and the neck ornament declines to a cord either raised or impressed, then to a mere nicked line, and finally is left out altogether, the last stage of all being a vertical plain white pot.

These different forms were not mingled together, though sometimes when a pot with well-formed wavy handles was found in a tomb, there might be others with rather poorer handles along with it, but never the latter painted or vertical jars. In the same way some of the very early or very late types were found with those of the transition stages. A large class of poorer graves, in which there were only two or three red and black pots, never contained any of these wavy-handled patterns.

24 *Red and Black pottery* —The red and black pottery was found in larger quantities and in greater variety of form, than any other class, and it was spread over every period except the latest. In the early tombs containing ash-jars, there were only a few examples of the red and black, but later on they became more numerous, and in the large class of graves which contained the coarser kind of basalt vases, they were the only pottery found.

The main part of each pot is red, usually with a black band round the rim. They are well made and smoothly polished, but the black is much more shiny than the red.

The colour was produced by a wash of hæmatite, lumps of which material were picked up in the graves.

The black must be the black peroxide of iron obtained by limiting the access of air in the process of baking.

This may have been done, Mr. Petrie suggests, by placing the pots mouth down in the kiln and leaving the ashes over the part which was to be burnt black.

The pottery was all porous, there was no real glaze, and the broken edges shew that the black colour goes right through the fabric, and is not confined to the surface.

The small bowls and egg-shaped pots are the commonest forms. These bowls are red outside and black polished inside. As might be expected from hand-made pottery, no two pots are of exactly the same shape, and the drawings given do not exhaust the minor varieties. In very few cases were these pots filled, and indeed sometimes they must have been put into the tombs empty, as they were found packed in nests, especially the shapes XVIII, 11 and 22. Where they shewed signs of wear, it was only on the lowest inch or so of the base, where they must have been worn by being placed in the sand. Very few pottery stands were found, if supports were commonly used, they must have been made of wood.

From most examples it was observed that the polishing must have been applied vertically, from mouth to foot. The bottle shapes (92, etc.) were rare.

Red polished pottery —The next large class, the red polished pottery, is identical in character with the last, but without the black patches, and the finish is often a little better.

The commonest shapes are the bowl (23) the barrel-shaped jar (40) the flask (57, etc.) and the smaller vases (93-95).

25 *The painted and decorated vases* —These are of a whitey-brown pottery, with the pattern laid on in red lines. The spheroidal series (61–64) with splashed markings, must have been made in imitation of the marble vases.

Wavy lines, horizontal and vertical, webbing patterns, and spirals with a dentate pattern and a continuous row of ostriches are the principal motives, these are combined in various ways. Another ornament is what seems to be a plant (36) growing in a pot, the plant has long leaves falling down at the side, and a single long spike of inflorescence.

The fan-shaped ornament in 44 represents perhaps a large leaf. In one case it ends in a spike, like the tree pattern. The paddle-shaped object in the lower part of 45 is not understood. It may be a skin stretched out to dry.

Last comes the "boat" pattern (44, 45, 47). That the object seen in 45 represents a large boat cannot be doubted. The curved branch at one end must be the shelter of the look-out. The large steering-oars are shewn in one case. Amidships are two cabins, on one of which a man is standing. On the side of one cabin is a mast with standard and pennant. Several standards were found, an elephant, a sign like a double scorpion, one much like the symbol of Min, one like a capital Z. Where two or three boats are shewn on one pot, each has a different standard. These, however, were rare.

26 *Late pottery* —The pottery classed as "late" is of two kinds —a hard and coarse kind, of which the larger pots are made, and a polished red variety, lighter in colour than the older red-polished pots, and with the marks of pebble-polishing running vertically from mouth to base. In the graves in which this

pottery occurred no red and black pots were found
Neither were there any good stone pots, flints, or
other objects, nor any signs of mutilation of bodies, as
in the earliest tombs

The conical ash-jars seem to be replaced by the
very long shapes (XL, 31–33) of a hard, strong ware,
pink to whitish in colour, and by types (34 and 35)
of a coarse brown friable pottery

The forms 36–46 are new   They are of a good
strong pottery, varying in colour from strawish white
to pink. One had scratched on the rim an inscription
of two Egyptian signs (XL, 46)   Shapes 50–54 have
a coarse strainer fixed in the mouth   The handsome
flask 64 is of good pebble-polished red ware   Numbers
72–78 are distinctly of Old Kingdom type   The first
was the only shape found at all frequently   The
presence of unbroken specimens or fragments of the
Egyptian bowls (XLI, 78) may be accounted for by
supposing that they were robbed from the Old Kingdom tombs, or else that, in the case of fragments,
they had been accidentally dropped into the later
graves

27 *Incised pottery*—These were small bowls of a
thick, rather weak, black ware, on which dentated and
zigzag patterns were worked by gouging short deep
scratches in the surface of the wet clay, and then,
after it was baked, by rubbing some white powder,
probably gypsum, into the marks   The bowls were
very rare, indeed, in eight hundred tombs at Ballas
only two bowls were obtained   In some fragments of
similar ware (PL XXX, 50) the pattern was produced
by smaller pricks, and there was no sign of smearing
with white clay or gypsum   These were on the
surface of the ground, or in utterly looted tombs, and
fragments of extra thin red and black bowls to which
the same mode of decoration had been applied, were
found in the same place

White painted pottery—Some of the ordinary unpolished ware was decorated with patterns in white
line   The white was gypsum and was laid on
thickly

Most of the designs were dentate and zigzag, but
foliage and animal forms were also used

Pattern on black—A few bowls and fragments of
the red pottery were found, in which a pattern was
burnished on the black lining

28 As to the distribution of pots, etc, in the tomb,
the rough taper ash-jars (XXXVIII, 81) are placed
either N or S, and quite rarely to the W. Those
with flat base (XXXVIII, 82) are nearly always
to the N, as also is the shape with a collar

(XXXVIII, 85)   These are either empty or full of
ashes

Of the later types, the jar of strong red ware
(XL, 36) is nearly always placed to the N (occasionally W), and is either empty or contains ashes   The
coarse form (XL, 34) generally found N, though
occasionally in all parts of the tomb, was used for
mud

The red and black pottery is found in various
positions, but more frequently N and S W

The wavy-handled jars are nearly always to the S,
and are found empty, or with mud, or with fat, but
not with ashes   The later forms of these, viz the
cylindrical jars, are also generally at the S, but also
found W and N, and are used for ashes as well as
for mud

The painted vases were found in all parts but the
N   Flints were in various quarters, but the finest
flints in untouched tombs were behind the body, as
also were the mace-heads

29 *The Figures*—In one tomb of the regular type
two female figures of clay were found (PL VI)   The
skeleton in the grave was in the usual contracted
position, and arranged around it were a red bowl with
a foot (F), a red bowl with a white pattern painted
inside, and a small red and black pot of the
commonest kind   Some bones of a dog were in the
filling of the tomb, and a model of a boat made in
unburnt clay (12 inches long) was on the west side,
but was in bad condition, it was photographed on
the side of the tomb, but could not be brought
away

A pot (XXXVI, 84) painted white, and with an
incised zigzag pattern above, and painted in red over
the white on the body of the pot, lay at the feet of
the skeleton, and beneath this were the two figures,
one of which was nearly entire, but in very bad
condition, while the head and half the body of the
second could not be found

The arms are not represented on these figures, and
the upper part of the body is slight in comparison
with the very bulky thighs   The feet are bent under-
neath the body, and to the right side, the position
being the same as that of the figures found at Hagiar
Kim in Malta

The great size of the thighs recalls the steatopygous
type of the Hottentot, and the Princess of Punt of
Deir el Bahri.

The figures are made of a light-coloured clay and
painted red   The complete figure also shews traces
of black paint over the red, on the breasts and thigh,

and down the side of the face there are four black stripes, which would be taken for a beard if the figure represented a man

The mouth is roughly cut, and the eyes were painted In the top of the head is a round hole 1¼ inches deep, ½ inch in diameter The height of the complete figures was 8 inches, the breadth across the back of the hips 5¾, and the length of the thigh 6¾

Three other steatopygous figures were found at Naqada , one, seated, of dark mud, and two, standing, of the light-coloured clay

One figure, however, was found of another and a slighter type, and tattooed, so there must have been two types of women existing together

Figures in ivory of the steatopygous order have been found at Brassempouy, with reindeer bones, etc (Piette, in L'Anthropologie, vi, 2)

We have therefore the series from N to S of Brassempouy, Egypt in the New Race period, Punt in the XVIIIth dynasty, and S Africa , and this is also the sequence in time

30 *The game.*—The set of lions, ivory rods, etc , (Pl VII) was in a small hole in the cemetery, surrounded by graves, and like a grave itself, but for the fact that no bones, or pottery, or any object except the "game" was found in it

The four lions and the rabbit of limestone were placed side by side, facing N

There were also sixteen small four-sided prisms, made in pairs, one pair being very thin, of pink-veined limestone, and well finished , others of coarser limestone , and one of bone Seven of these were behind the animals, and evidently arranged, the rest were in front, and before them were many small naturally spherical flints, the size of ordinary playing marbles, one being shaped like a small dumb-bell

East of these were the ivory rods, eighteen in number, and of four different forms. Two were made in imitation of lengths of reed—the joints, and the bracts at the joints being shewn , and another form has incised black lines This arrangement can hardly have been anything but a game, or perhaps two games

The use of the little blocks and of the ivory rods is not at all clear

Of the game shewn in PL VII, I, there were three imperfect sets (Tombs 489, 450, 867) In two of these syenite pebbles alone were left , in the third, one side of the little gateway as well

31 *Ivory*—Bracelets occurred in two tombs (183, 686) , one of them had been broken and mended by

drilling the broken ends and tying them with copper wire

Bracelets of shells, made by cutting a ring from the base of a cone, were commoner Horn and slate were also used, and one complete flint bracelet was found with fragments of three others

There were maces of hard stone in two shapes , a cone, and a flattened disc A conical mace of hæmatite, and another of veined limestone, were found in graves , and in the N town were two others, one of a soft white limestone, the other of a hard, fine quality

Smaller implements of limestone which were also found in the N town, were spinning whorls, both barrel-shaped and flat cones

32 *Copper objects*—Objects of copper were rare In one large tomb (100) was a hollow knob, with small projecting pins inside

Two copper adzes were found, one broken

33 *Lamp*—The lamp with floating wick (PL V, 23) was important The bowl was of rough granite, 2½ inches across, and ¾ of an inch in thickness It had been protected from the earth which filled the tomb, by a small red pot inverted over it On one side of the bowl is a black stain with sharply defined straight edges, and at the base of this stain is a patch of black organic matter, the size of a sixpence This was probably the floating wick, and the black stain is the smoke left as the lamp died out

Mr Spurrell points out that the pith of papyrus would act as an excellent wick

This is the only lamp known in Egypt before the Roman period, except the bowls found at Tell el Amarna

The pot placed over it was of an Old Kingdom shape The other objects pointed to a foreign origin

CHAPTER IV

SELECTED GRAVES OF THE NEW RACE

§ 34. The description of Pls III and IV has been already given in Chapter II The tombs PL V, Nos 17, 18, 19, are typical of the poorer graves of the earlier period Of these a large number were found in a bank of clean gravel No mutilations were observed The graves were quite small, of indistinct outline, and much crowded Very few pots were found, and these are all of the black and red, or red-polished types

20, probably a rifled tomb, is one of the extremely rare cases where the upper part of the body remains without the legs. The opposite mutilation was common

21 contained a skeleton and two heads beside It had probably been disturbed

22 had fragments of a typical Old Kingdom bowl below the two pots, together with a quantity of ashes which had probably fallen from the pots

23 The body was sharply contracted, the left arm especially being quite doubled The brain remained in the skull dried to a dark brown mass rather smaller than a cricket ball, in which the convolutions were still clearly defined Some fragments of wood were below the body To the W opposite the feet was an alabaster bowl, which had been broken and mended anciently Opposite the knees was a small sharp-edged bowl (of Old Kingdom type) inverted over a small granite cup. None of the filling of the tomb had slipped under the cover, in the cup was the charred wick, and on one side the black stain left by the burning lamp Near the head was a vertical alabaster jar, to the W. of this was a red pot, and in the S W corner lay a quantity of ashes, a small alabaster cup, a small shell with a cake of green paint inside, a pendant of gold foil (LXV, 16), and an ivory spoon This is a clear case of a mixture of Egyptian and New Race objects.

24. The skull was removed and placed N of the body There are no ribs or arms, and only the vertebræ The bowl in the centre contained a stone pot with horizontally pierced ears

25. The body was complete Before the face were two small slates, pierced for suspension, and with traces of leather binding round the tops There was also a large slate of fish shape

26 contains a double burial.

27 was a child's burial and contained several of the dumbbell-shaped flints which are often found, also three bone pendants with incised black lines

28. In the small alabaster vase were some malachite chips and a few beads The bowl nearest to the face contained ashes

29. The greater part of this tomb was empty, the body lay in the S E corner, fenced in by a row of ash-jars. Five hair-pins of ivory lay by the head Beads and pierced carnelian pebbles lay before the face, and other beads under the head and neck. These were then necklace and bracelets

30 may have been disturbed

31 had no head, but the body was otherwise complete, all the fingers and toes being in place

Under the body parts of a mat remained, and under the pots the section of the mat could be seen sloping downwards to the centre of the grave Ashes lay under the body. Two slates lay before the hands

32 is a child's burial—one of a rare class, for very few children's graves were found

33 The beads before the head were of carnelian and green felspar (?) By gently scraping away the earth, the arrangement of the necklace could be seen in one place, three or four red beads, then a run of green

§ 35 We take now the description of such of the tombs not figured as need description Most were so robbed and disturbed that few conclusions can be drawn from the state in which they were found

19 The limestone plaque with serpent carved upon it lay on the mouth of a pot at the N end of the tomb No bones remained except the head, a piece of femur, and some fingers The head was at the S., face W, the fingers before the face (PL XLIII)

23 Disturbed Head only remaining, no other bones Slate before the face. An ivory comb was between the bones of the head. Necklace of beads of peculiar shapes (LVIII, 23)

24 contained three pots of ashes to N, one to S, slate palette, and a small slate cup It was bricked round (as also was No. 35), and bricks lay upon the top, but it was not possible to determine whether these had been built into an arch or not

37 A few large bones were scattered in the centre of the grave. The skull lay close to the S end of the grave. It was filled with fine sand, and when this was poured out a deposit of yellowish mud, $\frac{1}{16}$ inch thick, remained The hair-pins had hair sticking to them, all the points of the pins were to the back of the head There was a green stain on both of the slate fishes Under one was a little cloth, very weak, but its structure was clear

34 shews the association of the tall late form of ash-jar with the later forms of the wavy-handled jars and a simplefied slate palette

37 The skull was filled with fine sand, which ran readily out, leaving a deposit of yellowish mud $\frac{1}{16}$ inch thick on the lower half, while the orbits were blocked with the stiffish black mud which filled the rest of the grave The pots lay upon their sides One at the N. end was full of ashes

40 Bones scattered   Under the jaw was a wooden bar (10 × 2½ × 2 inches) bound with red thongs of leather, probably the handle of a bier

49, a disturbed grave, had a floor at the N end of smooth yellow mud, as if washed down from above Of this mud there were two levels, one on which the pots stood, one 5 inches below it   The tomb must then have twice lain open

68 contained two burials   One was in the regular foreign position, the other, that to the W, lay upon the right side, head N, with face to the W The W skull was filled with sand, with a thin layer (1½ inches) of yellow mud below   Fragments of five alabaster dishes lay in the N end of the grave

70 The body was complete, it was very sharply bent, the head being between the knees   Three jars full of ashes were to the S, one behind the body, and six others in a row along the N end   The skull was a quarter full of mud

75 contained three skeletons side by side, the easternmost being a little S of the others   Two were complete the central body lacked a skull, but the skull lay over the hips, and a fourth skull was in the N E corner   A few beads were over the hips of one skeleton

80, probably plundered, contained skull and os sacrum in the centre, a few ends of broken long bones near this, a palette of black and white granite (?) and a large bowl with spout and sharp edge of the well-known IVth dynasty type   The grave was filled in with stones of 20 lbs weight

81 Skull was removed, and lay against the W side of the grave   The only pot lay near the hips, and contained a black steatite cylinder (an inch long) without inscription   At the W side of the grave lay a group of four oblong flints (LXXV, 97)   A horn lay at the S centre

87 Legs and vertebræ were in the regular position, the arm bones were disordered and the head was to the N of the legs, it lay with the face up, 6 inches higher than the body, two shells were above it, both with green stains   The atlas was found in the centre of the grave, at a higher level

Three of the coarse hand-made pots lay to the N, two containing mud, next to them to the E was a pebble-polished bowl, and under it a copper needle

93 was a large grave (11 feet long), with 42 pots The walls were well plastered with mud, and had been covered with mats, the imprint of which could be seen   The marks of the plasterer's feet were also

left in the N W corner, in which he had climbed out   This was a good example of a later grave with vertical plain jars

97 contained a very large jar of fat (XL 40), with the later shapes XL 35 and 51 and R 24

98 contained the later form of ash-jar (XL 30) with the coarse hat-shaped pot (R 24) and a large stand (XL 84)

99, PL III, 12, contained a cist, probably Egyptian, with pottery of the later foreign types.

100 was a very large tomb (about 12 feet × 8 × 6) and had been disturbed   The body lay in the regular position but at the W side of the tomb, much broken pottery lay in the grave   At the N end only was it undisturbed, where stood a great mass of pottery, 4 very large jars for fat (XL 40), vertical wavy jars (W 55), the splay bowl (R 24) and a ring-stand There was an anklet of beads, and behind the body a very fine vertical alabaster jar (20 inches high) with the raised-cord pattern round the neck   In the S E corner of the tomb was a copper object of thin plate with nails projecting inside

185 is described above

207 contained good red and black pottery, with a lozenge-shaped slate stained red, whereas the usual colour on the slates is green.

323 A sheepskin was laid over the body

337 contained wavy-handled pots of late forms (W 62 and 71), they contained mud, one also an ivory spoon

338 One pot full of ashes contained finger-bones among the ashes   The grave appeared to be robbed There was little pottery, and that only at the two ends of the grave   There were six large red carnelian beads in the centre   The skull, hip-bone, femur, and a few vertebræ were at the N E corner   There were lattice-pattern pots (W 62), the similar plain pot (W 61), and the late pots (XL, 30 and 36)

394 A small tomb with uncommon pottery and noticeable for the human figures

The body lay in the usual foreigners' position The two figures (PL VI) were at the feet (W of tomb), one statuette faced N, the other S   Close by was a shell   Next came a pot of the coarse, short shape (XXXVIII, 82, but smaller)   Close to the figures also was a red bowl with white decoration inside (XXVIII, 26).   Above these lay the incised and painted pot with a stand (XXXV, 76)

To the W of the body lay the bones of an animal, probably a gazelle, also the model of a boat in unbaked clay   This was too frail to remove   There was also here a small square pot of a ware black all through , it was pierced with holes for hanging

CHAPTER V

SUMMARY OF BALLAS

36 Parts of the extensive cemeteries of Ballas and Naqada belonged to a people who were not Egyptian This will be generally granted from the contracted position of the skeleton found uniformly in 3000 burials, the small statuettes shewing no trace of Egyptian style, the character of the drawings scratched upon pots, and the entire absence of objects known to be Egyptian

And that the foreigners who had possession of the country were not a mercantile colony or a mercenary army is probable from the large number of tombs of women, and from the absence of Egyptian objects which traders or mercenaries would have possessed And they must have occupied Egypt for a considerable time, certainly for many generations. We cannot suppose that the gradual degradation of their types of pottery can have taken place within a single century We had then to determine to what period in Egyptian history such an inroad of foreigners could be attributed

Fragments of the black and red pottery had been found at Koptos in the previous year at early levels, and on this ground alone we did not expect that any date after the New Empire would be possible

An intrusive burial found by Mr Petrie in the S town of the foreigners, contained a necklace of carnelian beads and scarabs of known XIXth dynasty type, shewing that only a date earlier than the XVIIIth dynasty could be accepted

The evidence from our N town pushes the date still further back This N town was a small settlement of the foreigners no brick walls remained, but the place was black with brick mud upon the brown pebbly desert, and scattered over it thickly were fragments of all the varieties of pottery that we knew from the tombs In the soft soil left by the decay of this settlement, arched brick tombs had been made

The bodies lay in them stretched at full length and with the head to the N , round the head lay pottery mostly of a drab-yellow colour, with a few rough vases and some small polished cups of brick-red ware (PL III, 5 and 7)

A few of the bodies had necklaces of disc-shaped beads and of shell and blue glaze

There was also a rough scarab and a button, neither of certain date, but the shape of the vases (PL. XLVI) was that of a drop of water, like some of the XIIth dynasty pottery found at Kahun (Petrie, Kahun XII, 16) Later on, in the ravine just below our house, a solitary burial was found (354) The body lay but six inches below the surface At its head were a bowl of coarse red pottery (XLV, 25 and Kahun XII, 6) and a vase of the drab yellow pottery exactly similar in shape (XLV, 35) and material to those found in the N town

On the body was a long necklace of many kinds of beads (PL LVIII, Q 354), including two inscribed scarabs One scarab (3) has the same pattern as a seal impression found at Kahun (Kahun X, 43), and Fig 4 is similar to another (X 36, 47), while of the beads, the crumb beads (6), the small figures (12, 11, 15), the blue glaze beads with black spiral (28), the cylinders with pinched ends and spiral grooves (25), the rosette beads (21), and a smaller variety of the spade-shaped beads (17), were all found in the XIIth dynasty town of Kahun, and none of the beads in this necklace are known to belong to other periods than the XIIth dynasty The necklace then may safely be said to be of XIIth dynasty date, and it carries the drab white pottery with it In some other tombs found in a ravine S of Mr Petrie's house, the same pottery was associated with the spherical amethyst and blue glaze beads characteristic of the Middle Kingdom

We may therefore safely conclude that the intrusive burials of the N town are of the Middle Kingdom, and that the town and the cemetery of the foreigners are of a period anterior to this

A mixture of foreign and Egyptian burials was found also in the stairway tombs Although not one of these tombs was found intact, the presumption is very strong that they were made by Egyptians of the Old Kingdom , for fragments of the coarse pottery and of the fine sharp-edged bowls of this period were found in most of the tombs, and enough brickwork was left to shew that the tombs had been mastabas

Now in one of these robbed stairways (522) was a stone vase of the foreign type, in another (764) a red and black pot, and in another (179) the body of a man buried in the regular foreign position with head S and face W

Therefore a man of the New Race was buried after

D*

the ruin of an Old Kingdom cemetery, and some if not all, of the foreign burials must be attributed to the period between the VIth and XIth dynasties Moreover it should be noted that certain forms of pottery of the XIIth dynasty the "salad-mixers ' (XXVI, 51, Kahun XIII, 50), the bowls with spouts (XXVI 58, Kahun XII), and the duck-shaped pots (XXVII, 69 and XLV, 22) are found among the foreigners and in the XIIth dynasty, but are not known in the IVth–VIth dynasties

The remainder of the evidence for the origin of the foreigners is discussed in " Naqada "

37 To conclude, these six classes of burials were found at Ballas —

1 Stairway mastaba tombs of the Old Kingdom

2 Pottery cists, which are apparently coeval with the stairway tombs in which they fit, but which were re-used for foreign burials in some cases (*e g* 99)

3 Burials in or under large circular pots , certainly before the Middle Kingdom, and probably Egyptian and of the IVth–VIth dynasties

4 Contracted burials in wells, with head to the N and face E, presumably the same as those found by Mr Petrie at Medum, and to be attributed to the Old Kingdom

5 Contracted burials of foreigners

6 Extended burials of the XIIth dynasty, with drab-yellow pottery

CHAPTER VI
NAQADA (P)

THE CEMETERY OF THE NEW RACE
THE DRAWN GRAVES

38 As the burials of the New Race have given the most conclusive proofs of its general character, I shall first detail here the selected examples of the graves, and the notes on the details of the burials

The graves differ from any known to us of the Egyptians So unusual are their characteristics that we walked over the cemeteries for some weeks without suspecting their nature In place of burying on a rising ground, or in the face of a cliff, as the Egyptians always did when possible, the new cemeteries are mainly in the gravel shoals of the stream courses Instead of placing the body in a cave or hollow, the typical tombs are vertical pits, with the body laid on the floor , and the pit in all wealthy graves was roofed over with beams and brushwood, a system wholly foreign to the Egyptians In place of preserving the body intact and embalming it, the bodies are usually more or less cut up and destroyed In place of burying at full length, with head-rest and mirror, the bodies are all contracted and accompanied by many jars of ashes In every possible detail of arrangements and of objects there is not one common point of similarity between the Egyptians and the New Race , and no connection with Egypt would have been suspected if the cemeteries had been found in any other country In speaking thus generally I exclude the later class of graves in which a copying of a few Egyptian forms may be noticed, and the copying by the Egyptians during the XIIth dynasty of the later forms of some vases of the New Race. So far as the whole of the earlier and larger part of the graves are concerned, there is not a single form, material, or detail which speaks of Egypt

39 We will begin by describing in the order of the plates the selected graves, of which plans are here published in plates LXXXII, LXXXIII while reserving to one view afterwards the comparative details of the position and state of the bodies When the earlier types are named it is to distinguish them from those of a later and deteriorated period of the New Race which is very different

T 4 This grave is in the small cemetery near the tumuli, which was thence called cemetery T It was a somewhat complex grave, containing remains of three periods, but all of the New Race type In the plan only the objects of the most important burial are shewn Beneath these, at a lower level, were three skulls about east of the skull drawn here, and one west of it, and remains of pelves and leg bones scattered east of the body here Over these bones and a few jars of the New Race types, came the interment here drawn A box was placed about 18 inches over the floor of the grave, containing a body with the head in place on the spine—one of the few cases in which such a condition was found Along the head end of the coffin were ranged a row of jars, of the red polished and black top types (marked R and B respectively), the numbers of which indicate the precise variety in the plates of pottery For instance, B 11 f will be found on PL XVIII, which contains solely B or black-topped pottery , and there such pans are numbered 11, and this sub-variety distinguished as f Further south in the corner were some strange objects Three slate figures, of the form shewn in PL. LIX, 2, were tied together by a cord through them, they lay crossing in the position here shewn They cannot have been intended to stand upright, as they have no flat bases, nor to hang, as the holes are at the bottom The only use that I can imagine is that they were intended for manipulation in some ceremonies, in the hand Next to these lay a crushed egg of an ostrich, and upon that two ivory horns (see LXIV, 81) Similar pairs of horns or tusks of ivory were found in several graves, and in LXII, 34, 35, the numbers of these graves are recorded One tusk is always solid, the other is hollowed for about half the length These will be considered further in describing the plates At each side of the grave was a slate palette on edge, one of the fish, the other of the ibex type Lastly, a grave was dug across the side of T 4, cutting through the western side, and completely destroying all the leg bones of the body buried in the coffin But this third interment had three jars of early type of the New Race pottery This grave gives us then some perspective in the period of the first part of the New Race history, before the deterioration set in amongst them We see that a grave might be disturbed and disused, re-used after some feet of soil had accumulated in it, and then, after that burial was forgotten, it might be cut into by a third burial, yet all of these belonging to one style and age, which must have extended over at least one or two centuries

40 T 5 The next tomb is one of the most important that was found, and one of the largest It shewed no signs of having been plundered, the valuable hardstone vases and beads being all in undisturbed positions The bones likewise shew that they were so placed while the grave was open and unencumbered, as their arrangement could not have resulted from any plundering of a filled-up grave They all lay on the floor, and were mostly heaped together in one pile, the consideration of these will be found in the discussion of the details of burials, after describing the graves Along the north end of the grave were stacked eight large jars, of the form shewn in the margin of the plan These were filled with grey ashes of wood and vegetable matter Such ash-jars were typical of the New Race graves, and occur in all tombs except the very poorest The ashes were very carefully winnowed by us at first, but nothing distinctive was ever found in them, except a few bits of broken bones of animals, no trace of human bone occurred, nor were any of the

human bones in the burials ever calcined or discoloured In every case we emptied out these ash-jars and looked over the contents, often of some dozens in a single grave; but amid the tons upon tons of ashes searched not a single object of human work was found These ashes then are quite different from the pits full of ashes at Gurob, under the floors of the houses, in which the personal possessions of the dead were destroyed We learn, however, that a great burning took place at a funeral, and the ashes of the vegetable matter, and even the burnt sand beneath it, were gathered up and buried in the grave In some cases a layer of some vegetable paste had been poured on the top of the ashes perhaps a libation of thick beer, of which the solid part lay on the top, while the liquid filtered down

Constant as the position of these ash-jars generally was at the north or foot-end of the grave, equally constantly another class of jar stood around the south or head-end These were of the wavy-handled type shewn in plates XXXI, XXXII In these jars nothing was found except fat, or its ceremonial substitute, mud In the early graves, with the well-formed wavy handles, the jars were full of strongly scented vegetable fat, details of which are given further on, in the middle period, when the wavy handles deteriorate, the fat gradually decreases, and a layer of mud fills the jar, apparently to prevent the fat losing its odour, in the latest forms, where the jar became a cylinder, and the handles disappeared, nothing but solid mud was found in the jars

At the ends of this grave then stood the customary series of ash-jars at the north, and fat-jars at the south Lying across the middle of the tomb were five skulls without any vertebræ attached, and a sixth skull lay at the south end (the normal place) upon a brick Amongst these skulls were three stone vases with flat bases, and pierced for suspension (H 25, 28, 29) and one oval vase with sharp edge (S 71), see plates VIII, XII These vases were all of the largest size usual in such hard materials, porphyry or syenite, the forms were of the finest type and they were quite perfect Moreover those with flat bases stood upright and had never been upset. In one vase (H 28) were hardstone beads, a necklace having probably been placed in it In another (H 25) was a brown pebble, which was an object constantly found with the slate palettes, and just the other side of skull E lay a slate palette of the double-headed bird type Beneath vase S 71 were chips of malachite, which was the material

D* 2

generally ground on the slate palettes Within and beneath skull D were stone beads and malachite We have here a grave in which the placing of the objects, the presence of valuable stone vases and beads, and the appearance of the filling all shew that it has not been disturbed since the burial, and yet the positions and conditions of the bones shew a very strange manner of dealing with them What conclusions we should draw from this are considered in the details of burials

41 T 14. In this grave the fat-jars are exceptionally placed towards the N end The interest of the grave is in the human and ox bones being laid together in parallel order It is certainly not disturbed, as a marble vase (H 25) stood by the interment , and on the fish-shaped slate (Sl 53, see Pl XLVIII) lay some malachite and an ivory pin

T 16 This is one of the rare examples of an apparently undisturbed burial, with the skull in place Yet here the 5th–7th vertebræ were displaced , and in the S E corner were parts of the pelvis of a young body Four stone vases lay in the grave three of them close to the undisturbed arm bones (H 29, H 32), the fourth, a small cup of veined marble (like S 49 but smaller), lay by the brown pebbles and a shell The N end of the grave was filled with ash-jars as usual , and the fat-jars stood along the W side The jar marked "B1" contained brown dust of organic matter, not burnt

T 19 was a grave which I specially noted as apparently unopened The ash-jars stood on the N E, and a single fat-jar on the W Three jars of brown dust, and one of gravel, stood also on the W The jars of gravel often found in the graves were doubtless filled with liquids, water, milk, or beer, and then became choked with gravel when the tomb was filled up The lower part of the spine, 12 vertebræ in length, and the legs were in place The rest of the body was dispersed, the arm bones lying together parallel at the S end

T 42 contained only a single jar , but the distribution of the bones was peculiar They were classified in a way which proved that they had been buried as separate bones the legs in the N W , the vertebræ in a group at the N E, together with a handful of ribs , the arms in the middle

The above selected graves all belong to a small but good cemetery near the two tumuli We now turn to the general cemetery in the wide shoal of the watercourse

17 This grave is of the later class of New Race remains The ash-jars are no longer of the wide-mouthed conical type, but have become longer and narrower, as shewn in the left-hand margin Another type of jar, almost egg-shaped, also is largely used for the liquid offerings, being filled with sand when found , and these jars are of a hard, smooth, light reddish-brown ware, which is unlike any of the earlier pottery A tall ring-stand, pierced with triangular holes in the side, is an evident imitation of a usual Egyptian type of the Old Kingdom, which is not known in the XIIth dynasty or later times At the S E corner were many jars of mud, the substitute for scented fat , most of them of the cylinder form, which is the later modification of the wavy-handle jar An ivory spoon lay in one of these jars A rectangular slate (form 100, Pl L) is another token of the later period Small saucers of malachite and galena stood in a pan, and such were the materials used for eye paint Only fragments of the body remained , but as the feet were in a natural relation, it appears that the rest of the body had been destroyed by plunderers The arms were found high up in the filling The sides of the grave were lined with brickwork, and a shelf of brick stands on the S W side

39 In this grave the bones are also broken up, and half a large pan lying with them, suggests that they were plundered Yet a copper adze or chisel, c (LXV, 6), lay by the broken remains, and two fine flint knives—white and black—of the type LXXIV 84, lay side by side with some sheep bones on the west The plundering must therefore have been very partial Along the south stood a row of wavy-handled jars, these had originally nothing solid in them as they were filled with the general gravel

112 This grave is another of the later type The strainer-jar, the tall ring-stand pierced with triangular holes, the table-stand, the rectangular slates, and the cylinder jars all shew the later period Here there was but one ash-jar, which lay 25 inches up, over the cylinders at the S E, two other jars were filled with sand (original?), and five with gravel from the general filling It seems then that the great burnings diminished in the later age The two slates here (type 106, Pl L) had green malachite ground on the upper sides, and brown flint pebbles lay upon them The cylinder jars were irregular in their contents, only one had the traditional mud in it , one had ash, one earth, one brown organic matter at the bottom, and three had sand from the filling of the

tomb Only two bones were left from the burial, probably owing to plunderers

177 This grave did not contain any bones, yet there were four slates, apparently undisturbed, malachite lying by the central slate, and the square southern one having the green patch of ground malachite upwards If the body had been attacked by plunderers, it is hard to see how they could have left the other objects so undisturbed, on referring to T 16 it will be seen that a body would have filled the whole space between the jars, and have overlaid the slates and comb Yet the whole body must have been removed without disturbing these Looking at the cut-up condition of the bodies, it seems as likely that little, if any, of the body was ever interred here The slates are of the types, XLVII, 24, XLVIII, 42, L, 102 At the middle of the south end, is a jar with pointed base (type R 76, PL XXXVIII), such form is often found in this position, never more than one in a grave, seldom in other positions, and never with any contents but sand or gravel of the filling

218 Here there have evidently been two bodies in one grave, both apparently broken up by plunderers, as many bones were scattered about in the space between the bodies The interest lay in the number of small objects Four flint lance-heads, (marked F) lay along the north, and behind the eastern body These are figured in PL LXXIII, 61, 62, 63 Two small arrow-heads of bone, and a copper band from a staff-end, lay at the N E A copper piercer (as LXV, 15) lay at the N W, by a stone vase, type H 70, PL IX One fish-shaped slate palette (XLVIII, 37) and one rough oval slate lay at the north, and a brown pebble was by the side of the fish slate A large red bowl contained the small red and black cups

263 Here again were two bodies, of which only twelve vertebræ remained of the northern, and six vertebræ of the southern one one skull lay about 16 inches up in the N E. corner, and the other skull in the middle of the south side Unless the tomb were almost empty when plundered, it would be very unlikely that the skulls would lie at opposite ends of it, close to the side of the pit, and no trace of arms or blade bones remain, which also seems unlikely if the skulls were left tossed aside in an empty pit The southern skull was partly hedged in by an oval pan on edge And the end of the vertebræ of one body, rested on the undisturbed toes of the other At the N W stood a large ash-jar, with

a cake of brown organic matter on the top of the askes.

42 271 This grave, though plundered, and not containing more than two shin bones of the body, was yet of much interest. The unique feature was a row of four ivory statuettes, of a rude peg-shape, shewn in LIX, 7, they were along the east side of the tomb, behind the body's position, placed upright at 3 inches apart. They stood in a bed of clean sand, with sand behind them Yet on removing this sand, I found behind the figures a piece of a forearm (ulna), and below them a fragment of bone At the south end of the row stood a red polished jar (P 59, XXIII) and beneath the jar was a fragment of a thigh bone and a finger It is certain then that a body has been dissevered, and the bones broken, before the bed of sand was laid, and the ivory figures and jar set upright at equal distances in it Behind the figures were remains of cloth painted with stucco in red, green, black and white And similar remains lay on the pottery at the W side. Here then there is absolute evidence of a body being cut up, quite apart from the later plundering of the tomb The later plunderers had dug a hole down on to the body, and had dragged the greater part of it out while the ligaments were still strong, so that it lay on a slope of earth, on the west side of the pit, the skull 45 inches up, the bones about 20 inches up

Of minor objects, there was a flint lance (LXXIII, 66) marked F here a fish-shaped slate (XLVIII, 38) with malachite on it, and an elaborate turtle slate, with the legs modified to gazelle's heads (XLVII, 11) with malachite on under-side a pair of ivory tusks like LXII, 34, 35, (one solid, one hollow, as in tomb I 4), and a slate figure (LIX, 4) placed together in a basket with some malachite, a flat cake of resin, and three stone vases of the types H 67, 70, 72, PL IX Also a large quantity of red coral (*Tubipora musica*) broken up into separate tubes and pierced, probably for threading as necklaces The pottery is sufficiently shewn in the plan, all the contents were sand and gravel

43 283 The peculiarity of this grave was that it contained three bodies, which had been laid in position on a wooden tray The remains of the tray shewed it to have been 33 inches wide, with upright sides 2 inches high, mitre-jointed at the corners Unfortunately the south end of the grave was plundered, and the heads were all lost, the longest spine having only fourteen vertebræ The feet of the southern body were under

the shoulders of the north-eastern   Whether this tray was used for carrying the bodies on as a bier, we cannot be certain , but from the slightness of it, about ¾ boards, with only a rim 2 inches deep, it would hardly bear the weight of three adult bodies, and it seems more likely to have been only placed as a floor to the grave   The wood was destroyed by white ants, and only traces of the skin of it could be found

326 This grave was robbed, only four vertebræ remaining, and two leg bones   But it is remarkable for the large quantity of pottery   Thirteen large ash-jars stood at the N end , six filled with sand or gravel (formerly with liquids) stood at the W side, all but one , six wavy-handled jars stood at the S side , beside many little jars and saucers in front of the body   The usual pointed brown jar R 76 stood at the S W

362–3, are two bodies in the very unusual position upon the back, with the arms straight down the sides, and the legs bent round beneath   The knees have been subject to violence to bring them into this position   the epiphysis of the thigh, on the right leg of the western body, was broken off and attached by the ligaments to the shin 4 inches from its true place   As it would be impossible for this to occur in the sharpest bending of a fresh body, it suggests that the body was partly dried before it was put in the grave , then the tendons had to be cut across to bend them, and a cut being too high up, the epiphysis broke off instead of the bend acting on the joint   The eastern body was old and large, the western young and smaller

400 This grave only contained three leg bones, and yet if plundered it is strange that a copper adze (marked c) should have remained (type I XV, 5)   It is of the later age of the New Race, as Egyptian forms have begun to be imitated in the stand , and the long conical jar with a collar-brim, the strainer-jar (XLI, L 50), and the cylinder-jars all shew the later age   The bones are those of a child, the thigh being only 11 inches long , and pieces of the skull lay over the pottery at the S end

414 Three fine flint weapons were found in this grave , a dagger 25 inches up at the N end (LXXII, 51), a forked lance 25 inches up at the S end (LXXIII 65), and a knife on the ground behind the place of the body (LXXIV, 84)   The grave had evidently been plundered, as there was no body, and a basalt jar was high up in the filling of the pit , but the flint dagger and lance were too close and flat against the side of the pit, to have been thrown there in digging   The contents of the jars are irregular,

the ashes being with the gravel jars at the S end, all the N end pottery being of fine red and black ware, and one wavy-handled jar

421 This grave contained an unusual amount of pottery, but none of the bones were left   The ashes burnt sand, and brown matter are all at the N end as usual, in eighteen jars, together with one jar of mud and one of gravel, originally of liquid   Five jars of gravel at the W, and two more at the S , were also filled with liquids   The three wavy-handled jars at the S end, contained neither fat nor mud, but only gravel   A peculiar double vase, F 42, and a spout-vase, F 25, lay with the others , and two stone vases, H 25 and H 29, stood at the S end

530 This was one of the less usual type of graves, with a recess hollowed out on the E side   The pit itself being 50 × 40 inches, the recess is about 10 inches back , the depth of the pit being 50 inches, the recess is rather lower than the floor, trending into the floor, shelving downward, and about 20 inches high, the top of it being thus about 35 inches under the surface   along the front of this recess a row of ash-jars of a lateish type, long and scanty, were ranged, touching one another, and leaning inward over the mouth of the recess   It was therefore impossible for any one to reach the body without moving the jars.   The body was in very fine condition, the tendons and much of the muscles remaining dried upon it, and all quite complete, excepting that the head was cut off and turned round reversed   The hair was all entire on the head, which was severed at the atlas, the last vertebra remaining complete on the spine   The arm bones were stained green from the malachite which lay by them   The pottery was unimportant

594 In this grave the bones were all placed loosely   They belonged to three adults and one child , the vertebræ were scattered   The leg bones were mostly laid parallel, but many inverted, in a row across the grave   The pottery is not important   This was recorded by Mr. Duncan

733 Here there were sixteen vertebræ remaining in line, while the upper bones and arms were all confused, and the skull upside down   Two large ash-jars stood at the feet, and one rudely-made pot, like those of the IVth dynasty, which may have been re-appropriated   A very unusual form of jar, for fat, stood at the middle of the S end, marked F

836 This grave was quite undisturbed, and the body was perfect and unmutilated   The hands were drawn up close to the face   Lying across the hip was a copper dagger (LXV, 3), which had stained the

bone green Around the skull had been laid a string of large beads of carnelian, lazuli, and other stones, which also lay round the neck Along the fingers were parallel lines of beads, which must have formed a beadwork mitten A small black pottery vase stood in front of the forehead At the side of the tomb, behind the head, was a bird-shaped slate (XLVII, 26) In the S W corner were bones of a gazelle, the same position as the gazelle head in No 17 In the N.W corner was an ash-jar, and a jar of brown organic matter, probably bread, with sand over it The jar, pan, saucer, and water-bottle at the S end did not contain anything

880 Here three adults and an infant appear to have been buried together, but the bones must have been all dissevered before being placed in the grave The pairs of thighs were reversed in the eastern side, end for end, and in the mid and western the upper ends were to the north, where there is no room for the body. The pelvic bones and vertebrae were all scattered irregularly, and only one skull was found A little vase of resin lay in front of the skull

CHAPTER VII

NOTABLE GRAVES

44 Having now described those graves of which the plans are here published, and which will enable the reader to realise the nature of the burials, we will turn to note the details of some of the great mass of the rest of the graves Plans were sketched of the position of all the objects in nearly three thousand graves examined But the great majority of these are so much alike that the important facts would be easily lost sight of in the wilderness of notes if they were all printed It would be impracticable here to classify all the notes under different subjects, as often the details are so miscellaneous So the best system for reference appears to be to place the noticeable graves in the order of their numbering, and to group together afterwards some details of the positions of certain classes of objects The initial of the recorder follows each description of a grave —D, Duncan, F, Flinders Petrie, G, Grenfell, P, Price, Q, Quibell The letters B or T preceding a number, refer to the small cemeteries—B, by Kom Belal, T, by the Tumuli—shewn in the plan of the cemeteries at the end of the volume To render this list more convenient,

references are given to those graves of which the plans have been already described

B 14. Box coffin, with contracted burial, head S, face W, as usual, the skull, arms, and one blade-bone thrown out of coffin on E, at higher level, apparently by plunderers Pottery, brown (R 81), red polished (P 40 c), and black-topped (B. 38 c) Therefore this is distinctly a New Race grave, by both the attitude and the pottery, although box burial is used A papyrus mat lay under the legs, and both wood and matting were found in the filling. Pit 95 × 65, 50 d F

B. 50 A complete body, with head on, and normal position, but a gap of one inch between fourth and fifth vertebrae A mass of small green glazed stone beads, in parallel lines on the fingers, with three large ovoids, apparently a beadwork mitten On the wrist carnelian and green glazed stone beads sometimes alternate, sometimes in long lengths of one colour Pottery, usual large jars, and the peculiar spout-jar D, 15, and ring-jar D 84. F

B 62 A normal grave, with an annex on the N W containing a child's body, and separated by three large stones The main body was complete from pelvis to right scapula and both arms But there was no left scapula, although that was the undermost side, and the head of the humerus was bare Though both arms were entire and in place, there were no wrists or hands The skull was removed, and placed in a corner of the little annex, with the child's body huddled round it Pit 70 × 45, 35 d Annex 40 × 24 F

B 99 A normal grave, ash-jars at N, one wavy-handled jar of sand at N W (type W 23), sand-jars at W, at the middle of the W side two shell pendants, one with turned-up hook (LXII, 21) North of these a line of parallel implements, starting from west, an ivory harpoon (LXI, 15), copper harpoon (LXV, 34), flint knife (LXXIV, 84), another ivory harpoon, a syenite jar (H 26), and another flint knife (LXXIV, 81) south of the jar In the S E corner lay a rude oval fish-slate At the mid-south was a decorated jar with spirals (D 67 c) The body was broken up, and much rotted Pit 85 × 70 P

B 102 A rudely triangular grave, body normal Sand-jars along the S W side, and two double-tubular jars (XXIX, 86, 91) in the N E corner, behind the heels, both filled with fine sand Pit 45 at sides P

B 105 Two bodies, one normal, the other along the E side, head S, on its back, the shin doubled back to the thigh Pit 80 × 40 P

B 107 A double grave, one body north of the other, the N skull at its feet—a young female, the S skull in front of its arms No pottery Pit 95 × 40 P

B 110 Body normal, but a mass of sticks lying on the upper part of the body, and the skull upon the sticks Pit 60 × 30 P

B 113 Skeleton of trunk and of each limb, wrapped closely round with a hairy hide Position normal Head separated Pit 35 × 35 P

B 117 Two bodies, positions normal, lying one in front of the other Below the eastern skull lay two ivory rings and a bead necklace Pit 45 × 40 P

B 121 Male body, wrapped entirely in well-preserved matting Skull at higher level Rhombic slate No 94 Pit 35 × 35 P

B 126 Two bodies, positions normal, lying one in front of the other, eastern one (behind the other) young Pit 85 × 60 P

B 133 Two bodies, positions normal, lying one in front of the other, the pelvis of the western resting on the middle of the thighs of the eastern Pit 85 × 60 P

45 T 4, T 5 See plans above described F

T 10 Male body, position normal, also a second skull, and a child's skull Along the W side of the grave a forequarter of an ox, the upper end S, and by that the head All surrounded with pottery Around the ox-head nine wavy-handled jars (type W 25) with scented fat and mud Pit 120 × 66 F

T 11, also, a blade-bone of an ox at mid-west side Square slate (No. 100) Pit 138 × 88 F

T 14, T 16 See plan

T 15, One of the most distinct of a class of tombs unlike all other New Race burials In the pit a vaulted brick chamber has been built, with door at E end of N side, opening into a smaller space, which was doubtless the well of access This is an Egyptian type of tomb, and in such tombs many bodies are buried together in a confused manner, with New Race pottery It seems, then, as if some older Egyptian tombs had been re-used as common graves for a group of poorer persons, for whom separate graves were not provided Similar brick chambers in cemetery B contain regular Egyptian burials, at full length, on the back, with typical pottery and beads of the XIIth dynasty F

T 19 See plan

T 22 Body normal, no skull In front of the knees lay two flint lances, side by side, head to tail (LXXIII, 62, 66) Remains of a second body lay to the N W, and before that a bird-shaped slate (XLVII 32), a fine syenite mace-head (XVII, M 1), and a small twisted piece of bronze like a model horn Pit 70 × 70, 10–20 d F

T 26. Spine in normal position, the leg bones all laid together, parallel, on the upper part of the spine Probably plundered A piece of brown and white woollen knitted stuff, and bird-slate (XLVII, 20), lying by the body We had to beware of modern stuffs being carried down by rats to form subterranean nests, many examples of which I found in the graves But in this case the knitted material was unlike anything I have seen in Egypt of modern or Coptic times, and its depth—50 inches—and the extent of the piece, made it unlikely to have been imported. Pit 80 × 55, 50 d F

T 36 Male skull, body all gone A late-period grave, with cylinder jars, long narrow ash-jars, barrel-jar (XXVI, F. 34 b), strainer-jar (L, 52), and table (L, 86) A gazelle's head lay S W of the centre, and a bird-shaped stone vase (S 80) at the N E F

T 42 See plan

T 52 Body scattered, legs normal, vertebræ solidified so as to form a hunchback An ox-head in the middle of the N end F

46 1 Deep grave, with ledges 12 inches wide half-way down Eight ash-jars at N end, two having baskets at the mouths Hair dark brown, turning grey Pit 92 × 67 at top, 80 × 42 below ledge, 70 d F

3 Large grave, with fifteen ash-jars, and many others The body had lain on a bed-frame, which was carved with bulls' feet, the hind legs at the S end, by the head At the W side of this bed-frame was a small table (traces of legs remaining), on which an oval red vase (F 31 d) had stood On the jars by this lay several copper needles, and others had fallen to the ground between the jars (LXV, 20, 21, 22) The skull lay at the middle of the S end, it was inverted, the base all broken out, and a quantity of small beads of garnet and green glazed stone lay inside it The wavy-handled jars had mud in them (type W 43, 47) A jar and a saucer contained barley Pit 123 × 66 F

17 and 39 See plan

34, 41 Wooden posts, 2¼ thick, occurred in the S E corner of 34, and in the N E and N W corners of 41 As the foot bones were in place on the legs, it is unlikely that the bodies were placed on bed-frames, as, if so, they would have fallen to the floor irregularly These posts may then be to support some kind of canopy over them In several cases, which we shall note, there is evidence of a roofing of beams and brushwood over the grave F

42 Here beneath the body a bed of ashes was spread out, and a papyrus mat laid upon the ash Two ash-jars lay under the legs The ribs were all broken off short, leaving the spine bare from pelvis to scapulæ Several ash and gravel-jars and a double-bird slate were placed here Pit 90 × 60, 77 d F

57 Body complete to shoulders Skull upright on a brick, with one collar-bone and half lower jaw close between skull and wall One neck vertebra in a brown jar Pottery intact, close to hands and to skull Lines of washed-in filling shewing from the top down to the level of the skull, as if the skull had been placed in an open pit, gradually filled by wind and rain Several instances of this wash-filling were seen, and dried wash of earth inside skulls, but most of these might be due to plunderers leaving a pit open In this case, the skull being upright on a brick, which would not have been there unless required, and the vertebra in a jar, make it unlikely to have been severed by plunderers, if so, the pit was left open after the skull was placed in it. F

124 Body normal, head removed to S end Ivory spoon (LXI, 8) in front of thighs Nine ash-jars stood at the W side, one containing a flint knife. Pit 65 × 50 P

162 Only a few finger and toe bones left by plunderers Six ash-jars along the N end, and close in front of them, flat on the ground, a fine flint knife, of translucent chalcedony (LXXIV, 86) The small pointed jar (XXXVIII, R. 76) stood at the middle of the S end, as usual Above the grave, at the side, were traces of the ends of beams in the gravel and brushwood roofing, with some charcoal upon the roofing F

165 No bones, pottery as usual The sides of the pit were lined with mats, of which a cast remained in the filling of the grave Over the pit, in the sides of it, were the ends of twelve poles, at intervals, shewing that there had been a wooden roof Pit 84 × 64, 52 d. F

177. See plan

178 Body all gone. On a shelf halfway up, mid-east side, lay a flint lance-head (LXXIII 61) and two flint knives (LXXIV, 81, 84), all parallel, pointing N At the N. end were three gravel-jars, one with a snake, the other with a gazelle (unfortunately lost after I left Egypt, and therefore not drawn here) Near the N. end, in the axis of the tomb, stood a black incised bowl (XXX, N 10), and such was the regular position of these rather rare bowls F

185 Bones all scattered The black incised bowl (N 6) stood the same distance from the N end, but rather nearer the W than in 178 A large quantity of rough clay beads were scattered a little N W of the centre of the grave, and three ivory combs lay in the axis, near the N end F

206. Bones scattered In S E. corner a black bowl (B. 11 f) lay almost inverted, and under it the bones of a calf's leg, doubled up Several fine red-polished and black-topped vases were in the grave F

207 A massive big skeleton in normal position, about 6 feet 3 inches high, in front of it a lesser, young skeleton, epiphyses loose, legs massive, spine slight. Photographed in position Pit 85 × 65, 55 d F

218 See plan

222 Robbed, legs only left At N end a child laid in a jar At side, pieces of a painted wooden box, red and black on white stucco, a gazelle's bones lay upon it Pit 90 × 70, 70 d F

223 Flint lance (LXXIII, 66) lying behind the pelvis F

227. Apparently unopened The skull removed westward, and a small jar lying against the top of the spine A young, but large body, with the thigh broken Pit 60 × 30, 50 d F

234. Body destroyed above third vertebra Young, epiphyses hardly set, but about 6 feet 5 inches high Red paint on leg bones Much pottery all along W side In S E corner a limestone top (VII, 5), in N E corner another (4) F

236 Body close to S end of tomb, usual attitude, but head S E, feet close to W side. Forearms both detached, and skull reversed, within the few inches between the undisturbed skeleton and the side of the pit It would be almost impossible to suppose plunderers, working down the edge of a pit, to reach the head and hands in so unusual a position, any ordinary plunder-hole would have broken up the skeleton F

238. Usual pottery, black-topped, etc Two lazuli flies F

240 The whole body was dragged up feet fore-most, on a slope out westward, the position contracted, and the neck sloping about 30 inches downward One arm and head broken off, the rest all together This shews that the ligaments were still strong when the tomb was plundered Very

E*

few bodies have at present the ligaments as strong as this implies, probably not more than a century or two had elapsed since the burial, when the plunderers worked in this cemetery   Pit 100 × 70, 70 d   F

260 Body normal, head and shoulders gone   On knees, an ostrich comb (LXIII, 62) on a piece of wood   N of legs another comb (LXIV, 73)   N E of feet a flint lance   Along E side a group of nine fig-shaped lumps of clay, mixed with clay rosettes, all originally contained in a papyrus box   F

263 See plan

267 In front of the knees lay a spindle-whorl or top of pink and white limestone, finely finished, and seven natural spheres of black flint laid in two rows   Pit 80 × 40, 50 d   F

268 An interesting group of objects although the body was entirely gone   In the N W corner (XXVII, F 69 a), over that a wavy-necked vase, like one here (XLVI, F 51 a), but with five waves   In front of that a slate elephant (XLVII, 5)   In front of the place of the knees an alabaster vase (S 268) containing the human-headed comb (LIX, 5)   Beside that an alabaster peg   In the S E corner a mace-head (type XVII, M 1)   F

271, 283 See plans

286 Body disturbed, seven vertebræ together, fingers and comb together   A patella beneath a jar under a pan   A square bottle of pottery (F 62 b) on west   And a dog's head   Pit 90 × 50, 50 d   F   In one pit in cemetery T dogs' bones only were found, apparently belonging to about twenty individuals

47 326 See plan

328 Feet, pelvis, and head all lumped together, without any trace of limb-bones, or vertebræ, in a small pit   The sacrum remarkably curved, as much as 120°   Recess 30 × 30, ledge in pit 25 wide   F

331 Flint dagger (LXXII, 56) on end, against S F of grave   Ivory rods and pins by it   Pointed brown jar at S W corner   F

343 A recess grave   Body normal, skull re noved to S W corner of pit   Slate fish, rough, by hands, on it a shell, a brown pebble, broken malachite, and powdered galena, E of it a packet of crushed malachite   Another packet of black powder and galena clenched in the right hand   A decayed decorated vase (XXXV D 67 c), containing scented mud (substitute for fat), N of the feet   Pit 70 × 50, recess 20 wide, 60 deep, recess 20 more   F

346 Only one leg left   On ankle a band of bead-work, lines parallel to the bone, long and short beads

alternately round bottom edge   A black incised bowl (XXX N 22) in axis, near N end, usual position   Pit 95 × 60, 60 d   F

350 A heap of rough clay beads, by the hands, two ivory bird-pins (LXIII, 47, 50) under the beads   Small clay beads with bag of malachite under the arm   F

355 A grave of the earlier style of New Race, cleared out, and pottery laid aside on a ledge on the E side   Then re-used for a burial of a later style, with smooth egg-shaped jars and pottery-stand   Pit 90 × 50, 80 d   F

356 Two bodies, only legs left, western lay on knees of eastern   The western was larger than the eastern   The eastern was old and had long strings of beads, green glazed stone, and carnelian, by its ankles   Pit 80 × 46, 50 d   F

362-3 See plan

369 An ox-leg placed along the western side in front of the row of jars.   A syenite mace (XVII, M 12) at mid-south end, with double-bird slate (XLIX, 82)   Pottery rather late, ash-jars long and scanty   Pit 80 × 50, 60 d   F

400, 414, and 421 See plan

430 A flint lance (LXXIII, 63) at mid-south end   A stone jar, like VIII, S 2, broken, in S E corner, by it a similar pottery jar (XXXV, 67)   A white limestone mace-head (XVII, M 9) at mid-east side   Pit 120 × 60, 90 d   P

530. See plan

551 Body normal   Legs wrapped round with brown fibre

534 See plan

654 Few bones left   Over foot at N E a black incised bowl (XXV, N 15)   At N W the other foot, and by it an oval bowl with foot (XXV, F 19 b)   Other pottery at N and S, of usual forms   Pit 80 × 70, 60 d   D

660. Male body, normal, skull off and reversed   Flint knife, and malachite behind the pelvis   Pottery along N and W sides   Pit 60 × 40, 60 d   D

664 Body and arms complete, no head   All wrapped in matting   Pit 50 × 30, 40 d   D

711 Body normal   A leather cushion, stuffed with vegetable matter (bran?) placed behind the shoulders   Pit 60 × 40, 50 d   F

721 Legs only left, normal   In front of place of hands a small rude oval dish of rough pottery, flat below   Beneath this lay four animal figures (LX, 12, 13, 14, 15), behind it a small decorated vase (D 67 c)   Pit 60 × 50, 40 d   F

722 Body normal, three jars lying beneath it A mat lay over the jars, and beneath the body

728 A mat laid over the body, and over a lock of hair, but the skull lying upon the mat If the grave were robbed, it is unlikely that the mat would be unbroken when the skull was dragged from under it and laid on it Also, if time enough had elapsed for the hair to become loose from the skull, it is probable that the mat would have become rotted already Pit 50 × 25, 50 d F

729 Body normal, no skull Mat and cloth laid under the body, and a mat over the body. Pit 50 × 30, 40 d F

733 See plan

743 One leg only left, and splint bone of this half gone, although protected by skin undisturbed Five hard limestone vases, finely worked, types H 34, 35, 41, 42, before place of hands, also a bone spoon, a pierced flake of obsidian, and malachite S of that a fish slate (XLVIII, 53), resin beneath it. In S E corner a log of palm-tree F

804 In front of the arms a group of beads, two ivory pins (LXIII, 47), a bag of malachite, and a lump of galena Malachite also under the shoulder Male skull F

807 Upper part of body disturbed In front of it two decorated jars (D 67 c, small), mouths down, and between them and the body a copper blade (LXV, 4) and small chisel (as LXV 11) A rough slate on the W side, half-way up Pit 60 × 45, 50 d F

822 An adult and a young body disturbed and mixed On one ankle a thread of minute beads of gold and lazuli In S W corner a fish slate (XLVIII, 51), with malachite ground on the under side Pit 70 × 50, 60 d F

824 A large number of univalve shells laid in front of the pottery at the S end, with one white and three brown pebbles Pit 60 × 35, 50 d F

827. Normal body, skull lying behind back, a mass of hair lying in front of the pelvis Matting laid over all bones, hair and pottery Pit 60 × 40, 50 d F

836 See plan

867 Male body, normal, skull in S W ; ivory rod and pin (LXIII, 47) E of skull In front of thighs a double-bird slate (XLIX, 86), a brown pebble, galena, and two flint balls Pit 75 × 50, 60 d F

869 Normal burial in a recess, body broken up A horn with a string of beads wound round it, some malachite, a fish slate, and brown pebble lay all

together in front of place of hands Pit 50 × 50, 40 d F

875 Normal burial, mace-head (type M 1) close to stomach In front, W, of this another body, with legs drawn up close to arms No skulls Pit 50 × 40, 50 d F

878 A mat lay in the middle of the pit, on it two tibiæ (heads W) and two humeri (heads E), arranged parallel A younger body, in normal position, to the N of this, without skull or lower arms, and vertebræ of the older skeleton were scattered over it Pit 80 × 50, 40 d. F

48 1037 Normal burial, male, head unshifted, arms complete Ivory bracelet on right arm String of carnelian beads round neck, small green glazed stone and carnelian beads on wrist (?) Gazelle head at W, in front of hands A rough slate before face Wavy-handled jar of M type Ash-jars rather late, elongated At E side a recess with another body, the arms and thighs in place, the vertebræ scattered, and the skull in the S W corner of the outer pit A brick in the pit measures 9 2 × 4 3 × 2 2 inches Pit 82 × 42, 60 d F

1206. Body gone Forty-nine jars at N end, ashes, sand, etc, thirty-seven jars, red-polished, etc., at E and S, total eighty-six Pit 140 × 80, 80 d G

1233 Later style, jars L 40 At mid-east side flint knife (LXXIV, 81), flint lance (63), and small copper chisel Pit 150 × 100, 60 d G

1241 Flint dagger (LXXII, 53) and two rough slates in N E corner Two stone vases (H 29, S 72) and a flint in front of place of head G

1248 Body complete, head in place W of hands a pottery ring-stand with alabaster saucer (S 50) on it. Close S of hands a saucer with alabaster cup (S 45) inside it, and an alabaster jar (S 1 c) with a smaller alabaster jar (S 3) inside it Large beads on the neck, smaller ones on wrist, a copper bracelet and an ivory pin under the hands Cylinder jars contained scented fat Pottery late (L 34 b, 64) Close W of the legs of this normal burial lay a skull and spine joined, with head at feet of other body and spine southward — i.e, reversed to ordinary position No pelvis, legs, or arms were found, though close to pottery and the undisturbed normal skeleton G

1247 Seventeen ash-jars and gravel-jars at N end At mid-east side slates 36 and 37, and alabaster jar (H 13) At mid-south end fluted limestone jar (S 64) In the N E corner syenite jars (H 29, H 33)

In the filling, fragments of stone jars and a tube of lazuli This tube is made of two pieces fitting with a sloping joint, slightly tapered to one end, and held together by an equally tapering tube, beaten very thin out of one piece, apparently of a gold-copper alloy Pit 140 × 70, 80 d   G

1251 One body complete, lower jaw and four neck vertebræ shifted, but head in place, position normal S of that the legs of another body, the feet under the previous head. At feet of N body two small slates (LXII, 42), a very short comb (LXIII, 52), an ivory peg (LXII, 19) and five painted balls of mud (VII 8) At the back of the head a saucer containing resin In front of thigh of the southern legs two pieces of clay, painted red Pottery usual, red-polished and black-topped Pit 85 × 60. P

1377 Body normal position wrapped in matting, head shifted, and pan lying on the neck Arm bones mixed together   P

1388 Body normal, head gone ; lying on a frame-work of wood covered with a mat At the feet, a flint lance with cord wound around it (LXXIII, 66) P

1401 Bars of a wooden frame under the body Along E side two long sticks with bark on, bound with leather, lying on them a porphyry mace-head (M 2), an alabaster mace (M 13), and a breccia mace (M 1) In S W corner specular hæmatite ore, and much malachite N of long sticks a loop of twisted leather, and other pieces At N E, a shell and flint knife At mid N an incised red bowl (N 6) In N W corner a basalt pot (S 1 c) P

1410 Body normal, but knees drawn up to elbows On the hip a flint dagger (LXXII, 53) In N W corner a basket with a ground flint axe, the only one found (LXXII, 59) A female skull and part of another body loose in the filling   P

1411 A very wide grave, with an adult at E end, and four children all in a line E to W , all in normal position The second child with another on its knees, and another child S of the westernmost In all, seven bodies A layer of matting lay over all the bodies Pottery along E side In S E corner a man-head comb (LIX, 1), a bird comb, (LXIII, 69), and a slate (97) Also an ivory vase (LXI, 11) The pottery was black-topped, etc   P

1415 Two bodies side by side Western, on left side, facing W as usual, but hips not bent, lower legs bent back sharply Eastern, face down, with lower legs bent sharply back Black-topped pottery, etc., at S end   P

1416 At mid-east a flint lance (LXXIII, 66), a syenite mace-head (XVII, 1), and a piece of a lime-stone mace Pottery black-topped P

1417 Two bodies, position normal, the smaller (a female) in front of the larger, knees of larger resting on lumbar vertebræ of smaller In N W corner large rhomb slate in a basket, mid N, a shell and a basalt jar (S 62), N E corner, two ivory combs (LXIII, 68), mid E, behind larger body, a flint lance (LXXIII, 65), and a painted limestone top (?) (VII, 3), in S W corner, four black-topped jars, and a syenite mace (M 1) in front of them   P

1418 Large rhomb slate behind body, and N of that two painted limestone tops (VII, 3, 6)   P

1419 Normal burial, skull reversed, lower arms displaced Female By the arms two anchor-bird slates (XLIX, 64, 66), two ivory horns (LXII, 34), an ivory crescent (LXIV, 91 ?), and ivory peg (LXII, 19) S of the knees, two ivory combs (LXIV, 72), some stone beads, another ivory crescent, and a turtle slate (XLVII, 15) The slates were wrapped in a leather cover (bag ?), and the horns bound round with leather thongs Pottery black-topped P

1426 Body normal, knees drawn up rather high, skull turned Some way to S W, rolls of hair separate In front of knees three ivory tusks, one solid, two hollow (as LXII, 34, 35) Much black-topped pottery all along E and S sides, many marks on it (marks 46, 383–389 425, 492)   P

1437 Normal body, no head, jar lying at end of spine Two ground double-edged flint knives (LXXII, 52), both broken in two, lying behind pelvis Frag-ments of a red and white line jar, XXIX, C 77, and of a limestone top   P

1480 Normal body, no head In place of head a broken ostrich egg, with two deer incised on it At knees, two rolls of thin sheet copper punched in lines, shewn unrolled in LXIV, 100, 101 Between chest and knees a bud slate (XLVII, 21)   P

1485 Normal burial, knees drawn close up Flint knife (LXXIV, 85), and two rough flint knives, wrapped in sheep's-skin, behind pelvis, copper pin and fruit pods by chest Five large bowls of black and red, three containing small vases, along W side   P

1487 Normal burial Incised black bowl (N 20) at mid west, with basalt jar (S 62), wavy-necked jar (F 51 b)   P

1488 Normal burial Female In front of fore-head alabaster mace (M 5), behind the back a syenite mace-head (M 4), and fragments of rolls (as

(LIX, 11), slate 98 before knees   Two horns in N W corner   P

49. 1507 Two bodies, one in front of the other, the eastern with legs resting on lumbar region of western. Comb at S end   Alabaster jar (S 4 a) before arms of western body   At higher level, a pelvis and legs of another body at N end   P

1563 Burial normal   Body tightly wrapped in a skin, which was tied round the femurs, and pieces of blue-painted skin before the arms, a parcel of leather by the hands wrapped round a cylindrical stone   In front of feet, two red vases with white lines (XXIX, C. 56, 63)   P

1579 Normal burial   Under the skull twenty-four large Carnelian beads, and a necklace of small beads over it   Cylinder jars   P

1583 Two bodies, normal, one in front of other, no skulls   Between the bodies two ivory tusks (LXII, 44) containing resin, with leather tied on over the opening, three alabaster pendants (LXII, 31), and a bone mannikin (LIX, 8)   Three black-topped jars at E. and S   P

1586 Body complete, male, normal   Over the head, beads, twelve to twenty white, and then black, also some leather mat (?), and two bags of leather 4 inches long   Two combs (LXIII, 58, 59) behind head   Mace-head below chin   Three large black-topped jars at W, with traces of a long object of ivory, red leather and beads   Small hedgehog-pot before face   Pit 70 + 60, 80 d   Q

1611 Only twelve vertebræ and one arm   Before body a coil of leather cord, bits of red leather N of it, a humerus and a leather-bound staff W of it, fragment of wood with red and green paint S of it, two femurs laid parallel N to S at F of it   A statuette at mid N side, and fragments of another in the filling   Black-topped jars   Pit 70 + 60, 70 d   Q

1615 Two bodies, normal, one before the other, between them, shoulder and legs of a child, in reversed position   Above western head a comb and beads   Behind eastern pelvis, two red jars with multiple necks (XXIX, C 81, 84), and a bob of red pottery with white lines (C 69)   A long, irregularly chipped flint at back.   Pit 60 × 60, 70 d   Q

1676 Two bodies, normal, one before the other, the head of the eastern under the western body   Behind eastern pelvis a flint lance-head (type 66), behind western pelvis two flint lances (LXXIII, 66) and a long, double-edged knife (LXXII, 52)   In front of E. shoulders a mace-head, in front of W shoulders a

red bowl with white lines (C 65)   Above W head a basalt jar   Q

1773 Male skull   Flint lance, 66, behind place of pelvis   P

1788 A child, position normal   Before hands the worked ivory, LXI, 4, the emery plummet, LXIV, 99, and a cup-shaped iron concretion   Three hair-pins behind the head

1790 Normal burial, but at S end a wavy-handled jar containing *ashes*   Leather knife-case (?) at back   Q

1820. Two bodies, eastern normal, western facing the eastern, i e, on right side   At N end three black-topped jars, and alabaster jar, S 4 b   P

1821 Body normal   Before chest a large rhombic slate and flint lance (66)   At S W, an ivory comb (55), a copper pin, and a considerable quantity of leather (LXIV, 104) coloured white, with zigzag lines of yellow edged with black   P

1848 On mid west a black incised bowl, N 31, and one broken one on each side of it   Q

1865 A fish slate, anchor-bird slate (XLIX, 64), a flint, and three hair-pins before the place of hands   Q

1899 Burial normal, male   Slate vase (S 72) before forehead   Six alabaster beads, a bracelet of ivory, and a bracelet of alabaster, by the hands   Behind pelvis a piece of a papyrus roll (like LIX, 11)   Pit 70 × 60   Q

1909 Normal burial, no head   Flint lance (66) wrapped in leather, between the arms   Pit 70 × 40, 70 d   Q

1914. Normal   Head on a mass of organic matter like seed, and matting below, probably a stuffed pillow   Q

1918 Seated figure of limestone at S end   Q.

50 We can now briefly sum up the positions of the usual objects   The large, coarse pointed ash-jars (XXXVIII, 81-83) occupy the N end   The wavy-handled jars (XXXI-XXXII) are generally at the S end, sometimes toward the W   The pointed jar (XXXVIII, 76, 78) is generally at the S end, only one in a grave   the positions recorded are, 7, S, 3, S S W, 5, S W, 1 each, W S W, W, W N W, N W and N E   The decorated pottery (XXXIII-XXXV) is found at every part of the graves, though mostly at the S and W   The incised bowls are usually toward the N, but not against the sides of the pit, 5 are 8 to 20 inches from mid N, 1 at 20 inches from N and E, 3 at 20 to 30 inches from N and W, in only one tomb were they against the

side, where 3 were at the W The slates are usually at the S , but are found in every position except mid N , they are equally spread E and W , those about the body are found at all parts, but most usually by the hands The flint dagger was on the hip, like the copper dagger The knives and lances are usually behind the body The bags and patches of malachite and galena are usually by the hands

CHAPTER VIII

DETAILS OF BURIALS

51 The first and most obvious difference between the Egyptian and the foreign burials is, that the latter are always in a contracted position The knees are always sharply bent, at 45° to the thighs, or else nearly parallel , while the thighs are always at right angles to the body, or even more drawn up, so that the knees touch the elbows The arms are always bent, with the hands placed together before the face or the neck In stating that this attitude is always followed, we must make note of a few rare exceptions, so few that they do not affect the rule of interment In a few cases the body is laid on the back, and the knees bent sharply, so that the legs are folded up together , or else both knees and hips are bent sharply, so that the legs are folded up on either side of the body That great force was used in thus placing them is evident , in one grave (363) the knee joint is separated so that the shin is 4 inches from the thigh, and the epiphysis of the thigh is broken off and attached by dried skin to the shin Such a mutilation could scarcely take place without the tendons being cut in the wrong place; above the knee-cap.

The direction of interment was as constant as the attitude There were but three exceptions found to the rule, that the body lay on the left side, facing the W, with the head to the S, and the feet to the N In one case the body lay at right angles to this (grave 667), feet W and head S E , in one case of an intruded burial in a grave, the head was to the N , and in the case of two bodies in one grave, they faced each other, so that one lay on its right side, facing E

The above constant attitude of burial is the same as that found in the earliest tombs of the lower classes at Medum, belonging to the beginning of the IVth dynasty ; while the upper classes there were buried at full length, and mummified like later Egyptians. This resemblance between the common people of the IVth dynasty, and the foreigners of the VIIth, may well be due to the Egyptian stock having a large element of the same Libyan race as appears to be that of the invaders , in short, we are comparing the customs of the western settlers in Egypt at two successive periods In one respect there is, however, a difference The Medum bodies, though on the left side, like the foreigners, are exactly in opposite azimuth At Medum they lie head N, face E., at Naqada they lie head S, face W

Though the attitude and direction of interment are thus regular, yet a number of complex questions are raised by the details of the bodies The main trouble is that nearly all the graves have been plundered in ancient times , and the bodies have been more or less disturbed—in some cases all dug out and dispersed, and in nearly all cases partly shifted. The original condition of the body can, therefore, only be settled by careful attention to special cases It will be best to state these crucial instances categorically, so as to shew the conclusions to be drawn from them

52 In one case (37) of the body being buried in a side recess of the grave, the head was entirely missing, and the neck vertebra butted close against the end of the recess, so that the head cannot have been on the body at the time of interment

In another case (227) the skull was missing, and small vases were lying intact above the neck, where they would scarcely be placed by a plunderer

Again (845) the body ended at the seventeenth vertebra (the twenty-four vertebræ are always counted here from the base upward) , a large pan, full of small vases all intact, lay where the neck would have been, and the skull lay on the top of the vases Here no plunderer would have moved a large pan of vases to and fro without upsetting them

In 1377, also, a pan is placed on the truncated neck

Another form of evidence is given by tombs which appear to be yet unrifled No 530 had the mouth of the recess practically covered by a row of long jars, stacked all along the opening (see plan) , and inside the space the body was intact, excepting that the head was off and turned round

Again (1105), where a later burial was over an

earlier, both of them in the normal contracted position, the earlier body had the head removed and placed by the legs, while the later was quite perfect above it   Here no plunderer later than the Xth dynasty can have been at work

A grave which appeared to be certainly untouched (315) had the skull and lower arms lying in the S W corner, with an upright jar standing against them

Similarly in B 107, the skull lay by the feet, a position not likely for a plunderer to transfer it to in an earth-filled grave

In 263, two bodies lay together, the truncated spine of one resting on the undisturbed toes of the other, while the skulls lay apart at opposite ends of the pit   Here it is hardly possible to suppose that the mutilation is due to plunderers

A like case of strange transference is in 1505, where two bodies were buried, one in front of the other, and the skulls of both lay together at the side of the grave

That the skull was intentionally removed is indicated by grave B 50, where, though the entire body lay together in place, a gap of a whole inch separated the twentieth from the twenty-first vertebra, shewing that the neck was severed, although the skull was put in position.

From the above instances it appears probable that *the skull was often intentionally removed before burial*

This leads to the question of the special treatment of the skull   In grave 1827 there was only a skull, without any body, and around the skull lay arranged seven pendants of clay   In the next tomb (1828) also only a skull was found   No plunderer would destroy an entire body, while leaving a skull

The same honour to the skull apart is seen in another custom   In grave 57 the skull stood upright upon a brick, for which there was no other purpose in the grave   In grave 18 there lay a pile of stones under the skull, which was detached   In 541 the skull again lay detached, on a pile of big stones   In 38 the skull lay on a pile of stones at the S end of the grave, the base upward, and broken   In 29 the skull was high up on a pile of big stones, laid upon the body   And in 54 the skull stood upright, jaw in place, facing S, on the top of a pile of flints, each of about 3 lbs weight, which pile stood on the bones, one blade bone was under the skull and the other upon it   All of these cases are entirely different from what would result from mere plundering of the graves   It appears probable, therefore,

that *the skull was separately placed in the grave, perhaps some time subsequent to the burial*

53 Special customs also attached to the fore-arms and hands   In grave 712 the pottery all stood undisturbed—two vases upright in place where the hands should have been , and it was specially noted at the time as an intact grave, by all its appearances   Yet there was no skull, and no trace of the lower arms or hands , while the upper arms and blade bones lay perfectly intact and in position, the spine ending at the eighteenth vertebra   In 548 the skull lay at the S side of the grave, the body ended at the eighteenth vertebra, the blades and upper arms were in place, but there was no trace of lower arms or hands   The grave was noted as undisturbed, by all its appearances   Again, in 540 the blades, collar bones, and upper arms were in place, but there was no trace of the skull, or of lower arms or hands, while a group of perfect jars occupied their place   This was also noted at the time as an unplundered grave   the body ended at the twenty-second vertebra   This same completion of the upper arms and body, while the lower arms and hands are gone, was seen in graves 236, 255, and 804   In 315 the skull and lower arms lay together in the S W corner , the rest of the body was undisturbed, and the grave apparently unopened   In 541 the arms were in place, but no wrists or hands, while the fingers lay under the skull upon the pile of stones   In B 62 there were no hands, and the skull lay in an adjacent grave of a child   And in 29, where the skull was on a pile of stones, the body was in position, except that the arms were scattered about the recess   In 878 a young body was buried without skull or lower arms, with its truncated neck resting on a mat, on which older bones are arranged parallel   Any digger would have destroyed this arrangement.

In one or two such cases we might suppose the hands had been dragged away, in order to secure bead armlets or similar ornaments, by plunderers   But such a series of total removals of the lower arms and hands, without disturbing the almost parallel upper arms (which lay articulated with them, and within a few inches of them), and instances where intact pottery occupied the place of the missing hands, compel us to consider that *the lower arms and hands were often removed before burial.*

That other mutilations of the body were practised is likewise shewn   In grave 29 the spine was perfect , but all the ribs lay in the recess of the grave behind the back, as if the sides had been cut off the spine   In grave 42, where the blade bones and fifteen vertebræ were all in position, the sacrum was missing from the pelvis, and the ribs were all chopped away short   In grave 32, which had a recess for the body walled across its mouth, apparently intact, the ribs lay in a handful high up behind the feet   None of these mutilations can be considered likely as a result of plundering   Probably therefore *sometimes the trunk was partly cut to pieces before burial*

But yet more thorough disseverment was practised   In grave 594 (see plan) the leg bones of four bodies were lying all parallel, while the pelves were scattered about, the legs must have been laid out as loose bones   In 880 (see plan) the same method recurs   In T 14 (see plan) some human bones, broken, were laid side by side parallel with ox bones

Beside parallel arrangement, we find in grave T 42 (see plan) all the bones of the body laid out, lotted according to their nature, the leg bones in the N corners, crossing just as grasped in a handful, the ribs laid in a handful, by them, the vertebræ ranged round in a circle, and the arms in the middle of the tomb

Other cases occur in which the bones are merely scattered apart   Graves 28 and 31 were recess tombs, with the body entirely walled in by stones and mud, and unopened, yet all the bones were scattered and apart, and the skull missing in No 31, and set on the top of all the bones in No 28   In grave G 2, a very narrow pit, the bones lay all loose in the bottom, the skull at the S, the spine to the F, and the hands under a bowl at the N, above the bones were six jars and bowls all perfect, and above them five jars neatly ranged in close order, head and tail alternate quite undisturbed, covering the whole area of the little pit, so that any later disturbance of the lower part is impossible.

In a large grave (271, see plan) which had been plundered, a row of ivory figures stood upright in the clean sand along the side of the grave, equidistant, and undisturbed, with an upright vase at the end of the row   At the same level, in clean sand, between the figures and the side of the grave, lay a piece of a lower arm bone, and below the figures another piece of bone, while under the jar lay a piece of a thigh and a finger   Yet this edge of the tomb was certainly undisturbed, as we see by the upright row of equidistant figures   We must infer, therefore, that *the whole body was sometimes dismembered completely before burial, and artificially arranged.*

54   But one of the most conclusive and important

graves is that marked as T 5 (see plan)   This grave is one of the largest, but had every appearance of never having been opened   The valuable polished stone vases stood in perfect order, upright on the floor, the stone beads still remained, the pottery vases were ranged intact along the sides, and the filling shewed no signs of disturbance   Six skulls lay in the grave, and a large quantity of bones, but not a single bone lay in connection with its fellow   The skulls lay on the floor, some close to the upright stone jars on either side of them   A mass of bones, mainly broken at the ends, and some split, lay together on the floor in a heap about two feet across, and seven inches high, while round the sides of the grave were many bones, nearly all with ends broken, lying scattered apart   Three arm bones and one thigh, broken, lay in the N W. corner, and in another place were ten shin bones lying parallel, with one thigh

Not only were the ends broken off, but in some bones the cellular structure had been scooped out forcibly, what remained of it being very firm and strong   and beside this there were grooves left by gnawing on the bones   That this disturbance could not be due to any animals that might have got at the bodies, either before or after burial, is proved by the scooping out of the cellular structure of the long bones, and by the heaping together of the bones in a pile, all dissevered and broken   The condition of the skulls is also important   Skull A had the jaw on it in place   Skull B had the face broken away, and holes in the under side   Skull D was young, broken, and with a splint bone stuck through it, yet beads and malachite lay in and under it   Skull E had an oval shell pendant under it   And skull F was sixteen inches above the floor at the S end, with a brick under it (like the pile of stones under skulls in other tombs), its jaw was behind it and a piece of the face of skull B (?) lying by it   These details shew that ornaments were buried with these skulls, both beads and a forehead pendant, although they were, according to our ideas, so maltreated

After these instances we must conclude *that bodies were sometimes—with all respect—cut up and partly eaten*

The conclusions from all this evidence—which it is necessary to give in such detail in order to draw any safe inferences—is that the head was generally removed before burial, perhaps kept for some time, and then interred at a later date, this would be exactly as many races now do from affection for the deceased person, that they may have something to talk to, and by which to remember him That the hands and lower arms were sometimes taken off, doubtless with a like motive And that very probably a portion of the flesh was eaten, in order to secure the transmission of the qualities of the dead to his descendants for we see that there are some extreme cases of complete dismemberment, and feasting on the remains, the very bones being broken and sucked out As it is stated that Osiris (who was probably a Libyan god) reclaimed the Egyptians from cannibalism, there is sufficient evidence that such an idea was remembered even down to the Greek period And the custom of feeding on the sacred ram of Thebes, and on the sacred Apis of Memphis, while burying the fragments of bone from the feast with the greatest honour, shews how such ceremonial flesh eating was combined with the utmost respect and reverence in historical times See also this question in the chapter on the conclusions

55 One suggestion, that has been made in different quarters, as explaining the mutilated state of the bodies, is that these cemeteries belonged to a colony of foreign mercenary soldiers This hypothesis is impossible when we look at the details The very meaning of a soldier-colony is that it is not a tribal settlement of families, yet we find in the cemeteries quite as large a number of women as of men, and in one cemetery a remarkable excess of women of a slightly varied type Hence these people were not a garrison That they were not foreign soldiers married to Egyptian women is proved by the skulls of an equal number of males and females being exactly the same in characteristics, and with the same proportion of minor varieties in different measurements That they were not soldiers at all, more than any conquering tribe is bound to be, is also shewn by the skeletons In all the hundreds of bodies examined scarcely one shewed broken bones Only three examples of fracture during life were observed, one thigh broken in childhood, and united so perfectly that only the alignment betrayed it, one arm, and one rib. These people were certainly not quarrelsome nor given to fighting And that the mutilated bodies were not of soldiers is shewn by two points First, no example of a skull smashed in or broken during life was noticed, and second, the noticeable cases of clear mutilation of which the sex has been determined shew four male heads removed, and seven female heads There seems, therefore, no possible room for the military hypothesis to account either for foreigners on Egyptian soil, or for the mutilations of the bodies

The tribe was fairly homogeneous, containing equal numbers of similar men and women, and was not addicted to fighting

Nor will the presence of even a tribe of foreign mercenaries account for the remains Any soldier employed by Egyptians must have had some contact with them, have used some Egyptian objects or weapons, and probably have been recompensed by some Egyptian products Yet not any Egyptian things, of any kind whatever, were found among these people, nor even the simplest Egyptian arts, such as the potter's wheel, they had no intercourse with the former inhabitants, but were entirely independent

CHAPTER IX

DESCRIPTION OF PLATES

By Messrs PETRIE and QUIBELL

56 PL I *Ballas to Naqada*—This map will shew the general relation of the places The belt of cultivation varies from $1\frac{1}{2}$ miles wide at Ballas to 3 miles opposite Nubt, while the desert plain back to the cliffs averages about 3 miles in width This desert rises in a low terrace to a plateau about 30 feet above the Nile plain, and then gradually slopes upward until it is broken into a maze of foot hills at about 2 miles back High above these rise the cliffs to 1400 feet, in many parts quite inaccessible, with ranges of precipices some hundreds of feet high These cliffs form the river front to the great Libyan plateau, which is intersected with stream-courses and valleys The valleys run down westward in the plateau, and open out in the Nile valley far to the north, while the valley-heads reach up to the cliff-face, and often break the outline of that with dips and slopes The plain below the cliffs is intersected with drainage lines or gullies, running down to the edge of the cultivated land, and thus cutting sections through the bed of old high-Nile gravels, marls, and mud, which form the edge of the desert

I A *Positions of cemeteries, etc*—The dyke at the extreme north of the map is a modern dyke which leads down to the river and divides the plain into separate areas for irrigation But it probably has descended from very early times, as the Egyptian cemetery centres around it, and it would be the natural road from the river or from Koptos to the

F*

westein desert Mr Quibell's house was close to this dyke   South of that he several early mastabas, scattered on the highei points of the desert edge, two groups of rock tombs with stairways leading down into them, and a cemetery of the New Race in a shoal of the wide valley All this ground was woiked by Mr Quibell, and is described by him

Further south is a pyramid built entirely of unhewn stones, on the cumulative-mastaba system Near that is the town and temple of Nubt, dating from the IVth dynasty, as shewn by the pottery of the lowest levels And to the west of the town are some tombs of the early XVIIIth dynasty, probably under Tahutmes III, cut in a spur of the rock These will all be described in the account of Nubt

At the mouth of a narrow and sharp valley, on a slight rise stand the remains of a town of the New Race, subsequently occupied in part under the XVIIIth dynasty On either side of the valley are several piles of stones, two of which are here marked, we opened some of these piles without finding anything Similar, but on a larger scale, are the two Tumuli marked here They are formed of natural blocks of haid limestone and flint, irregularly piled together in a conical form, about 65 feet across and the northein 9 feet high, the southern 10½ feet Both had been dug into about the top, but had not been really searched We ran a wide trench in from the east faces, as shrines or offerings are usually east of a tomb, and then a tiench into the northein tumulus from the noith face, as pyiamid entrances are from the north But nothing was found in the pile, and it did not appeai that the natural surface of the desert had been in the least broken before the stones were piled up, on placing the eye at the level of the desert, the undisturbed layer of surface pebbles could be seen at all parts of oui cutting, which extended through the surface mail down to hard soil Around these tumuli were many burials at full length of the Roman period, but none were seen beneath the stones

The several cemeteries in this region have all been surveyed, and the detailed plans of the positions of the tombs will be found on PL LXXXVI of Naqada The letters B and T were applied to two isolated cemeteries, one near Kom Belal, the other near the tumuli The outlines of the separate plans are here shewn on the map

57 II to V These plates of Mr Quibell's work are described by him in the earlier part of this volume, Chapter IV

VI *Figures from graves, and skulls* —In the graves at both Ballas and Naqada were found several figures modelled in whitish maily clay or in Nile mud These represent a iace which is otheiwise not found in Egypt, nor on works of the New Race The steatopygy, and the characteristic lumbar curve in the standing figures, seem to connect this with the well-known Hottentot type At first sight it may seem strange to adopt so distant a connection, but it appears that this race has gradually receded before the pressure of higher races This foim is shewn in two ivory carvings found in the cavein of Brassempouy, in the S W of France, about 30 miles fiom the Bay of Biscay and 50 miles fiom the Pyrenees (L'Anthropologie, VI, 129–151) These figures prove that a Hottentot type existed in that iegion at a period which is equal to that of Solutré (p 140), that is to say, the second of the four peiiods of the palæolithic age Another carving of a woman knocked down by a reindeer, found at Laugerie-Basse, evidently belongs to the same type, and shews the use of numerous bracelets on the foiearm, like the custom of the New Race In these carvings a full amount of haii is indicated on the body, shewing the habitude in a cold climate In neither Brassempouy nor among the New Race is this type the only one, a slender European type is associated with it A head and three ivory carvings (L'Anthrop VI, 147–149) shew this finer type in France, and the female figures tattooed or painted (LIX, 6, 11), shew it in Egypt Fig 6, it should be noted, is of the same whitish clay as the steatopygous figuie, but is left white on the surface, whereas all the steatopygous figures are coloured dark red

We may next note this same steatopygous iace in Malta The seven seated figures carved in limestone, which were found in the rude stone temple of Hagiar Kim (Adams' Malta, VII, 1), aie very closely like those in the graves of the New Race, there is the same monstrous thickness of the legs, and the same attitude of sitting on the ground with the feet both turned out to the iight-hand side, an attitude nevei shewn on Egyptian figures Then to the south this type is shewn by the Queen of Punt or Somali and in the XVIIIth dynasty, on the sculptures of Deir al Bahri And in modein times it is only known in the south of Africa There is thus a series of five regions in which the steatopygous race appears, and which lie apparently from N to S in the order of successive dates of the iemains

Below these figures are shewn some of the skulls of

the New Race, selected to illustrate the profiles Of these the most marked type is that with massive brows, deep-cut bridge to the nose, and a short but very prominent aquiline nose This type is remarkably like that of the Lebu, or Libyan, chief shewn on the front of the temple of Ramessu III at Medinet Habu, which is here given for comparison The details of the measurements of these skulls, and their comparison with those of other races, is stated in describing PL LXXXIV

VII *Games* —Some objects can hardly be other than toys or games In a large grave of a child (No 100) was found the group of stone balls, etc, shewn in VII, 1 They are here represented as being placed on a board, only to point the perspective of the group. Their original arrangement is quite unknown, as they were found loose in the earth and gravel filling of the grave which had been plundered They lay near the middle of the west side, at a few inches above the floor. I was present when they were found, and searched carefully so as to obtain them all The nine vase-shaped stones we thought to belong to a necklace at first, they are cut in alabaster and veined breccia, none of them are pierced for suspension, and they can only stand on their circular flat ends With them were four balls of porphyry, well made for such a refractory material This leads us to suppose that the nine vase-shaped pieces were to stand on end, and to be played at with the balls, which are just suited in size and weight for such a purpose With these were three square slips of veined grey marble, two exactly alike and one longer These naturally suggest a gate or trilithon to play through, and the width of it is such as to offer some little difficulty to the player in avoiding overthrowing the miniature trilithon in driving the ball through it So far I had restored this game of skittles the day I found it, and I was greatly interested to hear from Mr Carter, that in Norfolk skittles are played through a gateway of logs of wood which must not be upset by the player This trilithon type of the game therefore still survives What the history of skittles may be no one has yet ascertained, it appears to be a thoroughly European game, nor have I heard of it in the East In the same grave was a flint knife (LXXIV, 81) lying on two jars of gravel at the west side, and in the moved stuff two fine flint lances (LXXIII, 63) Another game was found by Mr. Quibell (VII, 2), with figures of a hare and four lions, rectangular blocks of bone and limestone, natural spherules of ironstone, and long strips of ivory, some

with diagonal lines, some with a carving of a leaf-bract in the middle, some rods with knots and a leaf-bract, and some plain rods There is an obvious similarity of idea between these slips, with a leaf-bract carved on one side, and the slips of palm-stick with one outer side and one inner, which are now used in Egypt for casting lots in games It seems as if the group of ivory slips would be cast on the ground, as the six slips of palm-stick now are used by the boys, and the number that lay with the bract side up would be counted as the throw We might even conjecture that such counted throws would be taken as steps by the lions chasing the hare, as the lion and hare game probably depended on luck and not on skill

Similar games appear to have been placed in other graves In 1215 there were 14 porphyry and 2 breccia balls, a bar (like that of the trilithon) of porphyry, 6 slips of ivory with a bract carved on one side and 1 slip with diagonal lines, with 3 or 4 rods of ivory In 1229 were 4 blocks of ivory 1 2 to 1 23 inches long × 27 × 16, 3 rods (one entire 5 045 long), and 1 slip marked with diagonal lines In 379 were 5 syenite balls (rude) and an alabaster bar In T 10 was a breccia bar, in 83 a slate bar, in 10 another stone bar Syenite balls were found in 1209 (5), in 1246 (2), in 1239 and in 472 Three syenite balls and 3 minute triangles of slate (from inlaying?) in 399 And in 267 were 7 spherules of iron-stone and 2 spindles or tops of fine limestone well polished Thus in fourteen graves (all plundered) more or less objects were found, such as seem to belong to games, and it is plain therefore that they are not merely isolated freaks, but that they belong to well-recognised amusements

Another class of toys seem to be shewn in figures VII, 3 to 7 These are at first sight like the stone mace-heads, but they differ from those in being all of limestone or soft sandstone, having, therefore, not the weight or strength to give a blow, and in being all painted with black sectors or dots, which shew that they were not funereal imitations of mace-heads As they were evidently fitted on to a stick, they seem likely to be spinning-tops, very probably derived from the familiar spindle That they are not actual spindles is shewn by their being different from the numerous spindles found in the town of the New Race, and by being painted in a manner that no spindles are On making copies in card and spinning them, a flickering effect is produced, and traces of the recently discovered chromatic effect due to alternations of black and white.

F* 2

58 VIII, IX *Hanging stone vases*—These vases were all found in the graves, along with pottery vases The types 1–4 are the origin of a usual form of the decorated vases, which are evidently derived from stone The types 21–35 are also the origin of another type of decorated vases As those decorated vases appear to have been imported, it becomes a curious question how far these stone vases have been imported Some of blotched grey and white marble are not like any known stone in Egypt, but the great majority are distinctly of Egyptian material. A breccia of limestone chips in a red earth base is a favourite stone, and I have found such among the low desert pebbles, the alabaster and brown basalt are characteristic of Egypt, and the other materials, as diorite, syenite, porphyry, slate, hard white limestone, etc, are all known in Egyptian work It seems, then, that these vases were made in Egypt, and were copies of types known to the race in their previous home, as they are seldom Egyptian in design The finer forms are the earlier, as in the New Race pottery, and the clumsy shapes of 47–74 are later in date

X, XI, XII *Standing stone vases*—These are in general later than the hanging types Type S 1 is copied from the latest and most degraded wavy-handled jars, as XXXII, 80, 85 And others, as 11, seem to be even later The forms 17–55 are all linked with Egyptian forms, by which they apparently are influenced, and in pottery the Egyptian influence marks the latest stage of the New Race No 20 is Egyptian, but 21–25 are from New Race graves The types 10–40 are not found at Naqada, but only at Ballas, where they may have been taken from Egyptian tombs At the end of this class, in PL XII, are some unusual varieties of stone vases The fluted, 64, is akin to the fragments of a fluted bowl (of outline 49) carved in red porphyry, found in a tomb at Ballas, and believed to belong to the Old Kingdom The oval types 71–75 are finely worked, and linked to the oval pottery (XXVI, 31) The circular form above in 77 tapers through oval to a wedge-shaped end below, spiral incised lines wind around it Two bird vases, 80, 81, are linked to the pottery birds (XXVII, 69) There are also two frog vases, 82 83, and a lid of a hippopotamus vase, 84

XIII, XIV, XV, XVI *Standing stone vessels, Egyptian*—These all belong to Mr Quibell's excavations at Ballas, which are described by him They appear to date from the Old Kingdom, as they are only found at Ballas in and about the Egyptian cemetery

The flat dishes (141–149) are restored from the 2 cwt of alabaster chips found in the large tomb (867) From this same tomb came the fragment 152, which is restored by comparison with Medum paintings The jar (154) came from a stairway tomb 153 and 156 are from New Race graves 187 occurs in both classes

It is probable therefore that all the forms of these three plates are really Egyptian, but that they were often found by the foreigners in the Egyptian cemetery close by, and were re-used by them

The flat dishes are of slate, limestone, and alabaster, and the cups are of alabaster

The tall alabaster vase (160) and the thicker form (163) are made up from the great heap of chips (867), and may be either foreign or Egyptian 161 was found in an Old Kingdom well, re-used for a foreign burial

The tables were only found in stairway tombs, and in the one burial plainly of IVth–VIth dynasties

The irregular one (170) is of limestone, with small pieces of granite and porphyry inlaid

XVII *Stone vessels, VIIth–IXth dynasties*—Three isolated forms belong to the New Race, a spouted vessel, a conical vase, and a rude cylinder

Stone vessels, Egyptian, XIIth dynasty—190 and 191 are probably of the Old Kingdom The four vases (192–5) are of alabaster, and were found in the same group of graves as the scarab of An, and the duck and monkey shaped pots of PL. XIV, and are therefore of the XIIth dynasty

Stone maces—These are of various hard stones, syenite, porphyry, basalt, hæmatite, hard white limestone, and hard breccia, a very few are of softer limestone and alabaster In general, the finer forms, as 1 12, 14, 17, are in the hardest materials, and are the best worked These are found lying by the skeletons in the graves No 23 is a pointed pick in hard pink limestone, with small holes drilled around it to insert shell rings as ornament No 25 is not pierced, but somewhat hollowed as a cup It has a groove and holes around it, apparently for tying it on to a skin, like the tusks in LXII, LXIV, perhaps these are plugs to secure the leg-holes of water-skins Other holes sunk around it for ornament, have shell rings let into them

59 XVIII, XIX, XX, XXI *Black-topped pottery*—This style is one most characteristic of the New Race, although it gave way in the later period of that people The pottery, and its facing, are identical in material with the red-polished pottery

(XXII–XXIV) The paste is reddish brown, fine, and moderately firm, but not hard, the surface is covered with red hæmatite, or rouge, which is highly burnished, so as to give a polished surface The difference of the black-topped pottery consists in the baking The red-polished was put in the upper part of the kiln, where it was exposed to air all round, and the red oxide of iron was preserved The lower stratum of vases was, however, partly buried in ashes, and so far as the charcoal covered them it deoxidised the iron from red peroxide to black magnetic oxide As the vases were stacked mouth down in the kiln, the black part is around the mouth, or in the inner side of the large bowls The limits of the black part is here indicated by a dotted line across the vases The remarkable mirror-like brilliancy of the black, as if it were black-leaded, is most likely due to the presence of small amounts of carbonyl, a gas which generally results from imperfect combustion, and which has a solvent power on magnetic oxide of iron This acting as a slight solvent allowed the black oxide to form a sub-crystalline face of a regular plane, quite different from the hæmatite face, however burnished that might be The stones of this black being due to smoke, or to the union of two kinds of clay, are quite beside the mark when the nature of it is seen in a large series It is precisely the same question of colour and composition as on Greek vases, where the black may become red wherever a draught of air has impinged upon it, and the black and red may be changed from one to the other any number of times by regulating the air supply

Although the preparation of red-polished and black-topped vases was the same before baking, yet there is some difference in the forms, according to the class that was to be produced The great upright jars B 25, are always black-topped, as also the large lipless jars B 57, 58 On the other hand the forms with almost equal top and base, P 34–42 are nearly all red The red-polished and black-topped are found usually mingled together in the graves, and appear to belong to the same range of time

XXII, XXIII, XXIV *Polished red pottery* —The types of this are generally less robust and more elegant than the black-topped The commonest form of all is the large wide pan, P 23, of which several were generally found in any grave containing pottery The little vases P 81–95 are also very common The burnishing of the red face is elaborate, and seems probably to have been done gradually and repeatedly during the drying, like the Kabyle pottery

at present The burnish lines always run up and down the vase, and the circularity of forms, as well as the profile, were entirely due to eye and skilled hand-work There is no trace of the potter's wheel in all the New Race pottery—unless in a few vases of the latest style, most affected by Egyptian influence The extraordinary variety, and the beauty of many of the forms is entirely the result of skill of hand, and the stone vases shew the same, being all hand-worked without any lathe

XXV, XXVI, XXVII *Fancy forms of pottery* — Beside the great variety of regular forms, there were many irregular designs which have been classed here as fancy forms The bowls with tabs all round (5), the oval bowls, nearly always black inside (11–17), the oval bowls with feet (19–24), the circular bowl on a stem (27), the oval jars, 30–31, the barrel jars (34), which recall a favourite Cypriote model, the strange double jars (40–43), which seem akin to the multiple jars still made in Kabylia, the jars with a long ringed neck (50–53), the jars with spouts (58), the cup with square base (60), and the square bottles (62), the fish-shaped bottles (68), the bird-shaped bottles (69), two of which were bought, from Abydos (?) (69 b, c), the heavy polished black pottery, apparently intended to imitate basalt vases (70–85), and small cups of stony-looking ware carefully smoothed (90–98)

This fancy pottery as a whole is of the early period of the New Race, as shewn both by its style and by the pottery associated with it Of the few types found with pottery of the later period, there are 17 a, 17 b, and 34 b, all found in grave I 36, which was certainly late, also 31 c and 31 d in graves 538 and 3, which were of an intermediate age, and the little cup 96 c also in T 36 All but the last are oval types, and it seems then that the taste for oval forms outlasted most of the other strange fancies shewn in this class of pottery

XXVIII, XXIX *Polished red pottery with white cross-lines* —This class is painted with a white slip clay, upon the base of the polished red pottery exactly like that in PLS XXII–XXIV The exact similarity of the body of the pottery, and of the red facing, in these two classes P and C, shew that they were both made at the same place and under the same conditions The great quantity of the red-polished pottery, and of the black-topped which is the same in material, but baked in the lower part of the kiln, shews that this pottery must be local, and we know that very similar ware with polished hæmatite face is still made at Assiut This decoration then with white cross-lines must be taken as characteristic of the New Race in Egypt But it is also, both in the material of the white slip, and in the patterns, almost identical with Kabyle pottery of the present day The fact that a white wash is hardly ever used, but hatching with cross-lines is the characteristic, points to its having been developed not long before fiom incised pottery The animals shewn are goats, kine, and a giraffe (91–98), shewing a people familiar with the fertile Nile valley and the desert. Some of the forms differ from those used in the ordinary red-polished ware, such types as 61, 63, 64, 65, 67, 68, not being found undecorated Probably they were developed with this sloping-in top to give scope for painting on a visible part The larger forms of red-polished are not found painted, and the use of this decoration is restricted to wide cups in which it can be all seen, or to upright cylindric vessels (as C 54, 75–79) which shew the whole height Some of the designs are probably derived from plaiting or basket-work, such as 34, 36, 46, 52–79 The tubes 85 are probably broken fiom gioups like 81, and the pattern 85 d is copied from a tube like the others, unrolled to shew the whole pattern around it It will be noticed that there is not a single point of Egyptian motives in the whole series, no lotus, no crocodile, no spiral, so that a foreign style, incoming without admixture, must be looked to as the source of this ornament

60 XXX. *Black incised pottery* —This pottery is rare in the graves, and in nearly 3000 graves only 30 examples, including fragments, were found The decoration is of a style quite unknown on any of the locally-made red pottery, and has no affinity with it in design, method, or material We must therefore regard this as imported pottery from some other source Vases of black ware, similar in material, incisions, and patterns, but more regular and very different in foim—having narrow necks—have been found in Egypt associated with remains of the XIIth dynasty (See *Kahun* XXVII, 199–202, *Tell el Yahudiyeh* XIX, 15–17) Such are obviously of the same family with these bowls, but of a more refined period

Very similar black incised bowls, with the filling in of white gypsum, have been found in a prehistoric station at Ciempozuelos, in the province of Madrid, and are there attributed to the earliest metal period (Boletin Real Acad Hist XXV, 436–450, XII plates, of which notice IV, V, XII, for similarity of design)

Other examples of this black incised ware have been found in the prehistoric station at Butmir in Bosnia, judging from photographs, some of these pieces are very closely like those here figured This station is attributed to the earliest metal age Pieces of a similar black pottery, incised with lines which are filled in with white, were found in the oldest city of Hissarlik (See Schuchhardt, Schliemann's Excav, 41) Here again metal is just appearing, but has not yet excluded the general use of stone tools In Egypt also the New Race remains shew the beginning of the use of metal, while stone is far more general, so that in each of these four instances around the Mediterranean this pottery belongs to the same level of culture We shall further consider this fabric in the Historical Conclusions

The motives of this pottery seem to have a basket-work origin, especially in the alternate slant of the rows of lines in 2, 15, 24, the separation between the rows in 12, the over-casting or lashing-down of the edge, to prevent the upper rings slipping off the uprights, shewn in 2 and 20, and the vandyke patterns in 30, 32 No 50 is very different in style to any of the others, the body is thinner, the paste browner, the incisions made much finer, and the pattern different But the basket motive iemains, especially in the base view shewing the square pattern with petals resting on its sides We have already noticed that these bowls were found singly and placed towards the N end of the graves, about 20 inches from the end, only in one case were there three together and placed at the W

XXXI, XXXII *Wavy-handled pottery* —This is a distinct class, separated from others by its form, by the wavy ledge handles, by its material, and by its contents In Nos 1–4 we have the rare and less constant forms, which seem to belong to an earlier stage, before a permanent type had been adopted The clay of these is far softer, flaking, and crumbling but both in these and in the later forms, the paste has frequently small white specks in it, different from the paste of any of the other vases These early forms are very closely like the types of jars of similar paste, with similar ledge handles, found in the earliest part of Tell el Hesy (see Bliss, Mound of many Cities, III, 84, 87) This connection is maintained in the later forms of the wavy ledge handles (as in Bliss III, 86, Tell el Hesy V, 42–47), which are the same as those in the moie developed forms of the New Race Thus both in vase outline, in material, and in this very peculiar type of handle, there is the closest connection between the pre-Jewish pottery of South Palestine and this pottery of the New Race graves

The regular type of this pottery, after passing the rare and transient varieties 1–4, went through a long series of changes, for it is the only pottery which belongs to both the early and late stages of the New Race age At first well formed, as in 14, 19, with even and smooth wavy handles of types A, B, C, D, E, it became next coarser, as in 25, and handles F, G, H, made by barring a ledge of clay with the finger, next it is influenced by the late type of pottery (XL, 40) in an ovoid outline, 31, 33, 35, on which the handle has receded to merely an ornamental outline arching, probably at the same time it passed into a smaller type, 43–47, on which the handles became rude ledges, as in forms J, K, L, M Here begins the second stage, when the handle has lost all meaning and becomes a mere wavy line round the jar, as in 51 (where the division in two sides still survived), and in 53 (where a continuous collar is formed) The jar became more upright, as in 55, 61, and the handle an ornamental arching design, as in R, T, this was followed by painting a cordage pattern on it, as in 62, imitating a network sling in which it was carried Then the arching pattern became reduced in size, and was put on apparently with the finger nail in 71 a, and with a stick in 71 b This passed to a mere dotting around in 80, while in these later forms the cylinder loses all its shoulder and becomes swelled out below In 85 a cord pattern has been evolved from the nicking or dotting, as in forms Y, Z, and this led to a type of alabaster vase with a cord around the neck (X, 1), which has no meaning except as a derivative from the pottery. Probably the latest form is a misshaped jar, 90, without any cord or line on it Thus we have every stage represented, of a long series of degradation of form, a series which wanders so far that three stages of it, 1, 51, and 60, would never be supposed to have any connection with each other were it not for the intermediate links

Side by side with this degradation of form there is a change in the contents of the jars One very large jar of the type 4, with slight rudimentary handles, as on 26, was found half-filled with a mass of vegetable fat (Oxford) The better class of jars, such as 6 to 19, generally contained this same fat, then in later types it has a layer of mud on the top to prevent the scent evaporating, next this layer of mud is increased in thickness, while a layer of fat still underlies it, and scents the whole, lastly the fat is entirely given up, and the cylinder jars, 55–90, have solely mud in them

The nature of this fat is not yet certain It is now porous—owing to the soaking away of the more fusible parts, thus leaving a spongy mass of higher melting-point. It is changed to a brown colour, and is greasy to the touch, easily polishing like wax when rubbed It has a strong odour, which resembles cocoa-nut, but which has been supposed to be due to decomposition A good example, taken from the heart of a large mass, was analysed by Mr J McArthur, of the Belmont Works, Battersea, his report is as follows —

"Our examination shews —

	Per cent
Water, volatile at 212° F	0 43
Mineral matter left on ignition, consisting principally of carbonate and phosphate of lime .	1 08
Dark resinous matter, insoluble in light naphtha, bulk of it soluble in alcohol, solution neutra lising alkalies	9 60
Fatty matter (by difference)	88 89

"The fatty matter consists altogether of fatty acids, it contains no neutral fatty or non-saponifiable matter A direct determination shewed 87 66 S P = 127° F. Saponification equivalent = 254 6 On saponification the S P of the fatty acids was raised to 128½, and the sapon equival to 266 5, these differences no doubt indicating the removal, in the process, of soluble fatty acids of low S P and sapon equiv The fatty matter would appear to consist principally of palmitic and stearic acids"

Dr Thiselton Dyer, at Kew, has also examined the question, including the débris of vegetable fibre in the fat He writes "The histological investigation of the débris has proved wholly inconclusive The large proportion of palmitine points to a palm But what palm? At the date to which you refer, the cocoa-nut (which seems to have been unknown to the Egyptians) had hardly come far away from its original home in the Malay Archipelago to be within reach of the Phœnician traders Still they brought to the West cassia from China, and it is not absolutely impossible that they may have got cocoa-butter The oil-palm is confined to West Africa, and is impossible Shea-butter is not a product of Borneo, but of West Africa, and is in the same category The castor-oil plant was doubtless cultivated in Egypt from the earliest times But would it yield such a fat? The Egyptians are known to have cultivated sesamum for its oil Is that a possible origin for your fat?"

In replying to this, I pointed out that the W coast

of Africa was far from impossible as a source, and more likely than an eastern origin for anything of the New Race I also described how the fat cannot possibly be the remains of any liquid oil, as the very stiff consistency of it at first is shewn by the thick pitchy flow of it when the jar was tilted in the burying, it appears to have been as stiff as butter or yellow palm grease would be at the Egyptian temperature Dr Thiselton Dyer stated further in reply "The oil palm on the W coast could not have been nearer than the Guinea coast It extends inland to the Bahr el Ghazal, but is nowhere found in the Nile Valley If your fat is 'palm oil,' your people must either have got it by sea from the Guinea coast or overland *via* Timbuctoo Both *Elœis Guineensis* (palm oil) and *Butyrospermum Parku* (Shea butter) do not extend beyond 10° N lat The latter was discovered by Mungo Park in Upper Guinea (kingdom of Bambara) It extends to the White Nile"

Here the matter rests It is obvious that we have to do with an imported product, no such material is known in Egypt in other periods It is more likely that it came from the W than the E It was not an oil but a stiff butter when buried, and from the quantity of vegetable fibre it is pretty certainly of vegetable origin The palmitine makes it unlikely to be a cocoa-butter, and the only source known for it would be one of the two vegetable butters, the Shea or the oil palm At present palm oil is packed in jars for transport to distances, as seen by Dr Junker, at about lat 4°, midway between Congo and Nile (Travels, ii, 324, English edit)

XXXIII, XXXIV, XXXV XXXVI *Decorated pottery* —This class is very varied, but it is linked together by uniform material and mode of colouring The designs, as well as the materials, are not found in any pottery of different classes, excepting that the paste is the same as that of the better quality of wavy-handled jars, which contain the foreign fat Another link to this last class is in the wavy-handled jars with decorated pattern (XXXIII 2, 3), which cannot be separated from the rest of such jars or of such patterns This decorated class must be looked on as generally imported pottery, for the spirals, as in XXXV, the boats, the ostriches and the deer, as in XXXIV, are never found on the distinctly local pottery of the white-line on red, the paste and the colouring stand equally apart from all the other pottery, except the wavy-handled And the foreign connection of the latter class gives the more probability

to both of these classes having been brought in as imports from some other people

The origin of the patterns on this pottery is varied When we look at 1, which is an evident imitation of the blotched limestone breccia so often used for stone vases, when we see 62 and 65 again marbled, and in 63 other varieties of marbling, we may well take 67b as an imitation of stone by spirals, which developed as a separate design into larger forms on 67a and 67c But a different motive is in the vertical bands, which imitate the network in which stone vases were carried They are sometimes crossing, as in 4a, 4b, sometimes wide apart and narrow, as at 4d, otherwise closer, as in 8a–8d, 68 and 70, or continuous all round, as 4e, or horizontal around as 7a, b, 17a, b The chequer of basket-work is indicated in 12, 29

These parallel lines were put on with a group of brushes varying in number, two together are seen on 21, three on 23, 24, four on 27, and perhaps six on 20 Thus the small waves and shakes are all parallel, and so imitate the banding of alabaster and other stones This same principle of using a group of brushes in a line is seen on the spiral patterns here, in which the brushes are shifted one line in going round, so as to make a spiral instead of concentric circles This is perhaps the earlier form of concentric circles, which are put on in exactly the same manner, with a line of brushes, on much of the Cypriote pottery The forms of most of this decorated pottery are copied from the stone vases, and the characteristic long tubular, horizontal handles are evidently due to a stone original

Regarding the subjects of these vases, apart from the structural decoration of marbling (modified to spirals), cordage, and basket or mat-work, there are some frequent subjects which throw light on the source of these vases The great boat, or galley, with a long bank of oars (see 40–47) shews that the makers of these vases were not an inland people of the oases, but dwelt on some large river or sea The ostriches (see 47–55) shew that they were familiar with Africa And the frequent lines of pointed hills (see 53 b to 60) which are shewn to be such by instances where the feet of animals rest on them, indicate that a hilly country was familiar, rather than the long level line of the cliffs in the Nile plateau One puzzling object is what looks like a tree (see 36–37) If it be such, it is strange that it never springs from the ground, but appears to be planted in a tub It may possibly be a sacred tree or plant, kept moveable in a shrine As these figure-decorations were found in the Naqada work chiefly, they are fully figured in the account of that (LXVI, LXVII), and discussed in the description of those plates

At Ballas some varieties of decoration occurred which were not found at Naqada, incised on brown pottery (see 74, 76), and which have little or no connection with the style of any other classes The form 76, with a bowl supported on a pierced ring of pottery, seems as if intended for heating liquids by means of charcoal burnt below No 75 a comes also from Ballas, and though it is in materials and decoration like the vases 2 to 20, yet its form differs from any at Naqada It was evidently painted with a group of three brushes

Other styles of painting are shewn on the large bowl 78, with red-painted figures of a crocodile hunt, the large one on the right being pierced with three harpoons , and on the vase 77 with a row of men (inverted), and similar men around the boat, 80 We see here the large paddles that they carry, and the narrow waistcloth, which does not hide the legs, but is tied in a knot in front, with the ends sticking forward These models of boats, 80–81, do not seem to have been copied from wood-built vessels, as the frequent lines of construction run up and down Such a type suggests rather a pliable, tough material, such as reeds, which could be lashed together by lines of rope from stem to stern The form 83 seems to be a model couch, as in grave 1470 one of the clay statuettes was seated on it Another example was found in grave B 120.

Another mode of ornament was by relief figures, which are found on No 87, shewing a scorpion and a lizard , but this was very rare Some strange forms are added here at the end of this class, though they might rather have appeared as fancy pottery The ring-shaped jar 84 has an analogy to Cypriote forms , and in the same grave, B 50, was the closed jar, 85, having only a spout at the side Both of these are of a rather soft brown clay, thick and heavy A double bird vase (90), a plain triple and double vase (91, 91 a), and a spout vase (92), are all of coarse brown ware Two curiously incised vases (93 a, 93 b) are made of smoke-blacked brown pottery , five examples of this style were found A fragment of a very rude figure (95) is explained by a part of another (96), which was bought (site unknown), but which is clearly of the same family.

61 XXXVII, XXXVIII. *Rough-faced pottery* —

This pottery is of a softish brown ware, without any facing or difference between the surface and body It follows the types of some of the finer ware in the bowls and small jugs But the commonest form is that of the large ash-jars 81, 82, of which dozens were sometimes found in a single grave, and which were almost always present with every burial In the later tombs, bordering on the late period, this ware is sometimes washed over with a slight coat of pinkish colouring This is the case mainly with the late ash-jars 83, 85, and some of the bottles 91 b, 91 c, 97, which are the later types of this ware The pointed conical vases, 75–78, were only used for some particular object One only is placed in a grave, and that is in nearly all cases at the S or S W

XXXIX, XL, XLI *Later New Race pottery* — We have often referred to the earlier and later styles of the pottery To the most casual view there is an entire difference between the product of these two periods In the earlier age there is an abundance of the rich, polished-red and black-topped pottery, while the fancy forms, the white lined patterns, the black incised bowls, and the decorated vases, all give variety and interest to the groups In the later age all this has disappeared, a poverty and ugliness of the forms are spread over all, and occasional links to the Egyptian pottery of the Old Kingdom and of the Middle Kingdom are traceable That this group really is later than the other is certified by the one class of pottery which runs through the whole period of the New Race, the wavy-handled jars with their strangely long sequence of variety The cylinder type of these always belongs to this later class of pottery And, to corroborate this, in one large grave the contents of the earlier period had been piled aside on a ledge cut in the side of the pit, when it was re-used for a burial of the later period

The characteristics of this later pottery are its absence of facing, its hardness, and a light salmon tint in much of it The bowls 2–4, 16–20, are generally thin, and burnished in lines in the inside , other forms of the bowls are marked by a turned-down brim in many (6–10, 25), or an internal ridge (26). The ash-jars became far longer (30, 31), then developed a deep collar (33) which ran lower until it formed a ring at the shoulder (34), which at the very basest style of all came to a fatuously ugly form (35) These are of coarse brown, like the earlier ash-jars Another large jar which came much into use, apparently in place of the large black-topped jars, is made of the

G*

hard pinkish ware, of an ovoid form varying in fatness (36–46) A very characteristic late type is the jar with a strainer in the mouth of it (50, 51), shewn in section 50 This is always of coarse brown pottery, and often accompanies the ring stands, 82–88 The bottles, 60–66, are frequent in late graves, the form 64 is of hard thin burnished pottery, and often accompanies the thin burnished bowls of type 17

Some forms are evidently copied from Egyptian, or perhaps Egyptian pottery taken from older tombs The rough hand-made jar 72 is probably Egyptian, as no New Race potter would be likely to form so rude a shape Moreover, nearly all of these examples were found at Ballas, adjoining the cemetery of the Old Kingdom This, as well as 74 and 76, are characteristic forms of the Medum pottery of the IVth dynasty The bowls 78 a–c are like those of the IVth dynasty, somewhat modified The ring-stands are copied from Egyptian forms, which are pierced with the triangular holes in the earliest period The latter vases, 92–96, are wheel-made— the only instance of the use of a wheel among the New Race, and evidently the most under Egyptian influence Thus, in general we see that this late style of the New Race shews itself cut off from the foreign objects—black bowls and decorated ware— which had been largely imported before, it shews great deterioration in the local pottery, and a decided influence of Egyptian models belonging to the Old Kingdom We may view it then as the product of the New Race settlers when declining in power, losing connection with the rest of their race, and coming into peaceful contact with the native Egyptians, who had at first been all expelled from the district by the rush of invasion

XLII Remaining pieces of New Race pottery from Mr Quibell's work at Ballas 26 is a fragment of a stone vase with the handle carved as a human head 27 combines the plain horizontal handle with the wavy ledge The bowl 32 and head-rest 36 are Egyptian, and come from stairway tombs

XLIII *Carvings from Ballas*—The ivory spoon (1) with handle representing an arm with an elaborate bracelet, was explained by another find, a child on whose arm were nine or ten ivory rings The lime-stone disc (2) with a coiled serpent in relief, was found on the mouth of a pot A similar object in green glaze, and larger, is in the Ghizeh Museum The small limestone stele of Set and Hathor was found amid the man group of stairway tombs, buried

a few inches only below the surface The limestone block (Δ) with the cartouches of Tahuti, is already described (sect 12)

62 PL. XLIV *Egyptian pottery*—In tombs of the Old Kingdom at Ballas burials were found in large bowls (1), and in square pottery cists or coffins, made in imitation of woodwork Mr Quibell states that the large circular pots (1) were found lying mouth up with contracted burials inside, and also were inverted over burials They occurred in the group of staircase tombs, and are similar to some pots found by the Gizeh hotel These also are probably of the IVth–VIth dynasties and are not known to be connected with the New Race

2 and 3 are specimens of the cists of rough red ware which were found both in the groups of Egyptian tombs, and in the later New Race burials. In the latter cases they had probably been re-used The model of a hut and the three tables of offerings (?) are all of the XIIth dynasty The three are of a rough red ware, the hut is of strawish yellow 5 and 6 are from the intrusive burials of the N town 4 and 7 are from the XIIth dynasty cemetery at the end of the embankment In the tombs of the XIIth dynasty are often found pottery trays of offerings (4–7) In the simplest form these are just a tray with a bull's head, a haunch, and some loaves of bread, while some semblance of a tank or trench supplied the idea of water Such offerings are apparently a survival of the orthodox offerings of the New Race, as in the finest of their graves a haunch and head of an ox are generally found The region of these pottery trays of offerings is closely that occupied by the New Race, about the Thebaid, especially at Gebelen and Ballas. Hence it seems that we have here a survival of New Race ideas into Egyptian times of the Middle Kingdom, which implies a blending of the people These trays developed into soul-houses, as in No 4 The tray became a courtyard, entered by a doorway, fur-nished with a tank in the middle, offerings of a bull's head and haunch, a gazelle, ducks, loaves, radishes, onions, and other food, while a stand for the water-jars occupied one side, a row of store-rooms stood at the end, and a flight of stairs led to the roof, on which was a sleeping-chamber furnished with a bedstead and table In this we may see the influence of the sets of wooden figures of servants and pro-visions which were made in the Old Kingdom

XLV, XLVI *Egyptian pottery*—This pottery is entirely from Ballas, though a few examples of the drop-shaped jars (34) were also found in the XIIth dynasty graves at Kom Belal. The fine bowls (1 a and b) are of the Old Kingdom type already referred to above as being known from Medum The small vase (2) is probably also of this early period

The two large pots (5 and 7) are probably of the XIIth dynasty, the first shape occurring at Thebes with the bowls with splashes of white paint, which are of that period They were found in a chamber opening from a tomb-shaft otherwise empty 8, 9, and 10 are ring-stands for vases (period undetermined) The fragments (14, 15) the strange inverted shape, the ape, and the duck-pot (20, 21, 22) come from the same tombs as the model hut in Pl. XLIV, and must be attributed to the XIIth dynasty The duck-shape is similar to some pots of the foreigners, though it is made in the hard drab-yellow Egyptian ware, and the others are of the smooth red pottery characteristic of the foreign work

The bowls (25) and the saucers (26-29) in drab-yellow ware, and in a softer red clay, come from the intrusive burials of the N town

The two last bowls are of uncertain period, as they come from re-used tombs

PL XLVI contains in the first three rows of pots (32-49) the types of vase found in the intrusive XIIth dynasty burials of the N town, while the last two (52-71) are from two XVIIIth dynasty burials in the same place. Of these last, 60 is of a smooth, and 63 of a rough-faced, red ware, the bowls (70 and 71) are also red, the rest are yellow and slightly rough

These are evidently of a different period to the drop-shaped vases, in the upper part of the plate, and they are attributed to the XVIIIth dynasty on the ground of their resemblance to the pottery of that period (see *Kahun*, PL. XX)

63 XLVII, XLVIII, XLIX, L *Slate palettes* — Strange forms of slate have been found in Egypt for some years past, but no account of their source was known, and their age and purpose were quite uncertain The cemeteries of the New Race have explained the whole subject, the slates were placed in the graves, and their purpose was for grinding malachite, and occasionally hæmatite, probably for face-paint That such forms should be used for palettes may seem almost beyond belief, but the evidence of the patches of malachite on them, and the worn hollows for grinding, are found on every class The monstrous rhombs (93-99) have been quoted as

impossible for merely grinding a little patch of face-paint, and have been suggested for shields But the inexorable evidence is plain on these as on any other forms, the patches of malachite are on them, and on some the deeply hollowed grinding-places (94-97, 99) stained with hæmatite and malachite, prove that the colour was not merely casual or ornamental, but had been ground on them for years during the life of the owner They run through all the periods of the New Race burials, both early, middle and late The general division is that the well-formed animal figures and the rhombs are of the earlier age, while the worst of the animal figures, 7, 53, 59, 60, 70, 82, 83, 86, and the squares, are of the later age, with late pottery and cylinder jars Associated with the slates are continually found selected yellow flint pebbles for using as mullers in grinding the colour The forms are very varied Of quadrupeds there are the ibex or the moufflon (1), indistinct species of deer (9-4), elephant (5-8), and turtle (9-19) Birds are common (20-27), and a curious double-bird type occurs in several forms (28-33) Fish are very common (36-61) The double-bird is made in an anchor form, with a long handle above (62-68), and also in a long form (69-92), in which the heads become lessened until, in 91 and 92, the outline is almost rhombic This passes into the rhombs (93-99) The squares are sometimes plain (100, 102), but more often scored around the edge with lines (101, 103-108) And many rough unshaped pieces are found (109-111) The degradation of many of the types is remarkable, especially the tortoise, where it acquires deers' heads for feet (11, 12) or loses almost all trace of feet (17, 18), the double-bird which becomes the shape of the *pelta* (32, 33), or a rhomb (92), and the fish, which become mere ovals (59-61)

The total numbers of the various classes (including rude ones and fragments) are ibex or moufflon, 1, deer, 3, elephant, 4, turtle, 13, bird, 11, double-birds, 60, fishes, 130, rhombs, 99, squares, 28, rough, 37 At Ballas the types belonged to the later styles, agreeing with most of that cemetery being of late New Race. There were 12 animals and tortoises, 39 fish, 14 double-birds, and 31 rhombs and squares

64 LI, LII, LIII, LIV, LV, LVI, LVII *Marks on pottery* —Many of the jars had marks incised upon them with a sharp point, probably of flint These marks have been fully recorded here, even to the rudest and slightest, because it is impossible to know what may prove of importance when compared

and studied   Most of them have been drawn direct from the pottery, but some (that were not brought away) are copied from sketches made at the time of finding, and have the number of the tomb (at the bottom right hand) underlined, to indicate that they are not exact facsimiles.   So far as possible these copies have all been placed upright, as on a jar mouth up   In some cases these marks appear to have been property marks, as where several jars in one tomb bear the same   They are usually upon the black-topped jars, less commonly on the red polished and ash-jars, only once on black incised (XXX, 20), twice (same sign ?) on wavy-handled pottery (XXII, 41, 55), once on a rough-faced pot (XXXVIII, 73), and once on a late jar (XL, 46), but never on white-line or decorated pottery

The subjects of the marks vary greatly   Human figures are rare, there being only three (1, 2, 7), the lion is also rare (6, 7, and perhaps 8), the hippopotamus occurs twice (9, 10), the elephant thrice (11, 12, 13), the ox is rarer (14, 15), but 14 is so very different in style to all the other figures, and so far superior that it should perhaps be reckoned Egyptian in origin, the giraffe may be attempted in 18, 19, 434, various kinds of deer are indicated (16, 17, 18, 20-24, 27), also the dog (25, 26 ?), agreeing with dogs' skulls being found in the cemetery   Some birds are shewn (28-32, 438 ?), crocodiles (33, 34), a scorpion (36), and lizards (35, 37).   The general result from this is that the people knew the Nile, by the hippopotamus and crocodile, that they also knew the desert well, by the lion, giraffe, elephant, and deer, that they were far more a hunting than a pastoral people, there being but one or two domesticated animals to twenty wild ones, and that their region was African rather than Asiatic.

The palm is the only tree represented (39–51), grasses or herbs perhaps being intended in other cases (52–69)   Two boats are shewn, somewhat like those figured on the decorated pottery, having oars, a tying-up rope, and a cabin, yet so far different in detail and style that we cannot suppose the painting and the incising to be done by the same people   It may be that these are attempts at copying the painting on the decorated vases   Two objects in relief on the pottery (74, 75) are known in Egyptian hieroglyphics, and might be copied thence, but on the other hand both of them may be African in origin, and be brought in again by the New Race, after having been introduced at an earlier date   An inexplicable sort of object is shewn in different forms

(77, 77 a), which can hardly be the fishing-nets, with long dragging ropes, which are often found (78–93, and perhaps others)   Of the geometrical marks, few are striking, or like any definite alphabetic series, nor are any found in sequence, to suggest that constant ideas were attached to them   The thunderbolt sign (117, 119–122) is one of the most recurring   The cross with looped ends (151) is remarkable   The pentagram (221) is known on pottery of the XIIth dynasty at Kahun   The crescent is one of the commonest marks, sometimes double (342, 343, 353, 354), but generally single, and turned with the curve upward (344–401).

65 LVIII   *Beads, etc*—Necklaces of beads were often found in the graves, but varied as they are, and great as is the variety of Egyptian beads, yet there are scarcely any of these which could be mistaken for Egyptian products   The materials used by the New Race for beads are gold, silver, hæmatite, carnelian translucent, carnelian opaque, agate, quartz crystal, amethyst, garnet, lazuli, slate, clay, red-brown steatite, transparent green serpentine, turquoise, white calcite, shell, blue glazed stone, green glazed stone, and blue-green glazed pottery   Some of these materials, the quartz crystal glazed, slate, clay, red-brown steatite, and green serpentine, were rarely, if ever, used by the Egyptians

The forms of the beads were also unlike the Egyptian types   Rough pebbles, pierced, were used, and especially cylindrical carnelian beads, ground by sliding in a groove on a block of emery   Several blocks of emery grooved for this purpose were found in the graves   This cylindrical form was not only for the long beads, but even short ring-like beads had a truly cylindrical polished edge, evidently made by tying a group tightly together and sliding them in the groove as one piece   Others were loosely connected, and so locked in the process of polishing, thus making a conical slope toward either face, and a ridge around the middle   This double-coned bead was looked on as a type to be copied, and the very small glazed stone beads were made of this form by hand   Another form, which might be taken for very modern work, is the facetted bead, such as the second in group 836   Imitative forms were frequent, such as flies (723, etc), bull's head (1289), claws (1st in Q 23), spear-head (8th in Q 23), and beetles (top of plate).

The most usual glazed beads are small ones of stone, of the flat disc and the double-coned form, these were far commoner than glazed pottery beads, but some of the latter are found in very small quantities in late graves, and of types verging on those of the XIIth dynasty. The use of glaze upon quartz crystal is another peculiarity of the New Race beads, and sometimes large pieces were glazed, as the hawk (LX, 18). A curious bead is made of what appears to be a base gold, hammered out as a very thin tube and then burnished in at the ends over a core of soft limestone or plaster. The garnet beads are generally rough chipped.

The scarabs and beads (Q 375, Q 188, Q 354), are all of the XIIth dynasty, from Ballas, of these Mr. Quibell remarks that the beetle-beads are not derived from the scarab, but from the long iridescent beetle whose wing-cases are sold in Egypt as ornaments. Rough pebbles of carnelian and agate were frequently pierced and strung, a crystal is seen in the top string.

A lion-head bead was found in carnelian. Small hippopotamus head beads in beryl occurred in Egyptian tombs (XIIth dynasty).

The necklace (Q 23) contains several characteristic forms, of alabaster the animal's tooth, of serpentine are the fly, spear-head, crescent, and the peculiar shape seen in the necklace below (Q 709, 9), and also in the slates and ivories. The spear is interesting as proving a shape used by the New Race.

The scarab (Z 10) comes from one of the intrusive burials of the N town, the next two are also from Egyptian tombs of the same period, viz, the group from which the duck-shaped pot, the model of a house, etc, were derived.

The necklace (Q 709) is of the New Race. The well-modelled frog (2), the face (5), and the long spike bead (13), are of serpentine, the long cylinder (1) of steatitic limestone, the tooth (8), the disc and globe beads (4 and 6), and the double pierced beads (7 and 9), of shell.

The last necklace (Q 354) is attributed to the XIIth dynasty, and on it the argument for dating the intrusive burials partly rests. Three examples were found of emery blocks, each with a smooth, deep groove produced by polishing the long cylindrical carnelian beads.

We may here note other instances of metals and minerals. A thin ring of gold wire (grave 723), a few small gold beads (1547, 667, 822), a thin silver ring (1770), hollow silver beads and jar cap (1257), bit of an armlet of white alloy, and lump of copper (1635), cupreous slate (484) and rock (1562), specular iron (1900, 1430); micaceous hæmatite (259), lump hæmatite (658), blende (1734), pyrites nodules

(1401, 1485), emery blocks for polishing beads, garnet pebbles (1271), malachite and galena paint (common), obsidian flakes (1260), serrated and pierced (743), mica (399), white felspar pebbles (211, 1471, 1677), blue glass pendant (1759), calcite ball (691), alabaster armlet (1899). The hawk (LX, 18) is of quartz covered with blue glaze. The eye sockets are sunk for inlaying, and there is a hole below by which the bird could be mounted, as on a staff. The long shape is characteristic of the foreigners' work, and is quite different to the Egyptian type.

Besides this, there was found in the N town a piece of glazed quartz, one inch long, semi-circular in one section, oblong in the other, perhaps the base of a figure, and as beads of glazed quartz were frequently found in the tombs, it is probable that most of the glazed quartz beads found hitherto may be attributed to the same people.

66. LIX. *Human figures.*—The few and rude examples of human figures are of the greatest value as supplementing our information from the actual skulls and skeletons. We have noted before, in describing Pl. VI, the presence of a steatopygous type, like the modern Bushmen, in this plate (LIX) we have the instances of a slender and higher type, with perhaps some trace of the steatopygous shewn in the massive breadth of the hips, which recall the Arab description of beauty, "a slender waist and heavy hips." The male heads shew in every case a long pointed beard, and from the majority of them we may conclude a high forehead, without much thickness of hair on the head, as the ears are so prominent. This type is much like the Libyan and Amorite figures on the monuments, and has certainly no negro character. The slate figures (2) are found two (in 1757) or three (in T 4) together, as described in the details of grave T 4, and the bone figures two or three together (in 276, 1329, T 24). The ivory figures with a vase on the head (7) were found in a row, as described under grave 271. The large female figure in hard white clay painted with black (6) is valuable as shewing the figures and decoration which was tatued or painted on the body. The animal figures (of goats?) are exactly like those on the white-lined pottery (XXIX 91–95) both in style, in form, and in cross-hatching, and as that class of pottery we concluded to belong to local manufacture, this figure should represent the New Race type. The zigzag ornament also is like that on the pottery (XXVIII, 34, XXIX, 77), and the branch like the pottery (XXVIII 48, XXIX, 85 d). This system of

tatuing in rectangular patches of line patterns is the same as that shewn on the westerns in the tomb of Sety I It is noticeable that none of these figures, however, shew any side-lock of hair, nor was any such plaited side-lock found among the hair in the graves They cannot then be identified with the Libyan tribes who wore the hair plaited on one side The Lebu (M Habu) and Tamahu (Sety I) had a plaited lock hanging before the ear on one side , the Tahennu, a loose lock before the ear (M Habu, etc), and the Mashuash (M Habu), a loose lock behind the ear, not prominent, and perhaps on both sides The figure 11 is of a reed coated with a brown vegetable paste, and painted red on the parts that are here black

67 LX *Animal figures*—Few animal figures were found at Naqada A group of four animals was found together the lion (12), the hippopotamus? (13), a hawk of wood coated with lead fastened with copper pins (14), the wood of which has decayed , and the limestone hawk A game was found with four lions (16) and a hare (17) And two hawks came, one from Ballas (18), made of quartz covered with blue glaze , the other (20) from the S town at Nubt Another bird is from a grave, and is made of green glaze on a sand body In connection with this glazing on quartz another piece of quartz an inch long, of semicircular section, was found at Ballas Beside these some figures were bought at Thebes—probably all found at Gebelen—which belong to this same style The man (21), hippopotami (22), and lions (23–26) A bird like (20) is in the British Museum Four more such figures were found at Koptos three lions and a bird, of large size in limestone (See "Koptos," p 7) And also from Gebelen are figures of lions and birds in hard stone, which I had watched for two years in the hands of a Luxor dealer at impossible prices, and which were at last bought by the Rev Randolph Berens This completes, so far as I at present know, the visible sculptures of the New Race The best of those we found are at Oxford, with the rest of the type collection of this people , and it is much to be hoped that other important specimens may be acquired there, so as to make the Ashmolean Museum the centre for the remains of this character

68 LXI, LXII, LXIII, LXIV *Ivory carvings.*—Ivory and bone was the favourite material of the New Race for small objects, and a great variety was obtained from the graves The spoons are always of the type with the handle below the bowl, and not

above it, as in most mediæval spoons The carving of the lion chasing a dog (2) is well executed, the best indeed of any animal figures by this people The dog has a rope collar fastened by a wooden toggle at the back This was found by a woman digging for salt at Ballas The animals on No 3 are indistinct, apparently pachyderms ; as the elephant is frequent among the marks on pottery and slates, while the pig is unknown, it seems more likely that these ivory figures are intended for elephants, although no tusks are shewn The oval bowls unaffected by the handle (8, 9) look as if directly copied from some compound spoon made with a shell or nut In (5) the bowl is modified to the handle So also in (6), where the bowl is of slate, with a copper wire fastened into it, on which are threaded beads of white limestone and black slate alternately Another spoon of the type of No 8 was found, about half that size, in silver, with a twisted handle , unhappily it vanished quite unaccountably while the things were laid out to be drawn in England

The little vases in ivory (7, 10, 11 105) appear to be copied from the types of stone vases, and are of course entirely worked by hand without a lathe. The strange object (4) is inexplicable , it does not appear to be an ornament, nor has any use been suggested for it

Bone and horn harpoons (12–16) are frequent, several being found in one grave They are of both types, with fangs on one or on both sides The small arrow-form (14) is stained and roughened in bands across it This use of harpoons can hardly be dissociated from the common appearance of harpoons in early Egyptian scenes

The small tags of ivory, bone, horn, or alabaster (1, 19, 20, 28, 29, 31, 32, 39, 45, 46, 95, 96, 97), are very frequent in graves, and often have leather attachments to the pierced part With them we must associate the conical knobs of clay, covered with leather, and secured to some 'arge leather object at the base also similar cones of stone which are generally found two or more together with leather fastenings, and one of which, reduced to a round form, is shewn PL XVII, 25 The constant presence of leather bindings with this class suggests that they have been plugs to close natural or accidental holes in water-skins Any people entering Egypt across the side deserts, as the New Race did, must have developed the use of water-skins to a great extent The rudest and most direct way of stopping a hole in a skin, due to either a limb or a perforation, would be to stick a small horn or tusk through it and bind it round , or to put a stone into the inside and tie the skin round behind the stone   The tusks (19, 29, 39, 95) shew the earliest stage, and the flat tags (1, 31, 45, 46, 96) a later form, on which the spiral ornament cut around the tusks (as 39) is imitated by a zigzag (as 46)   This is the plug development , and the stopping by a stone tied round in the skin is the origin of the cones of clay or stone   Thus these very rude patchings of the primitive water-skin became the source of ornamental fittings and decorations , and the projecting tags of polished ivory or stone, incised in patterns and coloured, must have been a prominent feature of the skins.

A class of ornaments formed of shell (both nacreous and porcellanous), thin copper, and grey marble, is shewn in 21, 22, 23   These objects are very light, and all pierced for hanging   They are found near the head, and in one clear case I saw the piece close in front of the forehead   On actual trial the curvature of such pieces fits the forehead very closely, and one can hardly doubt that they were forehead ornaments, like the gold tube worn by women of Middle Egypt and Cairo at present   The hook at the bottom of No 21 might seem against this explanation , but it falls in to the bridge of the nose easily when worn, and as the New Race had prominent foreheads and deep-cut features, such a hook would not be at all in the way   It would then be intended to support some other ornament on the face , or if a face veil was worn it would be exactly the thing to carry that

Some things here are puzzling   The two ivory sticks with holes sunk in the ends (17, 18) are like another such in alabaster , the plate of ivory with holes drilled in lines, and a zigzag pattern on the back (24), has no apparent use , nor has the T-shaped ivory with a cleft along the top and a socket below

The pieces with crescents or horns at the top, 37, 38, 40, 41, 42, 43, 89, are all probably symbolical   They are cut in ivory or slate, and resemble the human figures in slate (LIX, 2, 4) and in bone (LIX 8-10)   They have evidently been tied to something by the lower end , but their use or meaning we cannot guess

The long tusks of ivory (34, 35, 81) we have already noticed as being found in pairs together, one solid and one hollow   They were associated (in the grave T 4) with three of the slate mannikins (LIX, 2) , and the whole group appear as if intended to be manipulated, as the slate figures are not fitted

to stand or to hang   It is at least possible that they belonged to the outfit of a medicine-man, to perform enchantments , and the tusks remind one that the negroes of the Gold Coast believe that the white man can enchant their souls into a tusk of ivory, and carry them away, to be liberated in another country and made to work   It may be that the solid and hollow tusks were for some process of soul-catching of the sick or dying

Hair-pins are very common   Some were ornamented with lines (as 25, 26, 27), others plain (as 36), and others with figures of birds or animals (47, 48, 49, 50, 61, 75, 76, 77, 82, 83, 84, 87).   The little figures of birds (as 50) are among the best carvings   The full and long hair indicated by these large pins, and found in the graves, required much combing, and bone combs are the commonest objects of all   These were not mainly intended for combing out the hair, as the teeth have no depth through, and would be very weak for straightening a tangle of hair , but they were rather for securing the dressed hair, when coiled up on the head   The prevalent animal figures upon them also shew this, as they were for ornament to stand up above the head when the comb was thrust through the hair   We see the giraffe (60, 62), deer (59, 63, 66), and many kinds of birds (64–69, 72, 85), and double birds (86, 58, 56, 57 ?), reminding us of the slate palettes   The shorter combs, 51, 52, 53, 54, must have been for scratching or combing over the skin of the head , and one of these, 53, is neatly combined with a hair-pin, so as to have it always handy   Such an ornamental use of combs is almost unknown among Egyptians , in the XVIIIth dynasty a few combs have a horse or other animal on the back, but merely as an ornamental handle, and not to stand up as a fixed ornament on the head , nor is any such comb-ornament shewn in any statues or scenes of toilet

The rings of ivory are sometimes plain or with a knob (as 30), and in one case with two rampant lions at the sides (78) , and, beside rings, large numbers of bangles of ivory, shell and horn were found , they are not illustrated here, as they are perfectly plain   They were worn in rows on the forearm, a dozen or more together   One carving of an arm as a spoon-handle (XLIII, 1) shews them thus worn, and they are found on the skeletons   It is noticeable that the carving of a woman overthrown by a reindeer (L'Anthropologie VI, 2, PL. V), belonging to the steatopygous race of France in the palæolithic age, has the same system of numerous bangles on the forearm

The model tusks (91–93) appear to have been worn as ornaments The point (98) may have come from an arrow

We now turn to some other materials in this plate, LXIV The piece of dark blue glass (94) is so far unique in these graves It was in an alabaster vase placed between the arms of the skeleton The rest of the vases and objects were all of a good period of the New Race, red polished, black-topped, an imitation-marbling jar (XXXV, 63 c), and a spout-jar (XXXVI, 92) The grave appeared in good order and undisturbed, although the skull is missing The glass must therefore be placed as early as about the VIIth dynasty It appears to be Egyptian in origin , it is a head of Hathor badly impressed in a mould, with traces of a previous impress of the crown across the face That such glass was made anywhere before the XVIIIth dynasty was not before suspected Another strange object is a plummet of emery (99), it has been stained green with copper lying on it, and was found in the same grave of a child with the ivory object 4, and three ivory hair-pins The bands of thin sheet copper (not bronze, as it is still quite soft and flexible), ornamented with zigzag lines of punch-dots (100, 101), were found rolled up, and lying in front of the knees At the bottom are two examples of painted leather , 103 is part of a long belt, with patterns of branches, etc., done in black on the brown , 104 is whitened on the surface, with zigzag lines in black enclosing a yellow band Another piece with the same colouring and style (LXVII, 18) appears to perhaps imitate a row of skins of a small animal sewn together with the tail of one overlapping the body of the other These leathers are difficult to deal with, as they have been crumpled up, and are now too much rotted to unfold, and if wetted they turn gluey The only way is to break them into pieces at the folds, and then fasten down the bits in order on a card

69 LXV *Implements of copper, etc*—A lid for a porphyry jar, made of thin sheet-silver (2), and a few hollow silver beads (1), are almost the only traces of silver found Copper was well known, though not abundant Only one weapon was found —the dagger No 3 As the form of this might be supposed to belong to a later age, it should be observed that the skeleton was entire, and the grave undisturbed, while the dagger lay in place on the hip, which it had stained full green , any mixture of age is therefore out of the question The ash-jars were of the earliest type (XXXVIII, 81), black and red pottery appears,

and the slate is a fairly good bird form (XLVII, 26) So unless we are prepared to reject the whole evidence of this people being before the XIIth dynasty, we must accept the date of this dagger at before 3000 B C

The adzes (5, 6) are much like the Egyptian form, and destitute of any means of attachment Only five of these were found in the three thousand graves Two copper harpoons (7, 8) shew that the forms of the bone weapons were copied in metal Several small chisels (9–12, 14) shew—like the adzes—that wood-working was important A curved pick (13) and a pointed chisel (14) are the only examples of such known The gold foil pendant (16) covered with punch dots was found at Ballas, as well as the fish-hook (17) and copper binding (18) Several pointed pricks of copper, with a ring at the upper end to hang them by (15, 19) were found in the town and graves It seems that they were probably for thorn extractors, like the bronze pricks of the XVIIIth dynasty, and the iron sets of pick, knife, and tweezers of Coptic times. Needles of copper were made of very small sizes (20, 21), and a sort of bodkin was found with them, evidently of pure copper, as it is quite flexible A small knife (23) is the only instance of such a form in these graves, found in position in a grave of fairly early period

70 LXVI, LXVII *Paintings on pottery*—These copies were traced directly from the vases on tracing-paper, and then reduced by photolithography, so that the forms and details can be relied on No 1 is from the side of a model boat, shewing that these people were accustomed to rowing with many oars on each side The boats or galleys which are shewn on so many of these paintings (2–14) are of one type, with very slight variations , there is a high rise fore and aft , a bough is placed at the stem to shade the look-out man , two cabins stand amidships , an ensign on a tall pole stands either between the cabins or—more generally—at the hinder cabin , and in the most complete examples there is a tying-up rope in front (10, 13, 14), and three large steering-oars at the stern (14) These last effectually shew that this object is a boat, and not any sort of palisade or enclosure, as might be supposed Whether it be a sea or a river boat is important Nile boats are always mainly worked by a sail, and sails were used from the IVth dynasty onward in a well-developed form On the other hand, rowing-galleys have characterized the Mediterranean , the most reliable power of propulsion on that sea has always been

rowing, and the galleys of the sea-fight under Ramessu III, at Salamis, at Actium, of the Venetian Republic, of the Algerian corsairs, of the French navy, shew that oars were generally more important than sails Hence we should rather refer these galleys to the Mediterranean than to the Nile We have already noticed how the materials and methods of this decorated pottery are wholly different from those of the white-line on red, which was made in the Nile Valley, and that we must rather regard this pottery as imported into Egypt from elsewhere

The ensigns on the boats are of interest. The most telling is the elephant (on 14), which shews that it is to the African coast, and perhaps to the Mediterranean rather than the Red Sea, that we should look The two pair of horns appear on 7, 11, 12 , the branch on 9 and 10 , the bow and arrow (?) on 5 and 9 , the four scorpions (?) on 6 and 10 , the Z-shaped bolt on 3 7, 8, 11, 12 , the thunderbolt sign on 6 and 8 , and the hill signs, of two hills on 2, 4 and 5, of three on 8, 12, 13, of four on 10, and of five on 13   These hill signs indicate the purpose of these ensigns , they were local rather than personal, no individual would be likely to take a number of hills as his mark, but settlements would be very probably known as the " two-hill " or " five-hill " harbour That ensigns were used in the Mediterranean trade is shewn by Strabo's tale of a ship sign found in the Red Sea, and set up in the market-place at Alexandria for identification, where it was recognised by a Gades sailor The sign of a horse appears to have been general for Gades, though the special example of it was recognised as belonging to a known ship These ensigns, then, were like the letters on the sails of our fishing-boats, such as PZ for Penzance

Beside the galleys there are apparently trees or bushes, which are usually below the galleys, that is, in the foreground of the view Some of these trees have one or two branches rising from the middle, and such trees always have a base separate from the ground, as if they were in a box or tub A strange object, which looks almost like a mast and sail, is placed below the boats in 6 and 9, and appears again in 8 and 10   In 6 9, and 10, it has huts or cabins on either side Rows of hills are shewn as a line of triangles on 13, 14, 16, 17 , that such are hills is apparent in the last instance, where the feet of the man and animals rest upon them, like the animals on the hills of the Min statues at Koptos That these hills should be shewn both above and below the boats, as well as trees and animals, does not detract from the probability of these paintings having the idea of views with successive distances, for such galleys would be observed most usually when entering or leaving a haven or creek, where they would be seen with scenery both in front of and behind them

Men are drawn wearing a short waist-cloth tied in a knot in front—1, 4, 7, 17 , while women are distinguished by the slender waist and heavy hips on 8 and 14   The latter example, with the hands raised above the head—which also occurs on a similar vase in the Ghizeh Museum—is like the attitude of the tatued figure shewn here (LIX, 6)   The animals are two varieties of deer, one with curved horns (2 15, 16) the other with spiral horns (11, 17), and the ostrich, which is the commonest of all, and is shewn in troops.

To prevent mistakes, it should be noted that the square patches of parallel or crossed lines between the boats on many of these jars is the pattern on the projecting handle, and has probably no connection with the scenes

The drawing 18 is the pattern on a leathern belt, covered with a white ground, and outlined in black It may be imitated from a row of skins of some small animal

71 LXVIII, LXXVI *Palæolithic flints High level*—These flints were all picked up by myself when walking on the desert The Nile Valley is cut down a depth of 1400 feet through a limestone plateau, the edges of which are deeply channelled with drainage valleys In an earlier age the Nile had filled the valley to a much higher level than at present, and rolled down thick beds of gravel These in turn have been cut through, leaving edges of gravel beds along the borders of the present river mud On the top of the 1400-foot plateau are great numbers of worked flints of palæolithic type, such as Nos 2, 3, 4, 6 At a lower point on a spur of the hill at about 800-foot level, lay No 1 While down on the shore gravel, I found No 5 lying loose and possibly washed down from above anciently, or detached from the gravel , it had certainly not been exposed to the same æonic staining of dark brown or black which all the flints exposed on the desert have acquired How long an exposure is needful to make such a coloration is indicated by the flints of the New Race type that are exposed on the surface, where they have not gained more than a faint yellow-brown tint in five thousand years the black-brown of the palæolithic flints is at least ten or twenty times as dark That the high plateau was the home of man in palæolithic

H*

times is shewn by the worked flints lying scattered around the centres where they were actually worked The Nile being far higher then, left no mud flats, as at present, for habitation , and the rainfall—as shewn by the valley erosion and waterfalls—must have caused an abundant vegetation on the plateau, where man would live and hunt his game

72 LXIX, LXXVI *Flints from high Nile gravel* —The fringe of gravel beds between the foot of the cliffs and the present inundation-bed of the river, form a low plateau with an edge about 30 feet high, scored up with dry water-channels which are ploughed by the rare storm-rains rushing from the cliffs behind These gravels are interstratified with marls and Nile mud-beds, shewing that they belong to the time when the Nile might be more sluggish owing to occasional drier periods or changes of its course In these hard, cemented gravel-beds, at depths of 3 to 8 feet from their present top surface, I found the flints shewn in this plate Some have the true palæolithic principle of edge-working around a natural oval (as 11, 12, 19), while others shew the long parallel flaking (16, 17, 20), which is commoner in neolithic work, though by no means absent in older times It is quite certain then that these shore gravels of the old High Nile are of human period

73 LXX. *Ballas Desert flints* —These flints were found by Mr Quibell Nos 21, 22 lay together on a spur of the cliffs, with deep ravines on either side, at about 900 feet level above the plain This is just the same nature of site as that where I found LXVIII, 1 Along with Nos 21, 22 were some large rounded flints, all stained dark brown , it is from such that these worked flints have been formed, and the chips of working were scattered around The flints Nos 23, 24 were found on the gravel plateau at the foot of the cliffs, about 30 feet above the present inundation, and a few hundred yards from the plain

74 LXXI *Flints from settlements of the New Race* —Beside the graves, I cleared a small town ("South Town," PL LXXXV), and examined some detached settlements of the same people on the desert edge At first sight so different are the flints of these settlements from those found in the graves, that it would seem that they could not be of the same age and people But in the houses of the South Town I found pieces of almost every variety of pottery that we know from the New Race graves, the polished red, black-topped, red with white lines, and decorated, while not a single piece of Egyptian

pottery was found there, except at one end, where a small amount of the XVIIIth dynasty was added Several smaller settlements on the desert edge can be detected by the hollow sound in walking , this is due to the soil containing air which can vibrate, and shews the presence of ash-beds On digging in these places we found scraps of New Race pottery, and strewing over the sites were large numbers of flints of the ovoid types of PL LXXI, while nothing Egyptian was to be found

We must conclude then that these ovoid flints (31, 35, 36, 37, 40, 43, 44) were the common domestic implements of the New Race people. They are peculiar for their thickness, and the rude ridge in the middle of each face (see sections 31, 40, 43), while the outline is smoother than would be expected from such rough chipping

Beside these, many saw-flints were found from sickles (38, 39, 41, 42), shewing that the New Race reaped with flint sickles as did the Egyptians One larger saw-flint, 45, can scarcely have been set, but was probably used for hand-sawing

75 LXXII, LXXIII, LXXIV, LXXVI *Flints from graves, New Race* —The wrought flints found in the graves are the finest examples of such work that are known from any country or age The regular and systematic surface-flaking, as in 82, 86, and the notching of the edges in 52, 66, are of the most delicate style, surpassing even the Danish art of flint-work In very few cases was grinding used to finish a surface as in No 51, but it was an inter-mediate stage employed to reduce the mass to a regular form before the final chipping, as noticed by Mr Spurrell in his chapter To that account we must refer for all the technical description of the nature of the work That the use of these finely-chipped flints did not preclude other modes of finish, is shewn by the ground axe, 59, which was found in a basket in the same grave where the dagger, 53, was on the hip of the skeleton

The longest form of all, 52, appears to be a double-edged knife, but the pointed forms, 51, 53, 56, are probably daggers In all of these the lower ends are left rough, to be covered with the handling, and are not finely finished like the working part Three arrow-heads of the same work are shewn, Nos. 57, 58, 69

The most unusual type of implement is the forked lance, 61, 62, 63, 65, 66 The lower end is always less finished than the fork, and evidently intended for hafting, while the fork is elaborately worked to a saw-edge or a knife-edge In one case the lance had a long cord wound around it, with two alabaster knobs at the outer end, and the whole wrapped in hide From this we gather that these lances were used for throwing at short distances, and were checked by a cord from flying too far if they missed the quarry In this way these elaborate and brittle flint weapons could be actually used in hunting So far as we can see, it appears that the hunter must have lain in ambush, while the game was driven past him, and endeavoured to cut the legs, so as to disable the gazelles, or other animals, by means of the forked lance. The reason for aiming at the legs rather than the body may have been either for capturing the animals to keep them in herds, or to avoid piercing the skin, which was so valuable for water-carrying The use of forked lances is mentioned in connection with North African hunting, when Commodus shot ostriches on the neck with forked arrows in the colosseum, they also occur in mediæval arms, and are mentioned for deer-hunting by Shakespear (As you like it," ii 1) Strange, therefore, as they may seem to us, the type has not been an unusual one in the world

The knives vary greatly in finish, some are mere flakes but little worked, as 64, while the working was elaborated on the back before the edge was touched, as 68, 71 In more finished instances the edge was worked as well as the back but the main faces of the great flake remained All of these knives have a very thick back and a triangular section, as shewn in 81, with generally a considerable wind in the faces This back was the place for ornamental work, and some examples are elaborately treated, even more so than the example 81 a The highest stage of working was where the old triangular section was entirely subdued by flaking and grinding, so that the two edges were almost alike, when a final flaking all over the surface finished the work This is shewn on 82–85, while 86 still retains the grinding on the back

The photographs will shew the actual appearance and effect of the work, while the careful drawings by Mr Spurrell will give the detail for study, and the references to the graves

76 LXXV *Stone implements, etc* —These are some miscellaneous examples which do not belong to the foregoing classes The large stone axes with lugs, 91, 92, are evidently the prototypes of the later metal axes Another type, 93, is not for binding on, but for setting into a haft These are all worked

by hammering and polishing A curious flaked piece of hard limestone, 94 was apparently worked up for use And a piece of hard quartzose stone, 95, appears to have been used for polishing All of these are from Koptos. The square flakes, 97, 98, 99, are of the regular type of the IVth dynasty, as found in tombs at Medum, they come from tombs of the same age at Ballas Three other flints from Ballas, 96, 101, 102, are of unknown age, the last is remarkable for the high pointed form on the upper side, as shewn by the section below The formation of the delicate flint bangle, 100, is fully described by Mr Spurrell in his chapter

77 LXXVII *Ivory handle, and lintel of Tahutmes I* —This ivory handle belongs to a knife similar to that drawn in LXXIV, 86, which was obtained by Mr Greville Chester from Sohag, and is now in the collection of General Pitt-Rivers That the knife really belongs to the handle—although the cementing of the two is modern—is fully proved by examining the remains of the ancient hafting This handle opens an interesting question The knife undoubtedly belongs to the New Race, but the carving on the handle is far finer than anything found among the remains of that people, and has, moreover, the regular Egyptian style of the Old Kingdom tombs This then seems to point to the borderland between the Egyptians and the invaders, and to indicate that Egyptian work to order was obtainable by the invaders at a little north of Abydos As the photographs, which are admirably taken by my friend, Mr Frank Haes, cannot shew all parts of the rounded surface well, I have added outline copies, drawn direct from the ivory on a faint blue print, with the edge figures developed The lintel of Tahutmes I, and the plates concerning the town and temple of Nubt will be described further on, in dealing with the Egyptian remains

LXXXII, LXXXIII *Selected tomb plans* —These have been fully described in the earlier chapter on the published graves

78 LXXXIV *Naqada, skulls of New Race* —The present publication of results by these diagrams is only temporary, awaiting a fuller discussion. The skulls were measured by some friends, and I have expressed the results for the principal elements in curves, separating the male and female, and placing the names of other races at the points of their average values, for comparison.

The capacities, which are placed first, were measured with seed by Mr Herbert Thomson, but the well-

H* 2

known difficulty of getting concordant results makes him distrust the amounts for any minute accuracy. Still, however, we may feel a certainty that the general capacity is very much less than that of European, Mongol, or Egyptian, and distinctly different to the Guanche, which is against any idea of the connection of the New Race with those islanders In fact the Hindu is the only race of any culture which can be compared with the New Race This is an important indication, as it shews that they were not recent travellers from a northern or colder land   The size of the head is closely connected with the temperature of the habitation of a race, and this small size indicates that they had probably dwelt in the hot plains of Africa and the oases long enough to have acquired a thoroughly small head

79   The separation of male and female skulls was carefully considered in each case by Professor Thane, and the results are shewn in the curves   There is a considerable difference between the extent of the curve of male skulls and female skulls (broken line) That such differences are not due to accident is certain, as nearly a hundred were measured, the highest point of the curves here representing ten examples of one value   The numbers of male and female also differ considerably, though from one cemetery   But on looking at the curves we see that the general area of the female curve is the same as the male, over the same extent, while the exceptional part of the female curve is of unusually small capacity   In short, the difference both in numbers and in capacity curve between male and female, is entirely due to a large number of female skulls of very small capacity   It became, therefore, a question what other peculiarities there were among this exceptional group They only occur in one cemetery, the great one, and not in cemetery B, or at Ballas   The breadth index, or ratio of length and breadth, shews a long and narrow head   The bizygomatic breadth-absolute (in millimetres) is a fair average   The frontal height is nearly full average   The absolute maximum parietal breadth (in mm)—that is, above the base—is small   The length is almost full average   The height is small   Thus there is no deficiency in length or basal breadth, frontal height or orthognathism, but the smallness is in the breadth of the upper part, and the height   In short there is no lack in the framing of the skull, but only in the filling out and development of the parietals   This indicates that we have to do with a part of the same

race, which has been less developed in the brain, or has retrograded owing to isolation   And these are all females   This points to a raid on one of the oases, where the population was behindhand, and a carrying off of the women from there   Such an hypothesis would just account for this very peculiar group

80. Turning next to the question of the ratio of length and breadth   Taking the length as 100, the breadth at the widest part is shewn in the second diagram   Here it will be seen that the male and female curves closely coincide in most parts, this is after subtracting 1 5 per cent from the female index, to bring it into adjustment, as the average female skull is rounder than the male skull   Hence the scale of numerals below refers to the female curve, the scale of numerals above refers to the male curve After making this sex allowance the curves closely coincide, and indicate a division in two groups, one centering about 71, the other about 74   Here the relation to other races can be seen in the names above   The skulls are much longer than the European, Guanche, or Egyptian, while one group closely coincides with the Algerian, ancient and modern, and the other is longer than any race except the Veddah and Australian

81   Lastly we have the curve of prognathism, and here we see a remarkable agreement in detail between the male and female curves, indicating a mixture of several stocks with small variations   Three main groups are tolerably certain, those at 93, 97, and 100   The general character is very high, about the same as the Egyptian, Algerian, and European, while scarcely any are as prognathous as the Mongol or negro

The general conclusions, then, are that we have to deal with a race with a small skull, indicating a hot climate as their source, with a very long head but very upright profile   That they have no connection with the Guanche, but agree closely with the Algerian, both ancient and modern   That there was no difference in capacity or orthognathism between men and women, but the heads of the men were slightly longer in shape   The nose was short and prominently aquiline, but not wide

82   Having noted these general results, it will be well to look more in detail at the Algerian skulls, as they shew a close resemblance to the New Race, and from their locality they may, of all that we know, be the most likely people to be connected with the invaders   The best material on the Algerian side for

our comparison is in the measurements of skulls from the dolmens, which appear to belong to the pre-metallic and early metallic ages These were published in the "Bulletin de l'Académie d'Hippone," No 4, 1868, which contains a paper by General Faidherbe, entitled "Recherches Anthropologiques sur les tombeaux mégalithiques de Roknia" As this paper is rarely to be met with (I owe the knowledge of it to Mr Weld-Blundell), it will be well to give a brief outline of the results here Roknia is about halfway between Bône and Constantin, near the Tunisian frontier Great numbers of tombs remain there, formed each by a circle of small stones around the interment, and a great cap-stone covering the whole Fourteen tombs were opened by General Faidherbe Only scanty details of position of the body are given, but it is stated (tomb 3) that the bodies were generally bent in three, knees to chin, and heels to pelvis, that is to say, in the regular contracted position of the Medum burials and of the New Race In tomb 3 it is stated that the head was to the north, and the face west, but in tomb 2 the skeletons were on the left side, faces to east, and therefore heads to north This latter is the Medum direction, opposite to that of the New Race In many graves there were several skulls, in tomb 9 either seven or eight heads, though the space was only 4 feet long, 25 inches wide, 27 high In tomb 13 were bits of bronze bracelets, and in 14 a bronze ring consisting of copper 86 8, tin 10 9 These megalithic tombs are, in some cases, as late as Roman times, but they probably belong to very different ages The pottery is, some of it, like the forms of New Race pottery, such as (B 75 a, L. 12 c, 17 a, 17 b), other bowls have a ridge around, like the debased copies of IVth dynasty bowls (L 78 a, to XLV, 25)

83 Turning to the details of the skulls, many of the measures taken are unfortunately not of the same parts as those taken from the New Race. The comparable measures are the following stating the mid-example and mid of deviation

(1) Length absolute in millimetres, New Race, 180 5, mean deviation 8 5, Algerian, 184 5, m d 5 Extent of variation, and main group identical (modern Algerian, 179)

(2) Breadth, parietal, absolute, in mm N R 132 5 m d 3 4, Alg 137 5 m d 3 0, Extent of variation identical (modern Algerian, 133)

(3) Ratio, length = 100, breadth, N R 74 1, m d, 1·8, Alg 74·4, m d 1 7 Extent of variation

not quite so dolicho-cephalic in Algerian (modern Alg 74 3)

(4) Capacity in cub centim N R 1298, m d 70, or, excluding the low females who are redundant in proportion, N R 1315, m d 55, Alg 1310 m d 90 But the Algerian, only ten in all, seem to fall into two groups, one, containing six, from 1250 to 1330, the other, containing four, from 1450 to 1538 These might correspond to pure Algerian and Guanche (modern Alg 1346)

(5). Nasal height in mm N R 47 2, m d 30, Alg 50 m d 2 Less low variation in Algerian (modern Alg 51)

(6) Orbital breadth, in mm N R 38·4 m d 1·4, Alg 39 8 m d 1·5 Variation less in Algerian (modern Alg 39)

(7) Orbital height, in mm N R 32·6 m d 1 1, Alg 33, m d 1 Variation less in Algerian (modern Alg 33)

(8) Ratio, orbital breadth = 100, height N R 85, m d 3, Alg 83 5, m d 2 Extent of variation same (modern Alg 84 7)

Tabulating these for brief comparison, we have—

—	New Race	Algerian Dolmens.	Modern Algerian
Length, absolute, mm	180 5	184 5	179
Breadth, absolute	132 5	137·5	133
Length breadth 100	74 1	74 4	74 3
Capacity, cub cent .	{ 1298 {or 1315	1310	1346
Nasal height, mm.	47 2	50	51
Orbital breadth, mm	38 4	39 8	39
Orbital height, mm	32 6	33	33
Breadth height 100	85	83 5	84 7

(Sex was ignored in the dolmen series, and is therefore also ignored here in others)

In every particular the resemblance is very near The ancient Algerian skull has slightly more length and breadth, but the same capacity, indicating a slightly less height The ratios are, however, exactly alike The nose is rather longer, and the eyes a trifle wider, but the differences are in no case more than might be expected between two groups of the same people, being far less than distinguish them each from other races So small a divergence is remarkable between peoples 1,600 miles apart, and separated by 2000 to 5000 years in time We may then safely identify the race of the prehistoric Algerians with the

New Race in Egypt, so far as the comparison of the skulls proves the matter

84 LXXXV *Nubt and South Town* The plan of Nubt will be noticed further on in discussing the Egyptian remains The South Town was an instructive addition to the results from the cemeteries It was mainly built by the New Race, as nothing whatever but their pottery and remains were found in the greater part of it, and in no part was there anything older than the invaders It proves, therefore, that they were familiar with mud-brick building , and the occasional use of brick lining to their graves agrees with this It also shows the carelessness about squareness and angles which we see in their forms of graves The thick wall of the northern part appears to be a fortification with divisions within it This area was mostly cleared by our men, and many ovoid flints, pieces of various kinds of New Race pottery, small rounded spindle whorls of limestone, and bone netting spools, were found A feature of this place are the many pits and grooves sunk in the rock, some of which are shewn in outline on the plan The pits are generally about 15 inches across, and the same deep , and the grooves about 6 inches in width and depth To the S of this thick enclosure are other straggling buildings, and an area paved with large cobble-stones, as marked on the plan Farther S are buildings of a different size of bricks Those marked solid black are 11 × 4½ × 3 inches, poorly made, and are certainly of the New Race , those shaded on the plan are 14 × 6 × 4 inches, and from the greater regularity of the building I should incline to attribute them to the date of the pottery found here of the latter half of the XVIIIth dynasty

85 LXXXVI *The cemetery* —The position of this cemetery is shewn in outline on the map I A, and the detached cemetery of T, near the tumuli, and B, near Kom Belal, are inset here, with a statement of their true position relative to the general plan, as well as being marked in true place on the map I A It will be seen that the chosen position for graves is on the slight shoals of gravel in a wide valley, though not actually in the watercourses Owing to the closeness of the graves, it has been impossible to enter the numbers in some cases , these are lettered, and references given to the numbers below

86 *Weights* —Beside the objects figured, five rudely-formed blocks of limestone have been found in the graves, without any signs of wear (as if they might be implements) or any hole for suspension

Probably they are weights, and on comparing them they indicate the unit in grains as follows —

Grave	Form	Now	Orig	干	Unit
461	Conical, rough .	2774	2830	15	188 7
1773	Cylinder, round ends . .	7673	7690	40	192 2
1873	Pillowy form . .	588	590	3	196 7
1866	Dome, rounded base .	3986	3990	20	199 5
1563	Cylinder, rounded ends, a flat side	4213	4230	20	211·5

We cannot suppose 3990 to be a different multiple to 4230 , granting such a variation, we cannot well deny that 7690 — 2, or 3845, is the same as 3990 This amount of variation being certain, the relation of 2830 to these as 3 to 4 is clear, and 590 is ¼ of 2830 Hence the multiples arrived at The unit averages 197 8 ± 2 5 grains, = 12 82 grammes This closely agrees to the Aeginetan standard, which we know to have been the oldest in Egypt The Khufu weight shews an unit of 206, Amenemhat IIIrd shews 196 5, Amenhotep Ist 207 6, and Tahutmes Ist shews 197 7 As no other borrowing from the Egyptians is found among the New Race, we must rather look to this unit as belonging to the Libyans originally, and being used in Egypt before it was re-introduced by the New Race

One piece of New Race copper was analysed at University College, and gave copper 98 60, tin 0 38, zinc 1 55, total 100 53 , so that if we regard it as an alloy, and not as merely impure copper, it is rather brass than bronze. Other analyses of the metal will shortly be made. In general the elasticity of it, and freedom from deep corrosion or changes, point to its being nearly pure metal, and not containing any serious alloy

The woods, fruits, etc, found in the graves have been determined at Kew, by the kindness of Dr Thiselton Dyer, as being sycamore (*Ficus sycamorus*), sesame (*Sesamum Indicum*), male palm flower (*Phœnix dactylifera*), wheat straw, *Cyperus esculentus*, *Zizyphus*, and *Balanites Roxburghii*

CHAPTER X

THE FLINT IMPLEMENTS OF NAQADA

By F C J Spurrell

87 *The Palæoliths*—The chief forms are, those rounded at the butt with sides straight to the tip (LXVIII, 3) Ovoid, with a narrowing at the tip (1 and 5), this is chipped all round, thin and flat Conical, pointed with thick butt (2) Circular, and other less determinate forms occur (6) Large, coarse, flat flakes are abundant (LXXVI), some have been chipped into ill-shaped implements, others slightly used at one or both sides, especially of the smaller end, but none of the larger ones shew signs of being pointed for boring purposes, and certainly no flakes having suitable points have been worked up for that purpose Many flakes are chipped naturally

A part of the butt of the longest (3) is rough, having some of the original crust on it This has been struck repeatedly, producing little cones which have since been bared by weathering Although it is difficult otherwise to account for this circular pitting, it may not be the result of river or marine action Other implements have the rough crust without any pitting, and all the implements have sun-flaking occasionally They are all of a light brown on one side, and a deeper colour, sometimes amounting to black, on the other, which lay uppermost Mostly this black coat is without obvious structure, but some spots have a dendritic outline Potash has no effect on it, but hydrochloric acid instantly liberates all the coating, which is ferric oxide No signs of vegetable growth could be obtained The rust, which covers the whole upper surface, continues round the edges for about a quarter of an inch (*i.e*, where exposed to the air), all other hard stones in the same situation are equally covered with it

One of the large oval palæoliths (1) has been re-chipped towards the butt end in the palæolithic manner, leaving only enough of the old work here and there to shew that it was originally worked all round This later chipping is paler, and shews very much less iron oxide than the older surfaces

All these were picked up on the surface of the high level

There are other palæoliths found on the surface of a gravel terrace, whose upper level is about 25 feet above the Nile plain at present (its lower level reaching perhaps as far below it) The terrace on which these lay has apparently furnished them by denudation, they having been left behind when the smaller gravel was removed They do not differ greatly from those of the higher level previously described Some of the largest are thicker in section, while others are long and conical with thick butts There is one small example with a well-worked point, which is not, however, acute, its butt is ill-formed Some may have come from above, while others may be coeval with the gravel

These implements are nearly free from the dark, ferruginous coat, and are often almost white. Those which are softest on the surface have been much smoothed, so that the outline of the flaking is nearly obliterated, but in this there are all stages, from the soft chalky surface, which has been deprived of much of its soluble silica, to hard, unworn implements which apparently have suffered no solution, and certainly no abrasion whatever The softening and obliteration of surface-marking are apparently the result of oft-repeated water-action (5)

The gravel terrace on which the above were found contains implements and numerous flakes, of which figs 11–20 (LXIX) illustrate all the specimens brought over this year All are poor and imperfect examples, the larger kinds not having been met with *in situ*, and with one exception they are merely waste flakes which have received some chipping at the edges The exceptions are figs 11 and 12 Their mineral condition closely resembles those found lying *on* their bed

88 *Implements of the Alien Race*—There are found on the surface in the *débris* of the town, and around it, a very large number of chipped flints Mostly they are chipped all over, those that have any of the original crust remaining shew that they are made from local materials The majority are oval in shape, their greatest length varying from 1½ to 7 inches, with a thickness somewhat unusual in proportion to the size (figs 31, 35, 40, 43, 44, 96) The general outline is slightly more curved on one side than the other Some are longer than others, and some nearly round, but the chipping is very uniform in kind Many of the longer ovals are chipped to a sharp edge at one end by flaking from side to side, and not as usual from edge to centre Signs of use are seen on comparatively few, and

present an appearance of continuous hacking on one side or end, by which the general outline is little changed One only of this oval variety (36) was found in a grave—it was found in a pot, but there is no evidence to shew whether this was accidental or not Along with these is a distinct variety, triangular in form It is mostly made from a flat flake worked to a cutting edge at one end, and the two edges approaching to a blunt point

Some other shapes, apparently belonging to the same period of manufacture, are shewn (23, 24) That given at (23) should apparently be included with the above, although found at some distance away from the chief site

Hoe-blades also occur in the same places, some of which may be of the regular Egyptian make A hâche (59), ground all over, was found with a finely-worked dagger-blade (53) in the same grave "Thumb" flints, scrapers or sticking-knives also occur, flat, thin, and nearly circular (32, 33), bevelled on one side only A hollow scraper, extremely thick in middle section (34) is shewn

Sickle teeth have been found on the site of the town The evidence of use in the polish of the notched edge of each is clear, part of the setting still adheres (38, 39, 41, 42) Fig 45 is the coarsest notching and the deepest fang recorded from Egypt

There is no certainty that any implements from Egypt can be assigned to any intermediate period between the palæoliths of the gravels and the earliest historic or dynastic period, unless it be those shewn at figs 21, 22, 102, but the characters of many of the above surface implements belonging to the Alien Race which lived here, closely resemble European neoliths

Arrow-heads.—Tanged There is one beautiful little arrow-head with a well-made tang, the earliest example known, it is finely notched at the sides (69) *Shouldered* This also is a rare form, it is heart-shaped, the lines forming the edges being *straight*, it is not very finely made, but is thin (58) *Barbed* The barbed forms are more common, they are finely worked with thick rounded forms The barbs curve inwards in all cases (57) A roughly-made one is unusually long, it may be called straight (55) *Double-pointed* (65, 70) The smaller examples of the fish-tail implements are almost certainly arrow-heads, as they are too small for javelins, though the make and shape is the same as the largest It is quite likely that many of the large ones were used for arrow-heads, when it is considered how studiously

their weight has been reduced, contrary to the requirements of a spear-head

89 There is a class of implements which may be included under one head, viz., flakes, by which is meant that from their simplest to their most elaborate forms, the characters of a crude flake, as struck from the block, are in the main retained This class, therefore, differs from all those previously enumerated in that the latter have been so completely worked over as to retain nothing by which their first outline can be determined

All the large flakes on a successful cleavage from the parent block, after its preparatory trimming is completed, have a butt end, a point and three (rarely more) sides The three-angled flake is the commonest among the larger forms The intervening angle is seldom in the middle, and in the best is placed as near to one edge as is possible, so that the flake is like a razor having a back and two sides coming together to a thin cutting edge, this kind of flake is met with in all sizes up to 13 inches in length, its greatest width in proportion to the length rarely reaching one in three (64)

These flakes always shew some degree of wind at the thin edge, though the back may shew none One of the largest of them has been carefully ground on both sides, of which one is finely fluted The back is carefully chipped Notwithstanding all this work the essential form of a flake is retained with some of the wind The edge is notched

Another is worked in the best style in correction of the wind (81) The back edge is worked along the ridge, the obtuse angle, in an ornamental and complicated manner, having the appearance of two edges, such as leather, sewn together The impulse which started the several fissures was begun from a very small point approaching the vertical on the flat side It had the effect of making a deep pit, the distal edge of which rapidly returned to the surface again, but before reaching it the fissure suddenly extended parallel with the surface and continued travelling for varying distances at a slight uniform depth its direction at the same time changed also, the latter part of its course being backwards at an angle to the first

The even surface of the great flake enabled the fissure to travel steadily beneath it when once the right depth was attained, which differed in different flints Notwithstanding a common tendency to ripple it was overcome, and it appears in this matter as if there was a relation between the original impulse and the quality of the flint surface.

The surface being smooth, the flint free from flaws or irregularities, and a ridge or guiding-line formed by a previously lifted flake, the worker was able to dress a knife-face in fluted lines for a distance of two or three inches from the starting-point, extending sometimes completely across the blade Unless the surface is smooth, this perfectly regular fluting was not attainable, knives were therefore first carefully chipped over until the desired outline and equal thinning of the edges and point were attained, then they were ground, probably on some such stone as quartzite, as thin as possible, with due regard to the future force to be employed, and with as little winding as possible, then they were fluted, sometimes on both sides, though commonly only on one, the other being left smooth in consequence of the thinness to which the blade had arrived allowing no further reduction

The fissure travels less easily as the surface is convex, it is sometimes carried quite across much-curved daggers previously ground so, but the parallelism is always inferior and the length of the chip reduced

Remembering the variety of the operator's touch, and the thinness of the brittle blades and rings, it will be obvious that direct blows from a flint or other stone would be too clumsy a proceeding to be a satisfactory explanation of the accuracy of the work A blow might have been delivered through an intervening substance, such as a pointed stone, or metal, which would limit the area of impact and concentrate the force, but the smallness of the point, and the slowness of the action, appear rather to be the result of pressure Whether that was delivered direct, or by means of a lever, cannot yet be determined If we may judge from the present mode of trimming the edges of thick glass plates by pressure or "pinching,' whereby fine regular fluting two inches deep is obtained, it is likely that the flint-workers did something of the sort, anyhow, the modern and ancient results look much alike

The remaining forms adapted from simple flakes call for little remark Some are long and thin, rounded off at the butt end, and used along one or both sides, answering to the duties of our pocket-knives (64, 67, 68, 71) Some are chipped all round, answering to prickers or borers (54) A form with the butt end large and snubbed is common (101) Wasters are plentiful Small collections of minute flakes were found in some graves A few inferior cores from the gravel stones round about shew that a little poor work was carried on but the absence of suitable tools for flaking, of waste chips, so characteristic and abundant as they would be, and of great cores and masses sufficiently large to form flakes over sixteen inches in length derived directly from the rock, as was clearly the origin of some of the finest implements, is evidence that the working of these fine objects was not carried on at the place where they were found

Of Obsidian—the tip of a leaf-shaped hâche was found, also some small flakes

90 The finest symmetrically-ended knives are thin and narrow and as much as fifteen inches long (52) They have a central bulge from which the edges recede with an inward curve towards either end, which is rounded off, never pointed One end is less carefully finished, and was covered by the handle for about three inches The remainder of the blade is well worked, but is never ground or fluted Except the tang or haft end the edges are finely notched, the best examples being 03 inches apart and about 01 deep, it is very regular work made after the edge had been brought to a true line

The notching of these knives round the broad point end shews that they were not intended for thrusting, indeed the extreme finish of this type is all for show

Another kind of knife is pointed and curved to form a thin crescent (84) The butts of these knives are not fully finished Most of them are flaked in the ordinary way but some (among them the largest, eleven inches long by one and a half wide) were ground and fluted, though not in the best manner The back edges are smooth and mostly bevelled, the other edge is notched

A variety of knife or spear head, evidently strongly formed for thrusting, is shewn at fig 56, this was not ground before finishing, but another like it was ground and fluted Fig 51 is ground in facets meeting at the median line, and was made for a like use

The most admirable implements of the whole series have a recurved tip (82) For them the choicest and most homogeneous stone was reserved, and on them the most perfect elaboration was bestowed, yet although the present series of implements exhibits examples of the highest art in flint-chipping now known, it should be remembered that it came from one small village or town, where it seems no great men were buried What then may not be expected on searching the seat of manufacture, and the tombs of the chief rulers of the race ?

The shape of these knives is commonly a straight

I*

blade with the cutting edge recurved towards the handle for the distance of one-third of an inch or so, the blunt edge meeting it after turning to a right angle with the blade   The knives are ground very thin on both sides, and then chipped in fluted lines from both edges with marvellous exactness, and with the aim, often accomplished, of obliterating all signs of grinding on that side   Almost always one side was left plain ground, as though the operator feared to spoil his work by attempting too much   They are bevelled at the back and smoothed   The convex edge is notched   In the figs 82 86, the flaking is carefully mapped out, but it should be remembered that the meeting-point of two flutings from either side frequently requires the aid of a magnifying-glass to define the dividing line—the *general* appearance of the meeting-point is that of a line somewhat more regular than would be gathered from the very detailed drawings   The original intention was to make the fluting meet, and not to alternate, nor at any part to " mitie "—this applies to all the cases in which it occurs

One implement (82) is fluted on both sides, signs of grinding are nowhere seen except at the extreme butt , the work is very soft and regular, the depth of fluting being from $\frac{1}{100}$ to $\frac{1}{300}$ inch for $\frac{3}{4}$ of an inch together along the flake   It is bevelled at the back It is of a yellow semi-transparent Chalcedonic flint There is evidence of much gentle handling and usage in this unique example, the teeth being nearly worn out except near the handle , and the whole feels smooth, in marked contrast to the other work, which, in all cases, is rough to the touch, as all freshly-flaked flint is   It follows in the latter case, therefore, that the implements were procured new for burial purposes

91 The spear or javelin-heads (61, 62, 63, 65, 66) are characterised as having the effective end much the widest   The smaller end is rounded, squared, or pointed , it is the butt or handle end, being left half finished for insertion in the shaft to the depth of about three inches, where it was retained by means of gummy and resinous stuff   The outer edges diverge from this point sometimes in regular lines, sometimes curving outwards gradually until near the free end, when the widening increases rapidly   These outer edges sometimes end in sharp points, in others they are rounded gracefully   The cutting-edges then return inwards in segments of circles, or in straight lines to the centre, or in an ogee curve to a flattened notch A variety is figured with a tang and shoulders, f 62

This type is always the best worked of the whole series   In all cases, this termination reminds one of the tail of a fish   The largest of these blades have had the greatest care lavished on them, but (as might be expected, in consequence of the curved outline), the finest parallel fluting is not met with, although every effort at regularity is attempted   In some instances the surface on both sides was ground, and then flaked   Finally in several, the blade is polished smooth   Grinding rubs off the prominences and irregularities of flaking, leaving sharp margins   The polishing was done with a soft substance, and passes over the ripples down into the hollows   therefore the polisher must have been of wood or skin, and perhaps Nile mud was used, but not sand   By this means, one of these blades shews the least thickness for the same breadth of any implement in the collection

With the exception of the butt, these blades are finely worked to a cutting-edge all round   In a few the edge is coarse and obtuse , in others the work is regular, but rough to the finger with *irregular* notching , lastly, the best examples are regularly notched, and this is different from the last method, as it is very uniform in depth and spacing   The notches are produced in the same manner as those on the sickle teeth and saws, but much more carefully, viz , one notch is made towards one side, and another notch in its hollow to the other side   The notching tool was perhaps a flake of some very tough stone, so thin as to enter the first notch easily without blurring its sides   The best examples are somewhat less than 03 inch apart, and a little over 01 inch deep, very uniform over long distances   This notch-flaking is not abrupt, but prolonged inwards as much as a quarter of an inch, thereby thinning the edge gently

The notching was evidently, to a great extent, a refinement or ornament, seeing that it is carried round the splayed points and backwards where it could be of no service   These remarks apply equally to the notching of the long knives and other implements, as 52 56, 53, 69, 81, 82, 84

The smaller fish-tail blades resemble the larger, but with less graceful outlines and little finish , one, indeed, is roughly constructed by hacking a small flat flake (70)

The proportion of knives and javelin (?) blades brought to a fine edge, is slightly in excess of those truly notched, but notching is not applied more in one type of implement than another

92 *Rings*—One perfect flint ring, and portions of others, were found, they have all been ground smooth, and he nearly flat. The example shewn (fig 100) has a width of 2½ inches, and thickness of ·15 inch (see section at side). They were made by chipping rings of flint naturally formed. Nodules of flint are found in the limestone presenting a resemblance to Saturn with his ring. When the central boss could be detached, the ring would be used. Commonly, however, it appears that rings were found in the gravel already detached, or the division between the boss and the ring so much reduced by solution of the soluble silica as to admit of easy separation. The finished rings in section shew a great change at the surface, greater than their age would warrant if made out of flint directly derived from the rock, though just such an amount as might be expected from flint which had lost part of its silica by exposure in the gravel, and become porous.

After the difficult operation of chipping (examples of which are well known), grinding was comparatively easy, especially as we know that emery, in varying hardness and pulverulence, was employed by these aliens inhabiting Egypt

At one side of the bangle is a section of a similar bangle, also of black flint. The outside of both is weathered grey, and the section shews the depth to which this change has gone since it was finished. Other bangles are made of harder, translucent flint of the same colour throughout. The polishing in the interior of the ring is backwards and forwards and around, on the exterior it is finished in all directions.

CHAPTER XI

CONCLUSIONS

93 The first graves that I opened at Naqada shewed a position of the body which was obviously not that usual among Egyptians. The pottery and objects found were also different from any that we knew as belonging to dated periods in Egypt. So soon as I found that these were not casual and isolated peculiarities, but part of a large class, it seemed that we must regard them as belonging to an immigrant people. The longer we worked the more we marked the distinction between these immigrants and the regular Egyptians, and the longer we searched in vain for a single object of the many kinds so well known in Egyptian graves—the head-

rests, the canopic jars, the pottery, the amulets, the scarabs, the coffins—without finding a single example, the greater appeared the historical gulf between the two peoples.

The classes of remains now brought to light were, however, some that had for years past been a great puzzle to all who had collected antiquities in Egypt. The pottery was very characteristic, yet apart from all that of the Egyptians, and the fine stone jars, the brilliantly worked flints, the slate palettes, were well known from the working of several other cemeteries, which had been plundered without any note or description of their peculiarities of remains or of burial. Cemeteries of this kind have not only been worked by dealers, but were excavated by the native workmen of the Ghizeh Museum, but no description of the burials or record of the graves was made, and the history was destroyed, as it always must be when a recorder is not on the spot. In 1885, much pottery was obtained at El Khozam and Gebelen by museum work, but no other fine things, probably the fine flint knives which appeared about that time in dealers' hands at Luxor came from there. A tablet of the XIth dynasty found in the same cemetery led M Maspero to date all this style as belonging to the XIIth dynasty. In 1895, another cemetery had been plundered, yielding a few flint knives and slates to the museum, but ignoring all the pottery. A large cemetery of the New Race has long been known at Abydos, and has been worked by native dealers, last winter it was worked by M Amélineau, and though he did not get the flint knives, I have heard of some excellent ones from Abydos reaching a well-known collector through the dealers. Of isolated examples of these classes of things I may note from Kom Ombo, a splendid flint knife in Pitt-Rivers Collection, Oxford, from Silsileh, pottery (Brit Mus), from Hieraconpolis, a lattice-pattern cylinder jar, which I picked up, from Gebelen pottery (Brit Mus), large animal figures in hard stone (Rev R Berens), stone vases, knives, etc, from Abydos, much pottery (F P Coll), flint knives (F P Coll), gold-mounted and other stone vases, a large collection (Chicago), from Sohag, the ivory-handled knife here published (General Pitt-Rivers), from Tehneh a late cylinder jar (F P Coll). And this year Cairo dealers have sold to the Ghizeh Museum a magnificent flint knife with gold handle said to come from Tuneh, but perhaps from Abydos, while a fine flint knife has been in the Ashmolean Museum, Oxford, for some years past, and in 1873 a large

I* 2

flint knife and two flint bracelets belonged to Mrs.
McCallum (Proc Soc Antiq , Lond , 8th May, 1873)

Thus it is plain that *these classes of foreign things
are no isolated matter but belong to a large population
spread over the whole of Upper Egypt* Even if the
single example at Tehneh be a casual importation,
yet the instances are so many between Sohag and
Kom Ombo, 160 miles apart, that there must have
been a continuous occupation

94 That there is a complete break between the
Egyptian civilisation and that of the New Race is
best shewn by comparing the two in parallel order

Egyptian Characteristics	New Race Characteristics
Inscriptions	Rude marks, not grouped
Sculptures	Great incapacity for form
Chamber tombs	Roofed grave pits
Tombs in cliffs	Graves in valleys
Coffins	Burial in clothing
Extended burial	Contracted burial
Mummification	Cutting up the body
Head-rests	Head usually cut off
Skull capacity, 1460	Capacity, 1310.
Nasal index, 48 5	Nasal index, 53 7
Weapons, bows and arrows	Forked flint lances
Ground conoid axes	Oval chipped flints
Lug axes	Fine flint knives
Copper-edged stick	Quadrangular dagger
Amulets buried	Ashes buried
Beads, globular (mostly pottery)	Beads, cylindrical (mostly stone)
Mirrors of copper	Slate palettes
Scarabs	Fine flint bracelets
Canopic jars	Jars of fat
Pottery, wheel-made	Pottery hand made—
	Red polished,
	Red and black,
	White line on red,
	Decorated,
	Incised

Moreover, throughout the whole of the Egyptian
town and temple site of Nubt not a single piece of
New Race pottery was noticed among tens of
thousands of pieces from the IVth to the XIXth
dynasty Conversely in the New Race town no
Egyptian pottery of the Old or Middle Kingdom was
seen, and only some of the XVIIIth dynasty at one
end of it with different brickwork

We conclude, therefore, that *this New Race possessed
an entirely different culture to that of the Egyptians,
and had no apparent connection with them*

95 The date of these foreigners was anxiously
sought for both at Naqada and at Ballas So
common are beads, scarabs, and pottery in Egypt
that it seemed as if we must before long find such,
of the known Egyptian types, and so obtain a fixed
connection Yet in this we were totally disappointed,
and but for the evidence from unintentional interference of Egyptian and New Race objects of different
ages, we should still have but vague inferences to
guide us At first we maintained open minds for any
indications from prehistoric down to Arabic ages
One by one the following limitations appeared

A Burial with beads of XVIIIth–XIXth dynasty
and scarabs of Tahutmes III and Ramessu II , grave
cut through the remains of the South Town, in a
mound, well above its base Result, *New Race earlier
than XIXth dynasty*

B Graves with pottery and beads of the XIIth
dynasty , cut through, and built in, remains of the
North Town, as detailed by Mr Quibell Result,
New Race earlier than XIIth dynasty

C This is confirmed by pieces of red and black and
of white-lined pottery being found the year before at
Koptos, beneath the pavement of Antef blocks which
was laid down by the XIIth dynasty. Result, *New
Race earlier than XIIth dynasty*

D Tombs containing in nearly every case pottery
or stone vases of the IVth dynasty, have intrusive
burials of the New Race. No 524, Ballas, had an
Old Kingdom burial ruined in the chamber, and on
the entrance stairway a body in New Race position
No 764, Ballas had alabaster vessels of the Old
Kingdom in the chamber, and in the filling of the
stairway a red and black vase and a bowl of the New
Race No 179, Ballas, shews a tomb of Old Kingdom form with a New Race burial with vases in the
chamber, and another on the stairway Pottery cists,
imitating woodwork, which appear to belong to the
Old Kingdom because they are found fitting in
recesses of tombs of that age, and because coffins
were not made by the New Race, are yet often found
re-used for New Race burials Result, *New Race later
than IVth dynasty*

On looking at the few resemblances—though no
identities—between the Egyptian and New Race
products, we see the same results The pottery
tables, bowls, and stands, which appear in the later
style of New Race tombs appear to be copied from
the well-known forms of the Old Kingdom, with
which the New Race would become familiar by the
plundering of the Old Kingdom tombs which we have
just noticed That this adoption of forms was due to
this, and not to learning from living Egyptians, is
indicated by the copies all being made by hand,
instead of on the wheel like the originals This link

shews then the pre-existence of the Old Kingdom, while on the other hand the favourite great offering in the New Race tombs, a bull's head and haunch, is copied on the pottery tables of offerings common in the XIIth dynasty in this region. Here then the cheap substitute of the XIIth dynasty appears to succeed the actual offering of the flesh.

From the absolute evidence of interference, and from the inferences drawn from copying, we conclude that *the New Race entered Egypt between the Old and Middle Kingdoms*.

How long they lived in the Nile valley is vaguely indicated by the changes in the pottery. As we have often mentioned, there are two main periods, the early and the late, of which the pottery is almost distinct. The later style shews several imitations of Egyptian forms, and an absence of the Decorated and Incised pottery, which was probably imported. It appears as if the old traditions, crafts, and connections of the invaders had decayed, and degraded imitation had taken their places, while still clear of any intercourse and trade with the Egyptians. The many changes in the history of the wavy-handled jars, and the entire loss of the earlier notion of the form, point also to a considerable time of sojourn. Such great loss of styles and of principles of manufacture were not likely to occur in less than a century, and might well occupy a couple of centuries, while on the other hand the entire absence of Egyptian objects in even the later period could hardly be accounted for in a people settled for many generations in the same valley as the active, artistic, and productive Egyptians. Any peaceful intercourse would have led to trade, and the exchange of objects. We might then venture to say that two or perhaps three centuries might cover the sojourn of the invaders, before they became subject to Egyptian influence, but that as little as a single century, or as many as four or five centuries, would be unlikely for their separate existence.

The period in Egyptian history that is available for such an intrusion, is after the VIth dynasty, which ended about 3322 B.C., and before the rise of the XIth dynasty, which ruled the Thebaid in the Egyptian manner from about 3006 B.C. The Xth dynasty was contemporary with the earlier part of the XIth, until 2821 B.C, and that part is therefore ignored by Manetho, who only states forty-three years for the Xth dynasty, reckoned from the fall of the Xth, which he preferred as legitimate. There is then the space of the VIIth, VIIIth, and IXth dynasties, or 70+146+100 years = 316 years, from about 3322

to 3006 B.C., which might be occupied by the New Race invaders in the Thebaid. And from the total absence of any known Egyptian objects belonging to this age in Upper Egypt it seems not improbable that the dominion of the invaders covered these three centuries. *We may then approximately date their remains between 3300 and 3000 B C*.

96. The relations of these invaders with the Egyptians appear to have been completely hostile. The absence in even the later period of their history of any Egyptian objects, and the total disregard (by such artists in pottery) of the potter's wheel which was quite familiar to Egyptians, point not only to an absence of any trade, but to the complete extrusion of the Egyptians from the region. Had any remained even as captives, they would have leavened the invaders with some traces of their culture, as the Gauls latinised the Franks, and the Franks gallicised the Normans. A civilised people subjected to ruder invaders always carry on their arts and crafts with but little essential change for their new masters. We must then accept the expulsion of the Egyptians as having been practically complete from the Thebaid.

That the invaders were not employed by the Egyptians as workmen, or as mercenaries (as has been suggested), is obvious from these very considerations. Moreover, if workmen, they would not have so many rich people among them, as is shewn by the large burials and valuable objects, and if soldiers they would shew some signs of fighting, whereas none of them appear to have died violent deaths, or to have had bones broken or heads wounded during life. That they were a tribe, and not merely men employed by Egyptians, is also shewn by the preponderance of women, who have exactly the same physical characteristics as the men. Everything therefore contradicts the association of the Egyptians and the New Race, and the absolute exclusion of their remains one from the other, in both tombs and towns, makes it impossible to regard them as dwelling in the country together.

We therefore conclude that *the invaders destroyed or expelled the whole Egyptian population, and occupied the Thebaid alone*.

97. The remains shew that the New Race were a sturdy hill people, by the massive legs and tall stature often found. They were not fighters, or quarrelsome, as only about one in three hundred shew bones broken at any period of life, and not a single skull injured before death has been observed. They were great hunters, by the forked lance being

the most frequent implement, a form only useful for laming deer and cutting birds' necks   They were right-handed, by the position of a figure cut inside a bowl   The dog was valued or sacred, by the burial of dogs in the graves, and by a grave full of dogs in the cemetery   They knew spinning and weaving, by the spindle-whorls and the linen cloth found   They were fond of colours, as many traces of such remain— red, yellow, green, black, and white   They knew of the most usual metals—gold, silver, and copper, as rarities, but flint was their principal resource   They were addicted to games, of which traces were found in many graves   They had a very fine sense of absolute form, their flints being exquisite, and their vases, both of pottery and stone, being more true and beautiful in outline than those of almost any other people, although made without any of the advantages of the wheel or lathe , while they were strangely deficient in imitative forms, and fashioned men and animals in the rudest style   They had simple marks, which were probably personal signs, but never combined them to convey ideas   They had fixed beliefs about the future and the needs of the dead, as the order of the grave furniture is very constant, and the position of the body almost invariable   They had a great burning at their funerals, though the body was never burnt   But the bodies were often cut up more or less, and in some cases certainly treated as if they were partly eaten

This last conclusion is one which, from its distance from our present ideas, may be perhaps doubted But when we see what customs prevailed in the stage of early metal culture in other instances, such mutilation seems to be usual   In the Algerian dolmens bodies are associated with supernumerary skulls and bones   In the Balearic Isles Diodorus mentions (V, 1) that the people cut up the dead in pieces with wooden knives or axes, and put the parts in an urn, over which a heap of stones was piled , and these people had customs like the Libyans, such as bridal community   In Europe also the bronze age burials in Upper Bavaria shew partial burial and intentional severing of the body   Sometimes the head, or the femurs, or the trunk, is missing, or else the skeleton is divided and the long bones laid by or on the trunk Often the head is placed on the middle of the body Sometimes only the femurs, and the arms across them, are found   Such are the varieties of mutilation noticed by a trained observer (Naue in Rev Arch , July, 1895), and they shew what probably was usual in many other western countries, as in the Balearics

and Algeria, already noticed   There is then nothing at all unlikely in the various treatment of the body which we have noticed in the graves , and the ceremonial eating of portions of the dead in order to acquire their virtues is so common in early civilizations as to be almost the rule, and is not unknown in Europe in recent times   That human flesh was eaten by neighbouring peoples is noticed in the tradition that Osiris (probably Libyan) reclaimed the Egyptians from cannibalism and taught corn-growing , while Juvenal accused the people of this very region of cannibalism, after their fight at Koptos in the Roman times, shewing that the idea was not incredible even then

98 So far we have carefully abstained throughout this volume from any theories about the connections of this people, and avoided any terms which implied conclusions as to their origin   This might appear somewhat needless reserve after their relation to the Libyans has been openly accepted by various authorities , but I have only allowed that presumption to indicate where we may look for comparisons, and nothing would require alteration if they were proved to be Mexicans or Chinese   But here we must finally enter on the question of the relations and origin of this people, and in such a discussion I shall freely deal with hypotheses   If fresh facts may modify our views it is only from this point onwards that the present account will have to be recast

In the first place we notice a strong connection with Palestine   The wavy-handle vases are identical in their earlier form, in their pottery, and in the unique form of the handle, with the most characteristic Amorite pottery of the lowest levels of Tell el Hesy, about 1800 B C   The burnishing in narrow lines is also like the Amorite pottery , and the forms of mouths cut in a spherical surface without any lip or projection are also characteristic of Amorite as of New Race forms   The use of hæmatite and lazuli points rather to Syria as a source   And the great burning made at the funeral, though not for cremation, is like the burnings at the burials of the Jewish kings, apparently copied from Amorite custom   For Asa in 891 B C " they made a very great burning for him " (2 Chr xvi 14) for Jehoram in 861 B C " His people made no burning for him like the burning of his fathers (2 Chr xxi 19), and in 590 B C Jeremiah said to Zedekiah " With the burnings of thy fathers, the former kings which were before thee, so shall they burn (odours) for thee ' (Jer xxxiv 5)   What this burning was of we do not know, for the word ' odours ' is only supplied in the English, that it was not the body is shewn by the burning being for the king, and by the absence of any trace of cremation in Jewish ideas It seems then to have been a great pyre of offerings for the dead, and to have been analogous to the great burnings of which many hundredweights of ashes were preserved in jars at burials of the New Race

99 On the other hand there are many Western connections The square pit graves, roofed over with beams of wood, are like those found in the circle at Mykenae The black bowls with white in the incisions are of the class found in Spain (Ciempozuelos), in Bosnia (Butmir), and at Hissarlik, and seem very probably to belong to the characteristic black ware of Italy, although there are perhaps no examples known there so early, and in that stage of development The quadrangular dagger is like the blades of Mykenae and of Cyprus The method of laying on the spirals with a row of brushes is also like Cypriote work The seated steatopygous figures are almost identical in form and attitude with those found in Malta in the prehistoric megalith temple of Hagiar Kim The double-bird slates develop into the pelta-shaped form, and such is constantly figured among early tomb furniture in Central Italy It has been often supposed to be a shield, but no reason for representing a shield in tombs and on coffins has been given, if, however, such a form were a constant object for personal decoration, as the slates were among the New Race, it might become fossilized as a survival long after its purpose was forgotten It was later adopted from the Etruscans by the Romans, and variously ornamented with heads and figures, without a definite idea of any purpose or intention so far as we can see

100 We now turn to the more definite Libyan connections The use of the word Libyan has been objected to because it included many varied peoples, but that is precisely the purport that is desired, as we cannot profess to distinguish yet between different branches of the fair race which occupied northern Africa The similarity between the pottery of the New Race and the present Kabyle pottery has struck every one who has seen them both The character of decoration is the same, some of the patterns being almost indistinguishable one from the other The materials used, the rouge red and white slip, are the same And some of the forms still remain Further, the method of making without the wheel, entirely by hand and eye, is the same And the high burnishing

of the surface (by repeated work during a slow drying) is also a special feature of both That a primitive pottery should be continued till the present is not improbable, because—as Faidherbe has stated—the Kabyles form an indigenous population of the mountains which has never been dispossessed throughout history The pottery of the dolmens is most of it identical in forms with that of the New Race The absence of amulets or charms in the Naqada graves corresponds with the contempt for such things shewn by the modern Kabyle in contrast to the Arab And the activity implied by the well-developed limbs and the hunting among the New Race is in harmony with the activity of the Kabyle The tatu patterns shewn on the New Race figures are closely like those of the Libyans in the tomb of Sety I When we turn to the actual evidence of the skulls we have firmer ground The precise likeness between one of the skulls and the head of the chief of the Lebu under Ramessu III, is striking to a mere observer, and so is the general similarity of facial form between the New Race and the skulls from the Algerian dolmens And when we come further to exact measurements of the whole material, we find that the mean of the New Race skulls, of the dolmen skulls, and of modern Algerian skulls, is practically identical in each point, the differences being less than might be expected between branches of one race so far apart in place and in time Captain Lyons informs me that he has seen in Dakhlah Oasis pottery extremely like the forms of the New Race, and that a smooth polished red pottery is made there Here the connection is in the same direction, and it is through these oases that the approach to Egypt must have been made When we look at the position of the New Race, and see that they did not dispossess the Egyptian lower down the Nile, and cannot, therefore, have come from the north, while assuredly there is no trace of negro in them to indicate a southern origin, we are led to look to the chain of oases, each within two or three days' march of one another, as the natural stepping-stones across the desert for the invaders And it is noticeable that the main centres of these people are at the ends of the present tracks from the oases, Abydos and Gebelen

101 That Libyan invasions were not unlikely, we learn throughout Egyptian history The Egyptians were largely formed from Libyan immigrants to begin with, the basis of the race apparently being a mulatto of Libyan-negro mixture, judging from the earliest skeletons at Medum And Libyan ideas

probably entered largely into Egyptian religion and culture Neit was recognised as a Libyan goddess, her crown is that which forms the lower half of the double crown That this was the Libyan crown is confirmed by its phonetic value, for beside the letter *n* it has the value *bat*, interchanging with the other royal emblem the hornet Thus a royal crown and royal sign were named *bat*, and Herodotus says that the Libyans called a king Battus in their language Here then one of the two crowns and one half of the royal title is identified as Libyan In historic times the very sign for an archer or soldier on the earliest tombs is a Libyan The Themehu in the oases were employed by Pepy in his wars They were attacked by Merenra, and by Usertesen That they had a hand in the XVIIIth dynasty is shewn by the daughter of Aahmes being named "princess of the Themehu" In the XIXth dynasty the Libyans occupied the whole west side in the delta and up to middle Egypt, and sought to absorb the whole country, only checked by a desperate effort under Merenptah A little later they again worked into the country and were cleared out with all their allies, by Ramessu III Soon after they succeeded and founded the XXIInd dynasty, whose princes were named "chiefs of the Maxyes" Later, the XXVIth dynasty of the Psamtiks probably owes its origin to them In the Greek times Cyrene was a constant menace to Egypt So soon as the Arab power decayed that had broken down the Roman rule, it was the Fatimite dynasty of Tunis that conquered Egypt and founded the most brilliant of the mediæval kingdoms, and in recent times a strong migration has gone on from the west into Egypt Thus a Libyan invasion in the VIIth and IXth dynasties is only one out of many such influxes of population

102 There remains still the question of the connections between the New Race and the Amorites to be dealt with The similarities are too close to be casual, but they only serve to reinforce a view which has been put forward long ago The Amorites were a fair people like the Libyans, their physiognomy on the Egyptian monuments is alike, and both were great dolmen builders On these grounds Professor Sayce has proposed that they are branches of the same race, and the portraiture has long ago convinced me of the probability of this Here then is a solution of the identity of Amorite pottery and custom with that of the New Race, they are both parts of the same stock That they branch independently is shewn by the wavy-handled jars, had the New Race gone on into Syria from Egypt, the later modification of those jars would have been found in Palestine But both in Egypt and Syria they start from one type It is even possible that the Amorite invasion of Syria was a part of the same movement eastward as the New Race invasion of Egypt

103 One outstanding matter has not yet been considered The decorated pottery we have noticed as being quite different in material, colour, subjects, and style from the pottery made by the New Race And it appears to have been imported from a sea, probably the Mediterranean Now on that pottery, among the ensigns of the galleys is one identical with the Min emblem on a pole, that is engraved on the primitive Min statues at Koptos If, however, we give credit to the conclusions that have already been arrived at about these statues, we shall not be in difficulty about this emblem recurring We have noted in Koptos" that the internal evidence about these statues points to their being the primitive idols of the Punite invaders, a part of whom entered Egypt by the Hammamat valley from the Red Sea, while other branches probably pushed on up to the Mediterranean, and there founded the maritime power of Phœnicia, and settled along the African coast as far as Spain This much I have stated in the "History,' p 15, before I went to Naqada And this point of view completely explains the Min emblems on poles on this pottery The pottery, we concluded, was imported from the Mediterranean coast, which is where the Phœnicians settled, the galleys are then the Punic trading-vessels, and the Min pole reappears as an emblem in the Mediterranean as it did in the Koptite branch of the same people This is but an hypothesis, but it flows naturally from what was independently deduced before the present facts had come to light

We conclude then that in the New Race we see a branch of the same Libyan race that founded the Amorite power, that we have in their remains the example of the civilisation of the southern Mediterranean at the beginning of the use of metal, about 3200 B C And that probably in the galleys painted on the pottery we see the earliest pictures of that commerce of the Punic race, which was so important for some three thousand years later on that sea In short, we have revealed a section of the Mediterranean civilisation, preserved and dated for us by the soil of Egypt

CHAPTER XII

NUBT, THE TOWN OF SET

104 The first matter which attracted us to working at Ballas and Naqada was not the subject of the New Race, which, indeed, we did not discover till after some weeks of work, but the attraction lay in the extensive cemeteries of early age, a small pyramid, and a temple site The early cemeteries proved to have been only too well cleared out by dealers in recent years, a few tombs at Ballas yielded some objects of the Old and Middle Kingdoms, but toward Naqada no tombs were found undisturbed, except two or three under the edge of a slight cliff south of the town We cleared out many of the already-plundered tombs near the pyramid, but found only remains of probably secondary burials of the XVIIIth dynasty Yet some valuable results were obtained in the purely Egyptian line, and these we shall here notice in the order of their history

The temple on the spur of the desert, marked NUBT on PL I A, proved to be that of Set, from which he was known as Set Nubti The other town of Nubt, or Ombos, was sacred to Hor-ur and Sebek-ra, and not to Set Hence it is evident that Set Nubti must rather belong to the Nubt where the figures of Set are found

The well-known 15th Satire of Juvenal, describing the fight at Koptos between the people of Ombos and of Tentyra, is at last explained How it should be that people of the other Nubt, Kom Ombo, 120 miles above Koptos, should come to festivals there with the inhabitants of the town of Dendera, which is just opposite to Koptos, was hitherto inexplicable, and Juvenal has been said to be in error in calling them neighbours But when we see that Nubt-Ombos is the adjacent town to Dendera—Tentyra—and both just opposite to Koptos, where the festival was held, the story is obviously reasonable Probably neither the Nubtis nor the Tentyrites would venture into each others' territories, and the point of the story is that they could not even meet in peace on the neutral ground of the great shrine at Koptos, on the other bank of the Nile

105 The pyramid was probably the oldest work that we examined A section and plan of it is given on PL LXXXV, and the position is shewn on the map, PL I A It is entirely built of unhewn stone

The neighbouring desert must have been thoroughly searched for suitable blocks, and natural masses of limestone have been brought together for building the whole pile Not a single block was dressed or even cloven in any way The form is square, composed of a central core and three successive coats each about 81 inches thick, the whole structure being 724 inches (60 feet 4 inches) square at the base The side slope is at an angle of 5 horizontal to 28 vertical The coats being very nearly 4 cubits thick suggests that the usual cubit may have been known to the builders, and the slope being 5 on 28 or 5 digits recess on a cubit height, seems to point to the same The angles of Egyptian buildings are frequently an even number of retreat on a height of 28 The faces of the sloping coats are brought to a fair surface by careful selection of the blocks Near the middle is a pit in the rock, which passes through the coat of gravel into the sand beneath, as all the surrounding tombs do The pit had evidently been attacked before, as the centre was all dragged out, and a great crater left amid the stones We removed the loose stones and reached the well, and cleared it down to the sand, but without finding anything whatever The sand was hollowed away on all sides of the pit, but how much originally, and how much by plunderers, we could not determine The unmoved sand stratum is so soft that it is difficult to distinguish it from the moved sand, but I made certain, by hand-grubbing on all sides, that we had really reached unmoved sand all round, the slight concretions running through it distinguishing it to the touch We have then no proof of the age of this pyramid, or rather, cumulative mastaba, but from the rudeness of the pit, and the complete absence of all trace of tools, it seems as if it belonged to the pre-metallic age.

Another very perplexing yet prominent object was a pair of stone tumuli to the south of the main cemetery, marked "Tumuli" on map I A These stood in a prominent place on a slight rise of ground Both had been dug into a crater on the top, but not apparently down to the base, and the very rounded nature of the stones, which were natural blocks of limestone and of flint of about 8 to 12 inches across, made it impracticable to have mined down to the bottom The northern tumulus was 60 feet wide at the estimated original foot, and 9 feet 10 inches high at the maximum, implying probably that it was about 14 or 15 feet originally The southern was 63 feet 4 inches across, and 10 feet 7 inches high,

K*

implying about 14 or 15 feet originally I began by working into both of these from the east , as, had they been tombs, there might have been a place of offerings on the east Nothing was found but the same class of blocks of stone We reached the middle and went somewhat beyond it I hen on the northern tumulus we made a trench in from the north until we reached the central space All without any result These trenches were carried down to hard undisturbed natural beds of calcareous marl, about 6 inches under the desert surface, which is loose marl and flints On lying down with my eye at the desert level, I could see the original line of weathered flints which strew the desert, denuded of all soil, extending unbroken beneath the tumuli all round our clearance , and no heaps of earth or rock lay over it, as if any pit or excavation had been made near by The desert surface was untouched where the blocks of stone were piled up That these tumuli are pre-Roman is shewn by the ground around them being thick with late burials, extended full length with iron objects, while not a single such burial lay in the ground which we searched within the tumuli Smaller tumuli of rough stone stand on the desert near, marked " Stone Pile ' on the map I A , and some which we examined contained no burial The purpose of these tumuli is therefore not yet known, nor their age But as they each contain about 1000 tons of stone, collected from a considerable space, they have not been piled up without serious labour of a large number of persons

106 The oldest dateable remains here are of the IVth dynasty, of which many pieces of pottery were found in the lowest levels of the temple area , these are very satisfactory as proving that the varieties of pottery found at Medum were not merely local, but characterised a period throughout the whole country We have already noticed in "Koptos," how both pottery and flints are the same at the lowest levels of that site as at Medum Of a very early age also are two clay sealings LXXX, 1, 2, the first of which seems to bear a *ka* name *sahu*, perhaps a play of words on the *sahu* mummy This seems to be of the same class as the single-sign *ka* names found by M Amelineau at Abydos Another seal of the same class, which I bought a few years ago, has *Antha* on it

107 Of the XIIth dynasty more pottery was found in the temple area, lying above that of the IVth, and below the XVIIIth dynasty level This again confirms the styles found at Kahun as really belonging to the whole country Several scarabs of this age were also found by the *sebakhin* digging in the town ruins around the temple, and were bought by me A unique one is of Usertesen I, in wood, the first in so perishable a material that I have seen A fine amethyst scarab with incised gold plate, 7, of a royal favourite Mu-en-ab, and another in black jasper, 67, with an impressed gold foil cover, are very rare , it is strange that two gold-covered scarabs should be found in one town within a couple of months, and it suggests that many such may be still stripped of the gold when found, which would account for their great rarity I only remember two such being preserved, the heart scarab of Akhenaten, and a fine one of Sebekemsaf The scarab of Mu-en-ab contains in the gold the first specimen of Osmiridium yet known from Africa Most of the scarabs here figured are only known from the clay sealings which were found in the low levels of the town The cylinder impressions, 27–35, are very probably older than the XIIth dynasty

Some early constructions were cleared out by me, to the south-east of the temple (see plan, LXXXV) To understand the age of these we should note the sizes of bricks used

Dynasty					
IVth	Lowest in temple, with pottery	20	7 × 10	3 × 7	
VIIIth	New Race, South Town	11	× 4½	× 3	
”	I ow level building at S E	13	× 6	× 3¼	
”	Higher level ,, ,,	19¼	× 9½	× 6½	
IVth or XIIth	Low in temple	{19½	× 9½	× 6½	
		{20½	× 10½	× 6½	
XVIIIth ?	South Town, S end	14	× 6	× 4	
XVIIIth	Temple	{15	× 7	× 4½	
		{16	× 8	× 4¼	
	Granaries	16	× 8	× 3	

Here we see that the standard size of early bricks here was one cubit by one half, 20½ × 10¼ inches The New Race interrupted this by a smaller size, though the larger were probably continued by the XIIth dynasty Then the XVIIIth dynasty adopted about 15 × 7½ inches as a standard Hence we should conclude that the low level building at the S E of the temple was probably of the New Race age, and the upper wall of the XIIth dynasty It is, however, remarkable that in all the extensive digging by the *sebakhin*, extending down to the lowest levels, and in my own clearances in and around the temple, I never saw a single potsherd of the characteristic New Race pottery The absence of this from the temple is as marked as the total absence of Egyptian pottery from the graves of the invaders

Before leaving the early period we should notice one possibility Among the cylinder impressions is one, 28, reading "Prophet of Persen, whose name is the same", *i.e*, a prophet of some divine person, presumably a king, who was called after his god The only known king whom this could be is Perabsen, of whom Shera was prophet at Sakkara This name might be abbreviated as Persen, and if so, a prophet of his being at Nubt would suggest that the rough stone pyramid was the burial-place of Perabsen If, however, it might read "born of the same," it would then be only the name of a prophet Persen, who was son of a previous one of the same name

Of the XIIth dynasty were some tombs cut in the south side of the small ravine immediately south of Nubt The chambers had been dug in a soft sand stratum beneath the hard gravel But they had soon filled up by the caving of the sides, and the bodies were intact Owing to the damp the bones were quite soft, but by careful working in the sand I recovered some necklaces of amethyst and garnet beads, some pendant shells of silver (like those found at Dahshur of the XIIth d), and a small mirror

108 An interesting group of small cast, copper or bronze, cups with long handles, was found in the south part of the south town (pl LXXIX), each of them double the capacity of the next smaller cup Whether they belong to the New Race, or to the XVIIIth dynasty, is therefore uncertain from the locality, as objects of both those ages were mingled together there The use of such cups cannot have been for anything but measuring very precious or very poisonous material, it cannot have been for liquids as the two smaller sizes hold only about a drop, and half a drop, and cannot be emptied when wetted, and therefore they must have been intended to gauge a powder No such very poisonous material is known to have been used in Egyptian medicine, so as to require measuring to the nearest grain, and it seems therefore that gold dust would be the only material likely to be measured so minutely The long series of doubling ratios is also unlikely for any substance unless considerable quantities had to be exactly gauged I therefore applied to Messrs Johnson and Matthey, who very cordially undertook to guage the contents of the cups with actual gold-dust, both when struck and when piled, but without shaking down The following results were communicated to me by Mr George Matthey, F R S

Weight Struck	Weight Piled
Grammes	Grammes
572	681
1 366	1 753
2 535	2 943
4 893	5 783
10 235	13 307
20 103	23 081
41 008	48 113

Of these two series the struck amounts agree closer together than the piled, the average variation of the struck being 1 23% from a mean scale, and of the piled 3 15% So far the evidence would be in favour of their being used as struck measures, but on looking at the amounts the mean scale of the struck measure gives 40 674 grammes (=627 72 grains) for the largest, while that of the piled measure is 48 208 (=743 97 grains) The first is not in accord with any regular unit, but the second is just the half uten or *deben* If then we accept this latter connection, we may say that these are *a set of measures containing binary divisions of the uten of gold-dust from* $\frac{1}{2}$ *to* $\frac{1}{128}$ *when piled.* And this result gives us exactly the Ethiopian unit of gold measure the *pek*, or division of the uten into 128 parts (Stele of Horsiatef, front, L, 26) These were therefore measures on the Nubian system of dividing the uten for the gold trade

Probably of the XVIIIth dynasty are two weights found in the temple One a hippopotamus head marked at the mouth with "10" and 5 lines on either side, counting 10 This is to express apparently the 10 kats separate, and the 10 united in the *deben*, as the weight is 1397 grains As this weight is finely wrought, and the animal was the emblem of the divinity—Set—in whose temple this was found, this is probably a standard *deben* weight of the temple It agrees with the lighter standard of the *deben* known as belonging to Heliopolis Another *deben* weight is a thin square slab of hard alabaster weighing 1427 grains

109 The temple had been built as early as Tahutmes I, as is shewn by a magnificent lintel in white limestone (LXXVII) on which Set is represented giving life to the hawk, which is perched on the *ka* name of the king This is a good evidence of the nature of that hawk, it is not the god Horus, nor Ra, nor the deified king, because in such cases it would not need to receive life from Set It rather seems that it is the *ba* bird of the king, which was said to fly up as a hawk to the sky when the king died (see Sanehat and Anpu and Bata) This lintel

K* 2

was left buried at Nubt for the Ghizeh museum, as its transport was beyond my means, but it has not yet been removed I fear that it is now destroyed With it were fragments of jambs of the same doorway And near it was a sandstone jamb of a doorway of Tahutmes III, on which he is called "the beloved of Set, the bull in Nubt, lord of the south" All of these sculptures were found face down built into the bottom of a wall along the south side of the temple Who thus re-used them we can gather from a cornice with the cartouches of Ramessu II

The foundation deposits of Tahutmes III were found in the middle of the temple area in three pits (LXXIX) They were in no regular order, but strewing loose in the dust The alabaster vase and model shell, the alabaster cup, and the pair of corn-grinders, are all inscribed with ink, the model axe of thin copper is punched with the same inscription, "The good god Men-kheper-ra, beloved of Set of Nubt" A little girdle tie carved in ebony is the only unusual object in these deposits

Amenhotep II seems to have worked much here, the bricks of the great temenos wall are stamped by his father Tahutmes III and by himself The enclosure (LXXXV) has a pylon front to it, and places for masts before it On the north half this has been covered by building another wall against it In the temple itself but little remains to shew its arrangement A doorway of Ramessu II, with a line of added inscription of Merenptah, is not in the middle of the face Within are some brick foundations outlined, then a stone foundation along the east and south, and some of the general foundation sheet of rough stone left toward the W A long row of granaries stood at the S. and S W of the temple Within the temple, in the most N W chamber, were a large quantity of fragments of blue glaze After getting these to England, we at last found them to be parts of a gigantic uas sceptre, about 7 feet high (LXXVIII) This could be mainly restored, and has been erected at South Kensington Museum It gives a fresh ka name, vulture and uræus name, and golden hawk name, though too much broken to be all restored with certainty It was made by baking the sandy core in 8 or 10 separate pieces, each made on a centering of straw twist These were engraved with all the devices, placed in one column, with the head-piece separate, covered with glaze and fired in a kiln, which was capable of baking a length of five feet upright,

without letting the glaze become burnt or unequally heated It is the greatest triumph of glazing known in ancient work

110 Of the same age is a cuboid seated figure of Sen-nefer carved in black granite, headless, inscribed with the cartouche of the king on the arm, and a dedication on the front (LXXVIII) The top line of the inscription has been much erased, owing to being on the edge of the cuboid from knee to knee, and it is cut slighter than the rest, as is also the cartouche on the arm. It appears as if after the figure was cut the king had presented it to Sen-nefer as a royal gift, and added the line of presentation and the cartouche The inscription reads "Given as a reward from the king in the temple of Nubti to the prince of the southern city Sen-nefer," and below, "May the king give an offering and Set of Nubit, son of Nut, very valorous, at the front of the sacred bark, and all the gods who are in Nubt, may they grant the receiving of food that appears upon the altar, of every good and pure thing, the offering of frankincense on the censer daily, to the ka of the hereditary prince, the watchful overseer, who loves his lord, the steward of prince of the southern city Sen-nefer, devoted to his lord, makheru" This is the same Sen-nefer of whom there is a fine tomb at Thebes, mentioned by Baedecker, and photographed by Beato and the Rev C H Sutton, whose plates are published in the *Building News*, 7 March, 1890

The presentation of a memorial by the king was not unusual in the XVIIIth dynasty, the formula occurs on the gold bowl of Tahuti in the Louvre, and on a large wooden ushabti of the chief of the archers of Zaru, the keeper of the mares, Aanuna (F P Coll) The phrase of Set being in the front of the bark, refers to Set in the bark of Ra, see Pleyte, "*Set dans la barque du soleil*" A fine tablet of Set was also found (LXXVIII), dedicated by an official Anhotep, and with the engraver's name added below, "made by the priest of Amen, chief of the engravers Nezem" A piece of another tablet, also signed by an artist, was found at Nubt

111 Beside these remains in the temple, much pottery of the XVIIIth dynasty was also found in the town, of the various kinds already known The pottery of the foundation deposits (LXXIX) is just like that of the deposits of the same king at Koptos, but smaller Few scarabs of the XVIIIth dynasty were found, compared with the number of the XIIth dynasty It is a curious reversal, that there is no trace of sculptures and little of buildings here of the

Old or Middle Kingdom, but a large amount of the Empire, while there are more scarabs, and far more sealings, of the earlier than of the later period

Although the older cemeteries are all near the edge of the desert, yet in the early XVIIIth dynasty tombs of great people, were set back some distance in the desert About half a mile behind Nubt is a small rise of a stratum of hardened marl, and in this a façade was cut which was common to half a dozen tombs, all facing E These tombs appear to be all of one period, though we can only glean details of the southernmost They had all been plundered in early times, and were later the resort of Koptic hermits These brutal fanatics had destroyed the splendid work of their ancestors, hacking out the brilliant scenes of domestic life with which the tombs were covered, and finally plastering the walls over with an obscene coat of filth I looked at the tombs more than once without suspecting that anything could be recovered of their subjects, but in some parts I found that coloured stucco still survived under the mud, and that it was so hard that it might be cleaned I wished, however, to avoid calling the attention of the Arabs around to what colour remained, so I went up after dark (my last night at Nubt) with two of my best lads from the Fayum, carrying a bucket of water After gentle experiments, I found that the stucco was so strong, and the colours so firm, that wetting did them no harm, and I was able to slush the walls over, and scrape them with a steel straight-edge, without the least injury to the waterproof stucco below

The plan of this tomb which I cleaned is given in No 1 of Rock Tombs, PL LXXIX The piece of inscription given in that plate is in the outer chamber, on the south of the entrance door, it shews that the tomb belonged to the prince, chief prophet of Set (?) Nubti, Bak, or, as the name is probably shewn by traces on the W wall, Baky The scenes are, W wall S half, chariot, servants with offerings in 4 registers going N toward figure of Bak adjoining the doorway, now lost

S wall 3 or 4 registers of servants with animals, etc, going to W In base line a chariot, with chequerwork bow-case; at W part a great table of offerings piled up

E wall, S half Inscription copied on PL LXXIX Figure of Bak toward N lost The funeral feast, 4 women seated, servant waiting, below that, 5 or 6 men seated, and servants, below, the same, one man drinking from a jar Toward S, the piled up table of offerings, a fine goose painted

E wall, N half Reapers cutting corn with sickle, men winnowing with pairs of boards, ears of corn carried in a net The other walls are hopelessly defaced

The style of the work is perhaps the finest that is known for delicacy of outline and fine handling, and it belongs evidently to the brilliant age of the early XVIIIth dynasty The subjects also are exactly those belonging to this age at El Kab and at Thebes These tombs are therefore distinguished as the "Thothmes tombs"

The inner arrangements are—an inner chamber beyond the outer painted one, this inner part has also traces of coloured work Across the inner chamber a step up in the rock, and in the raised part a well large enough to let down a coffin horizontally This well is only about 10 feet deep, and opens into a sepulchral chamber towards the west. Two of these sepulchres I had cleared out by trusty lads, but nothing was found in them, excepting a globular false-necked vase of Aegean pottery, which by its early type might well have belonged to a burial of the Thothmes period.

112 Coming to the XIXth dynasty we found when digging in the mounds of the South Town a burial of the early part of the reign of Ramessu II A slight brick grave about 3 feet deep had been dug into the mounds of New Race dwellings, probably it was deeper originally, before denudation had reduced the mounds Over the coffin lay a quantity of thorn bushes, a familiar device now to hinder men or animals from easily digging into earth, and one which was effective still against my own fingers The coffin had been of wood 1½ inch thick, now all decayed and eaten by white ants The body lay with head west, half turned over in the coffin At the feet outside the coffin stood a jar, with a small hemispherical cup of alabaster in it, two lesser jars and a dish stood at the head The forms are those given in Kahun XXI, 60, 64, and a finer example of the type Illahun XIX, 2 The body was mummified, and has been brought to England In front of the collar-bone lay a mass of carnelian and blue glass beads, and two ivory strips pierced with holes, which had held the threads of the collar apart Some carnelian lotus pendants were with these Behind the waist lay a mass of carnelian beads and pendants enough for a bead girdle On the wrists were some beads and scarabs, including one of Ramessu II

Two hollow gold earrings were on the head   This is an unusually complete outfit of beads (all now at Univ Coll, London), and as the boy fetched me from a distance the moment he found beads to be on the body, I was able to settle the positions by examining them myself   It is curious to see the caution with which such discoveries are let out. A boy will come over to where I am at work and loiter until he catches my eye, when he beckons me aside, and then alone he shews a few beads that have been the first noticed in the dust, or whispers that there is something important, without letting any one else have any idea of it   One reason is, that for large finds I let the bakhshish remain a secret with the finder, so that his sheikh and neighbours at home may not know what he has earned, for fear of being bullied out of a part of the money

113 The temple was rebuilt, perhaps entirely, by Ramessu II   That it was refounded after Tahutmes III is certain, as a jamb with his name lay at the bottom of the foundation of the south wall   That it was not later than Ramessu II is certain, as his name was on a block of the cornice, and as an original inscription down the sides of the entrance is of him   So there is only a chance that Amenhotep III, as a great builder, might have rebuilt the temple, while Ramessu appropriated it   All over the site (see plan LXXXV) there are remains of early walls which do not seem to belong to any design like the later buildings   Probably of Ramesside date is a dark blue glazed lotus cup, which was found quite perfect, on the first stage of footing of the wall, 50 inches E 10 inches S of the S W corner (Univ Coll)

A line of inscription dated in the 5th year of Merenptah runs along the side of the stone gateway   The base of a column is 44 inches across, and 15 inches thick, and two pieces of sandstone columns are 24 5 and 25 9 in diameter

Under Ramessu III some reconstructions went on, and a priest Userhat made new lintels to doorways of the chambers in the N E corner of the temenos   One lintel of his (pl LXXIX) shews Set and Amen seated back to back over the intertwined Nile plants. On the left side Userhat is "Beloved of [Amen lord] of the thrones of the two lands who is in Karnak [Giving praise] to thy ka, Oh Lord of the gods, that he may grant long life and a good old age   in Karnak to the ka of the prophet of Set Userhat, makheru"   On the right side is, "Set Nubti lord of the South land, great god, lord of heaven, fair child of Ra   Giving praise to thy ka, Set, the very valorous, [that he may give]   in Thebes to the ka of the prophet of Set, Userhat"   And behind the figure is, "made by his son, who makes his name to live, for the ka of the prophet of Set, Userhat"   On another lintel are the cartouches of Ramessu III in the middle   On the left, "Beloved of Set Nubti, lord of the South land, great god   Adoration to thy ka oh Set   . ," and on the right, ' Beloved of Nut the Great who bare the gods   Adorations to thy ka, Oh Nut   "

After this there is no trace of construction in the temple, and only a fragment of a blue glazed vase of a Sheshenq serves to shew that it was not quite deserted till after the Bubastite age   Nothing of Greek or Roman period was found over the whole site, which seems to have stood quite untouched for over two thousand years

INDEX

L*

LONDON   PRINTED BY WILLIAM CLOWES AND SONS, LIMITED, STAMFORD STREET AND CHARING CROSS.

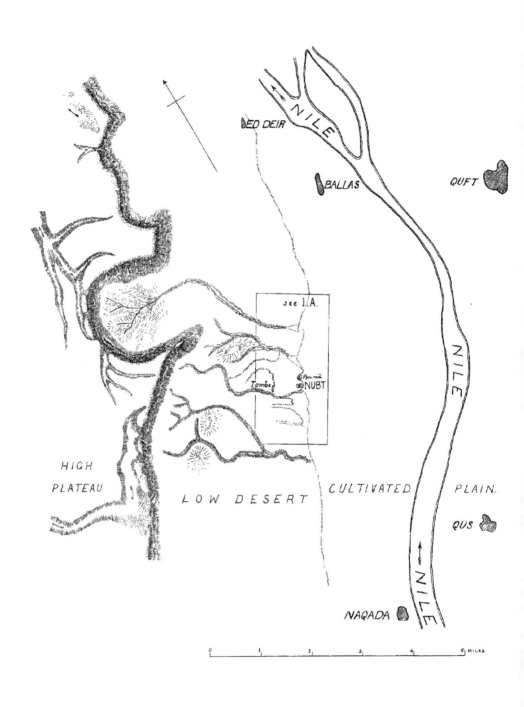

ED DEIR

NILE

BALLAS

QUFT

see 1 A.

Pyramid
NUBT

Tombs

HIGH
PLATEAU

LOW DESERT

CULTIVATED

PLAIN.

NILE

QUS

NILE

NAQADA

NILE

0   1   2   3   4   5 MILES

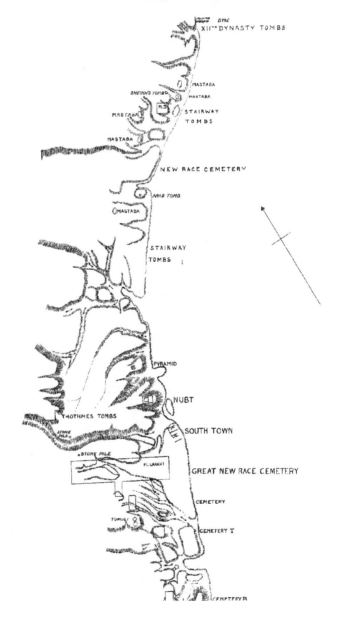

DYKE
XIITH DYNASTY TOMBS

MASTABA
MASTABA
SHEIKH'S TOMB
PL.35
MASTABA STAIRWAY
TOMBS
MASTABA

MASTABA

NEW RACE CEMETERY

ARAB TOMB

MASTABA

STAIRWAY
TOMBS

PYRAMID

NUBT

THOTHMES TOMBS

SOUTH TOWN

STONE PILE

STONE PILE

PL.LXXXVI GREAT NEW RACE CEMETERY

CEMETERY

TUMULI CEMETERY T

CEMETERY R

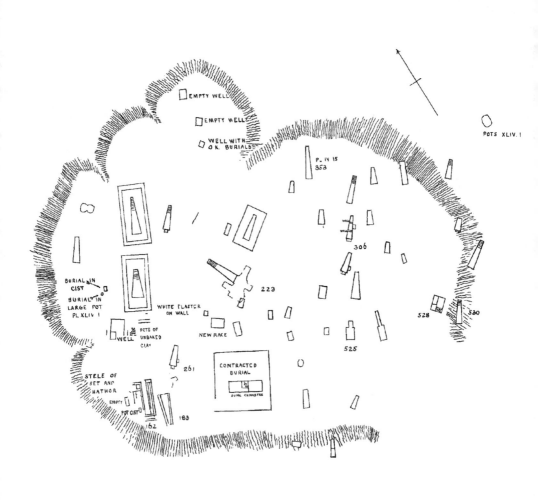

EMPTY WELL

EMPTY WELL

WELL WITH
O.K. BURIALS

POTS XLIV. I

P. IV 15
353

306

BURIAL IN
CIST

BURIAL IN
LARGE POT
PL XLIV I

WHITE PLASTER
ON WALL

POTS OF
UNBAKED
CLAY

WELL

NEW RACE

223

528

530

525

STELE OF
SET AND
HATHOR

261

EMPTY
POT CIST

162

183

CONTRACTED
BURIAL

BURIAL CHAMBERS

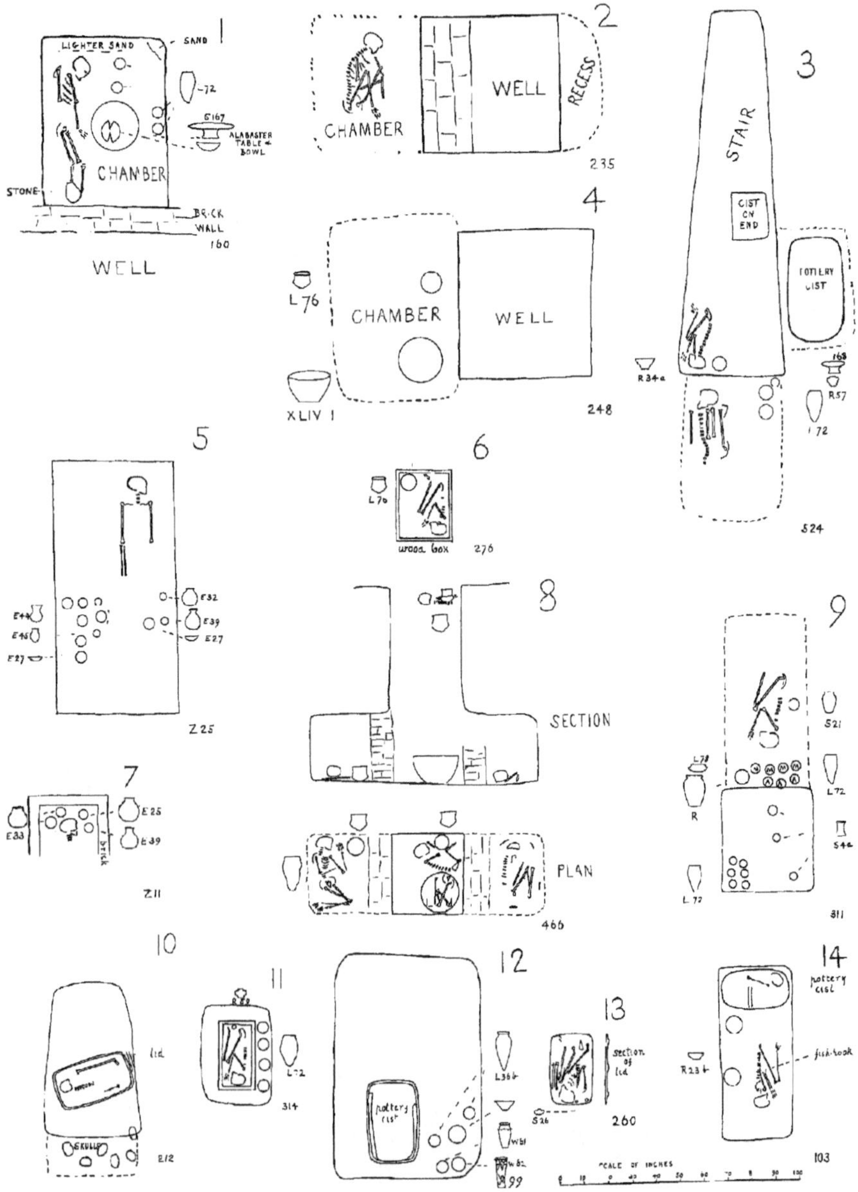
1
LIGHTER SAND
SAND
72
S167
ALABASTER TABLE & BOWL
CHAMBER
STONE
BRICK WALL
160
WELL
2
CHAMBER
WELL
RECESS
235
3
STAIR
CIST ON END
POTTERY CIST
R34a
168
R57
L72
524
4
L76
CHAMBER
WELL
XLIV 1
248
5
E44
E45
E27
E32
E39
E27
Z25
6
L70
wood box
276
7
E33
E25
E39
brick
Z11
8
SECTION
PLAN
466
9
S21
L78
R
L72
S4a
L72
311
10
lid
SKULL
E12
11
L72
314
12
pottery cist
L366
W61
W62
99
13
section of lid
S26
260
SCALE OF INCHES
14
pottery cist
R234
fish-hook
103

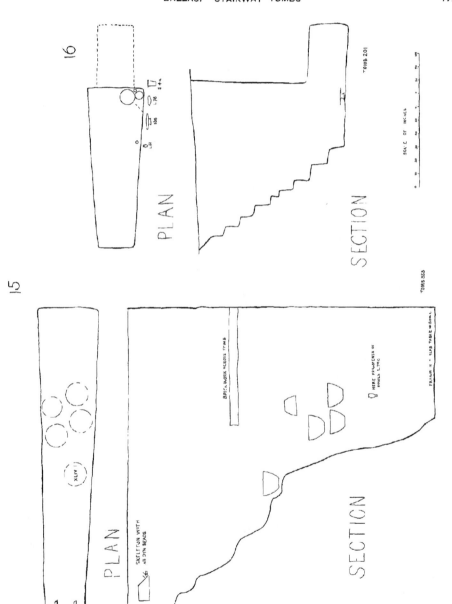

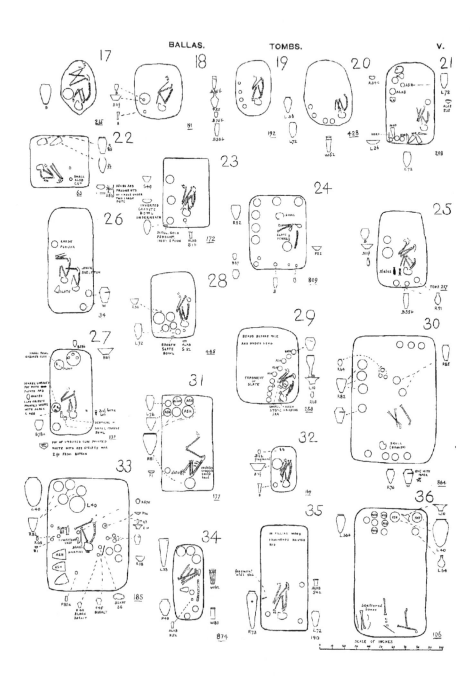

BALLAS.   TOMBS.   V.

1

2

3

VI

STEATOPYGOUS FIGURES.

4

5

LIBYAN CHIEF
MEDINET HABU.

6, 7
8, 9

10, 11
12, 13

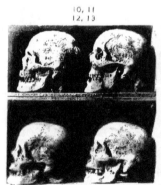

14, 15
16, 17

18, 19
20, 21

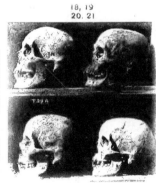

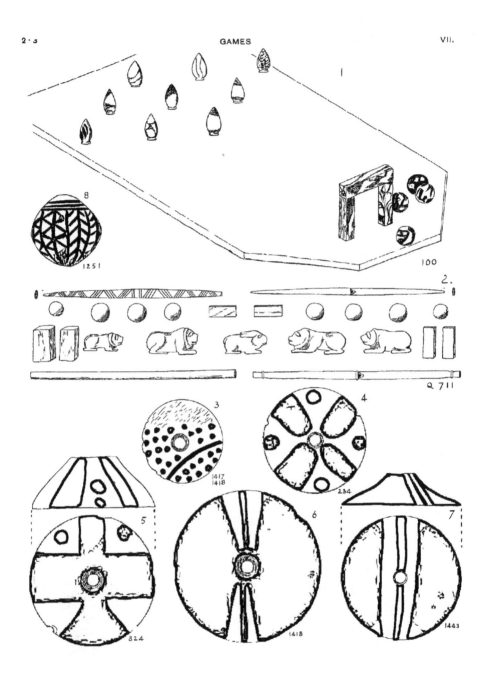

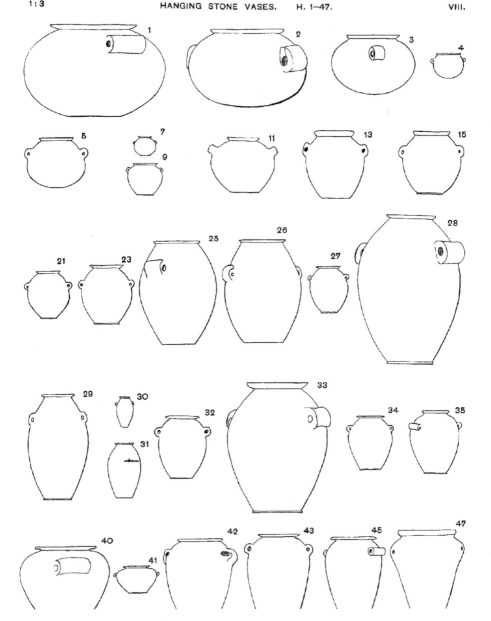

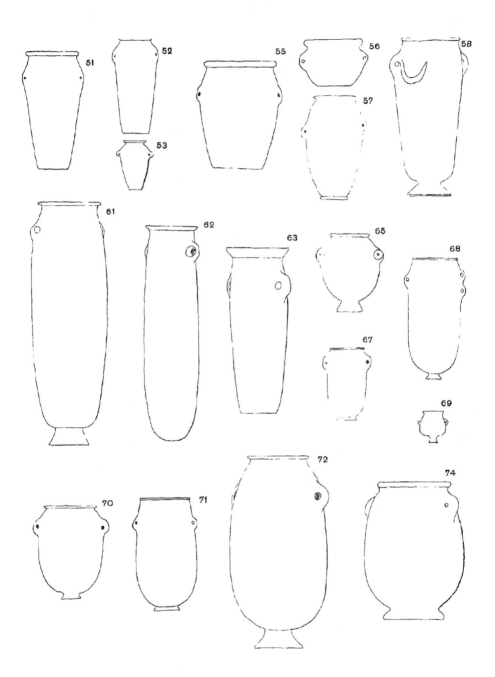

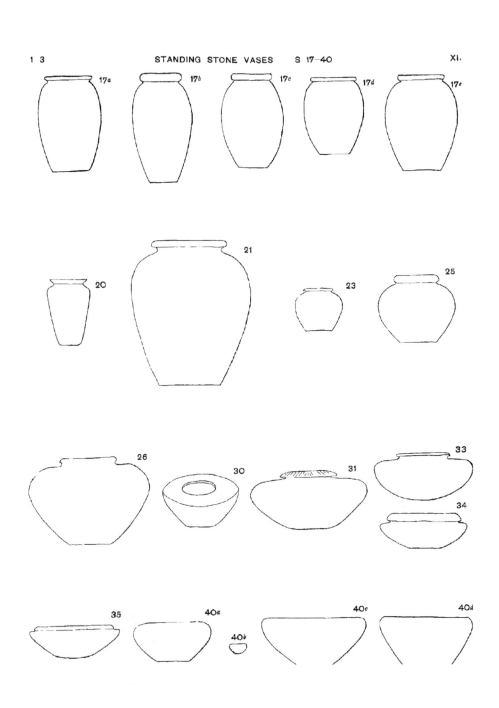

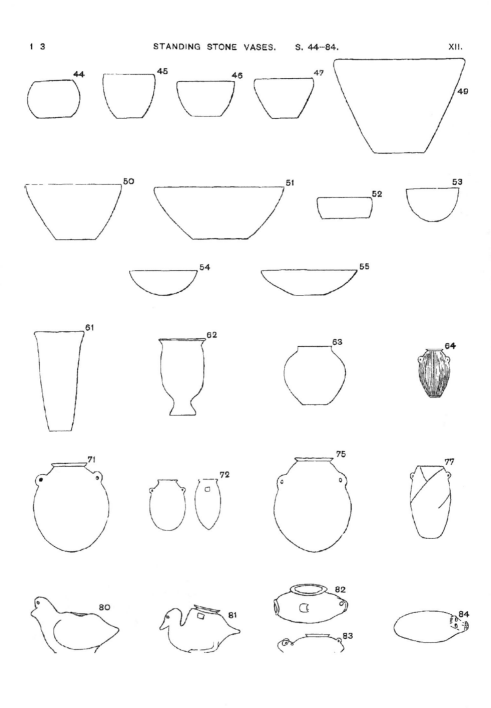

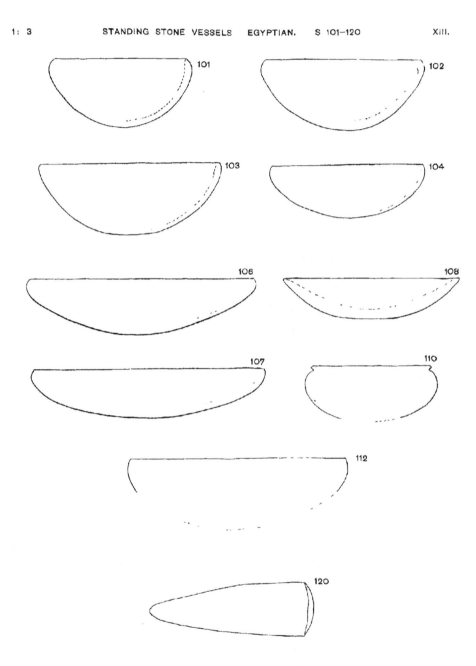

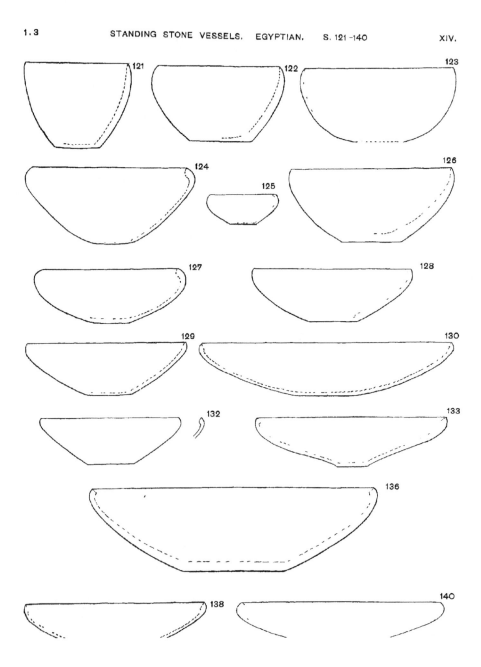

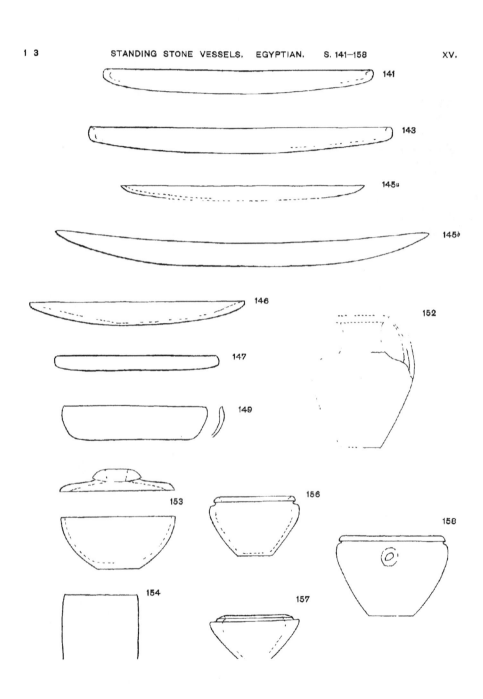

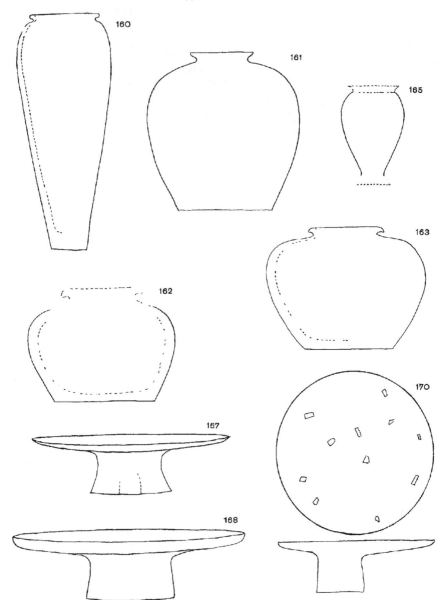

STONE VESSELS. VII–IX DYN.   S 185–188.

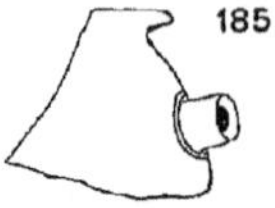

185

187

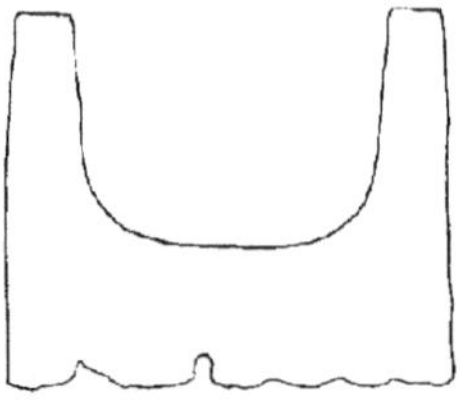

188

190   STONE VESSELS   EGYPTIAN. XII DYN   S. 190–195.

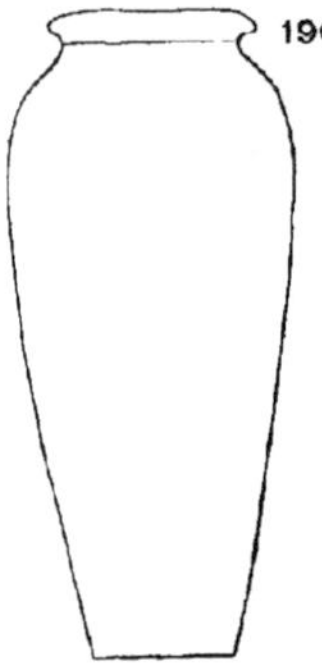

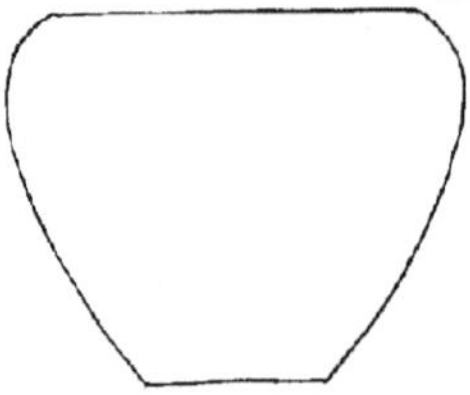

191

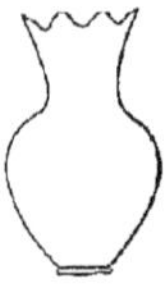

192

193

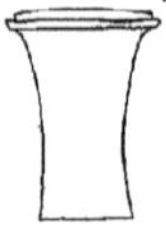

194

195

STONE MACES   VII–IX DYN   M 1–19.

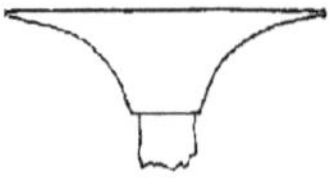

1

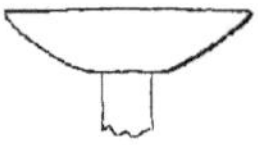

4

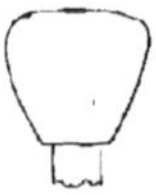

5

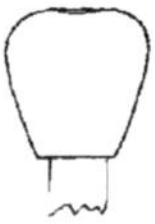

6

7

8

9

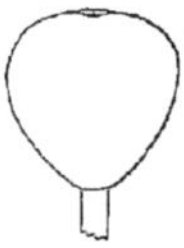

12

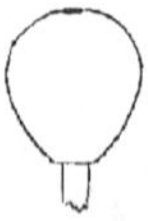

13

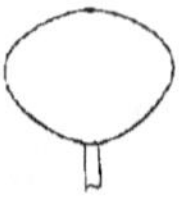

14

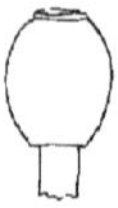

15

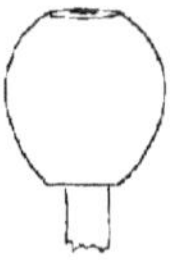

17

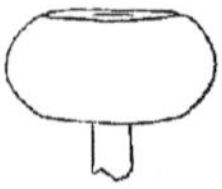

19

23

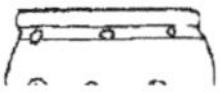

25

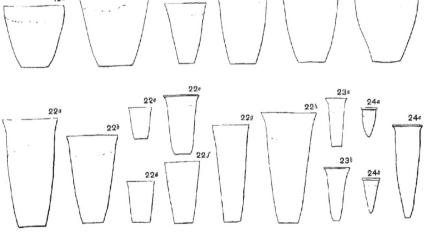

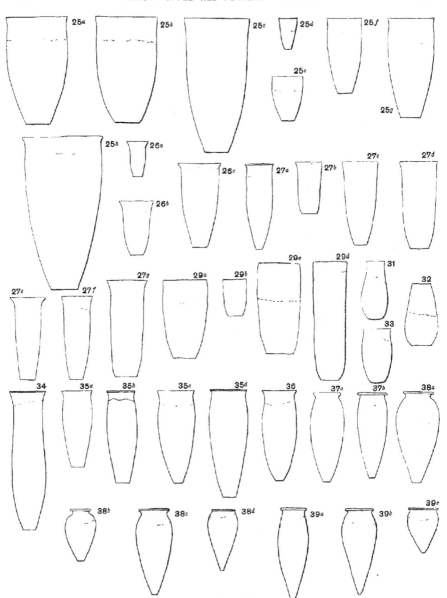

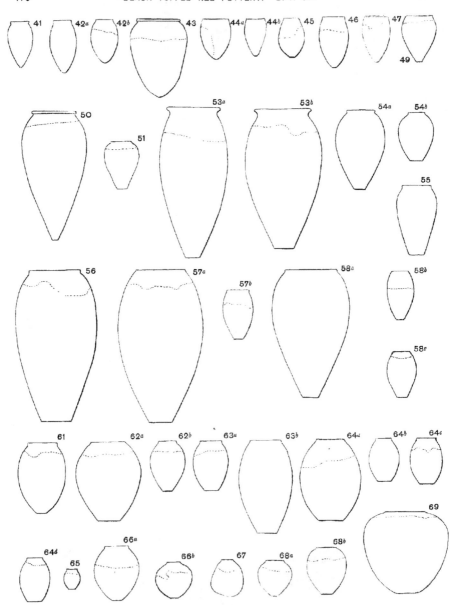

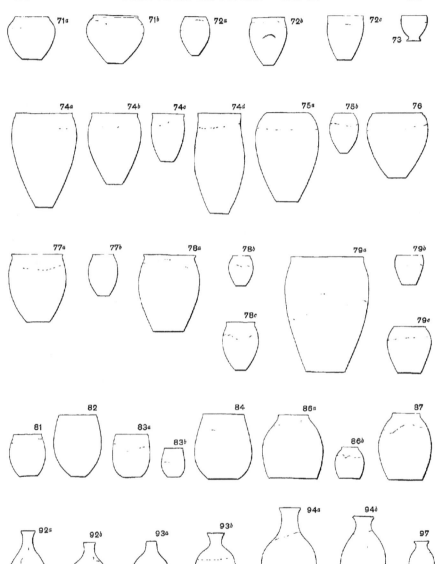

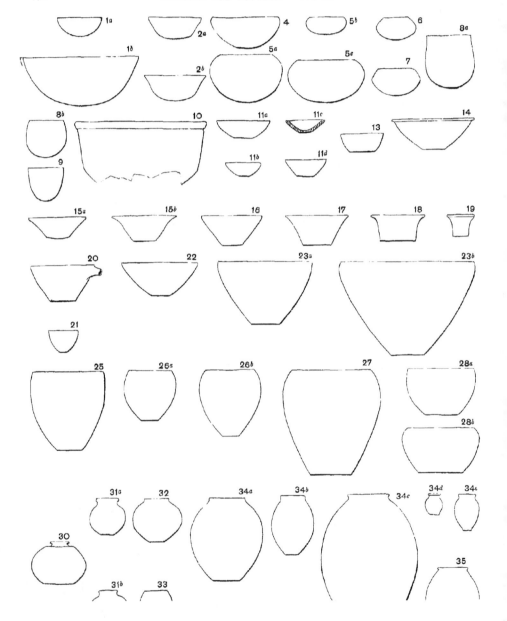

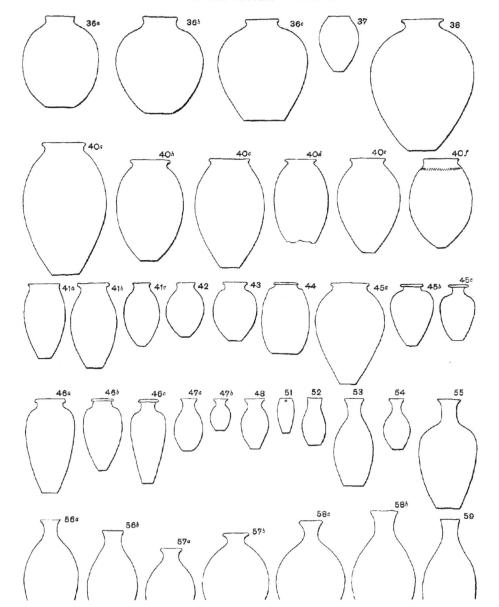

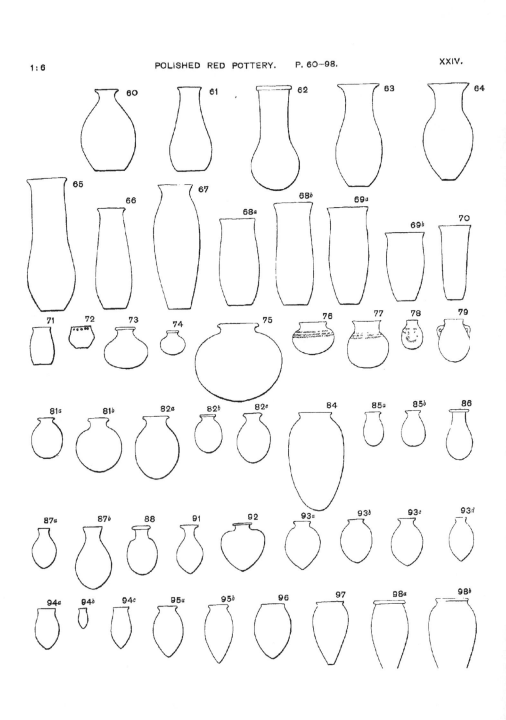

5a

5b

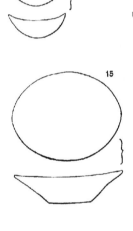
11a 11b 12 14

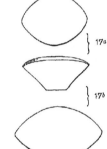
15 17a 17b

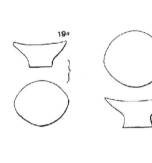
19a 19b

20

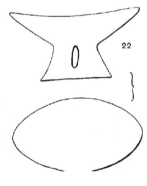
22

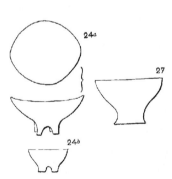
24a 24b 27

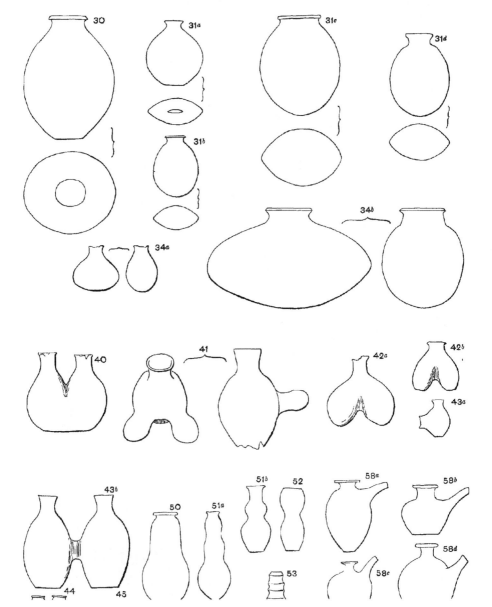

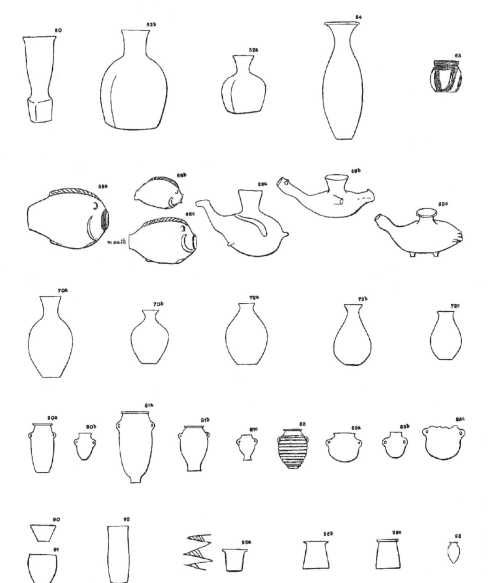

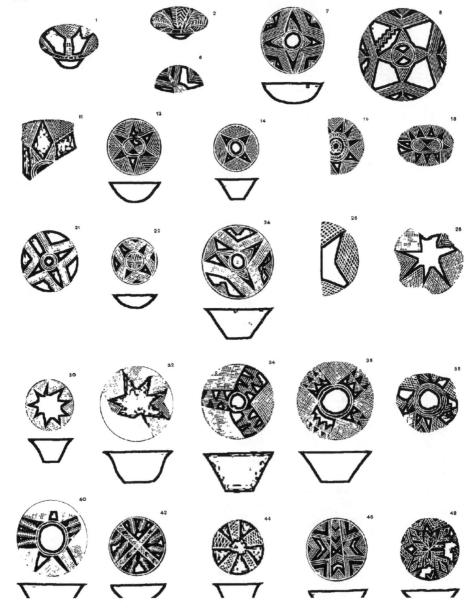

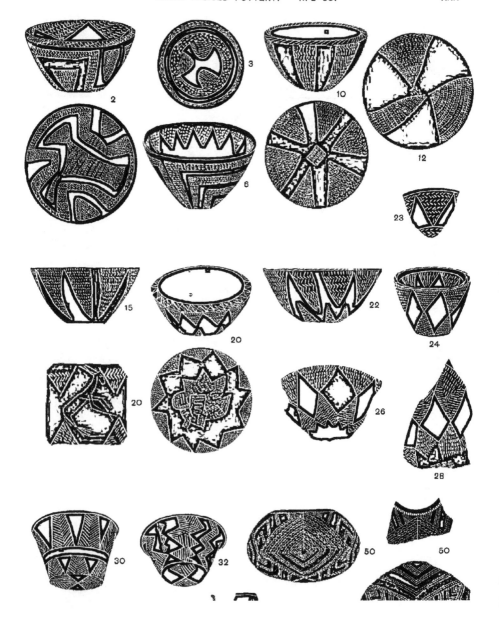

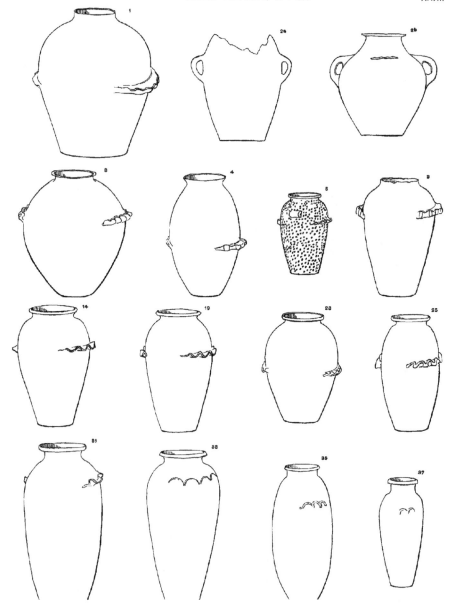

A B

C

D

E

F

G

H

J

K

N

O

P

Q

R

S   cordage painted
T

U

V

W

X   plain

2 3   Y   incised

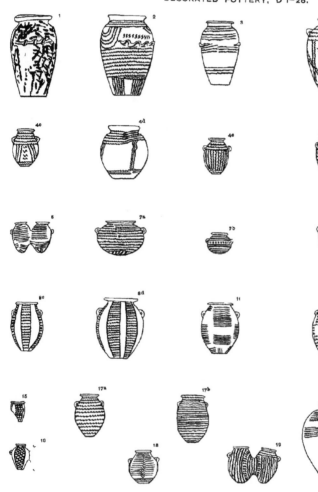

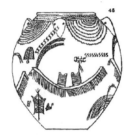
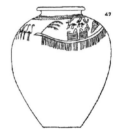

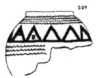

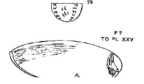

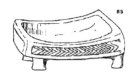

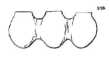

2 3   95   2 3   96

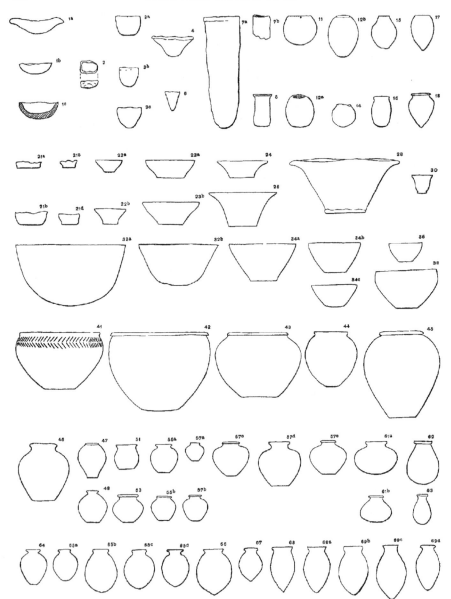

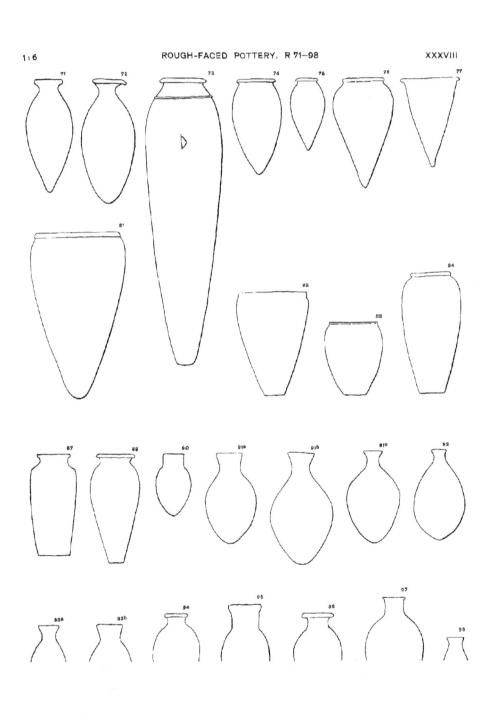

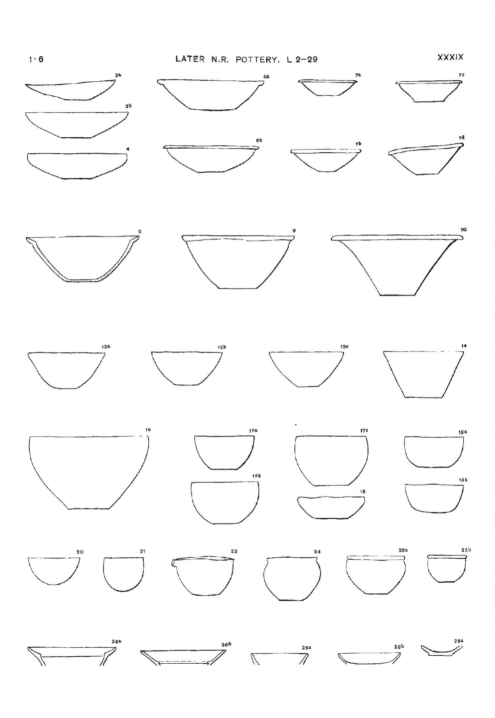

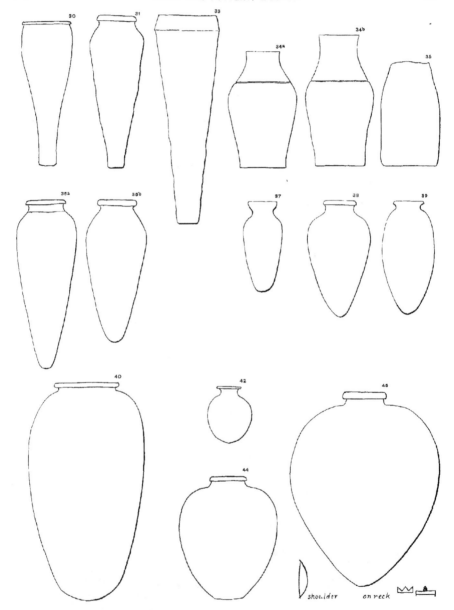

shoulder   on neck

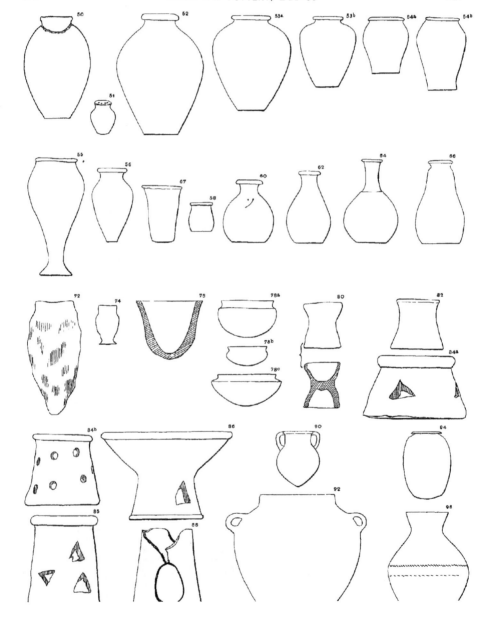

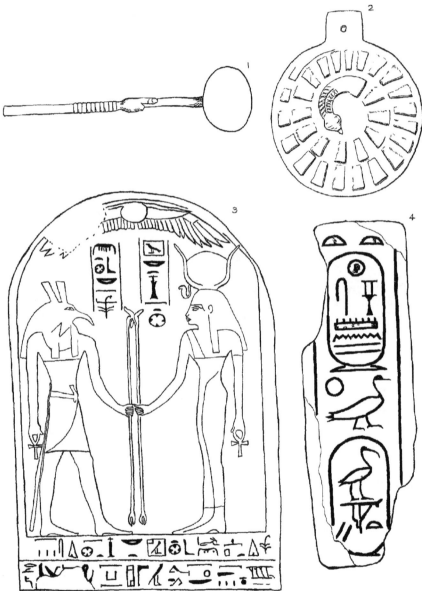

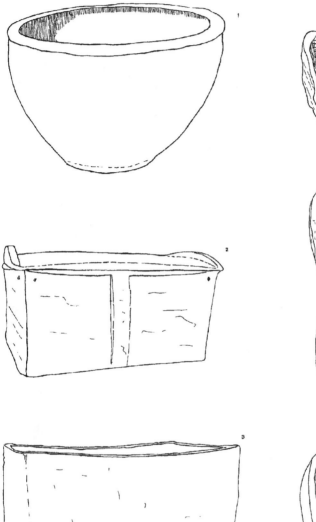

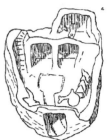

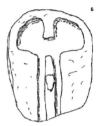

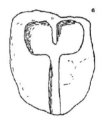

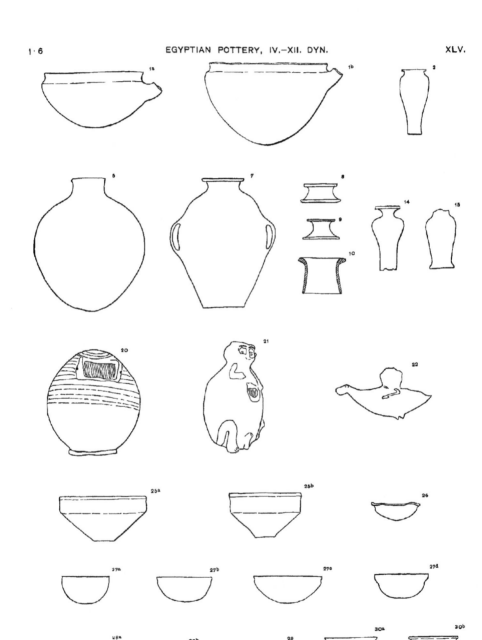

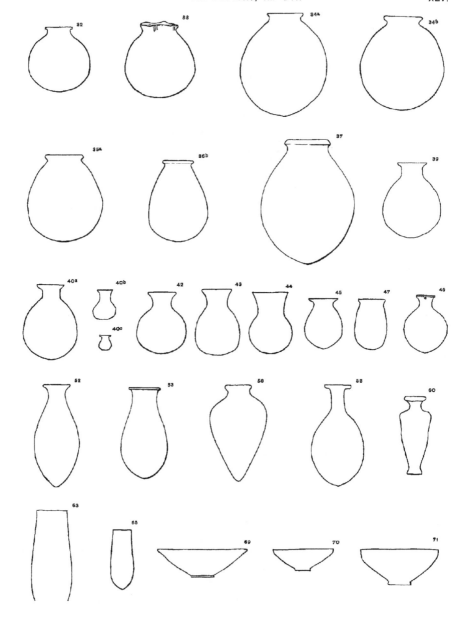

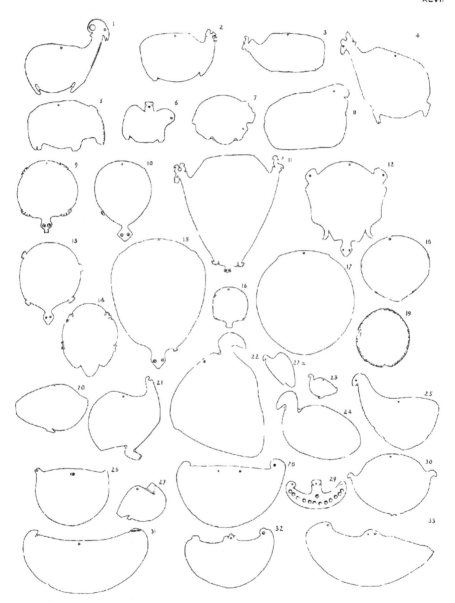

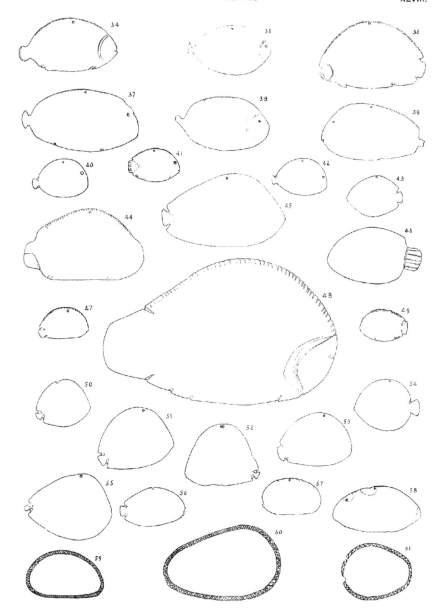

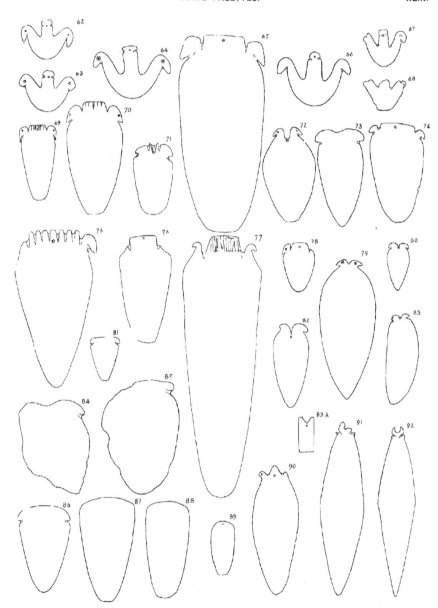

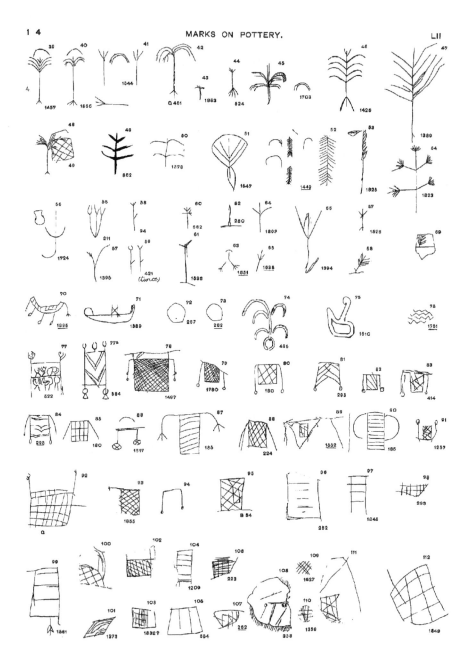

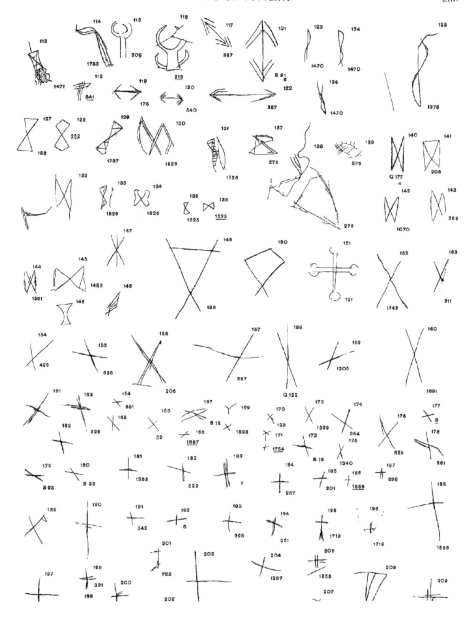

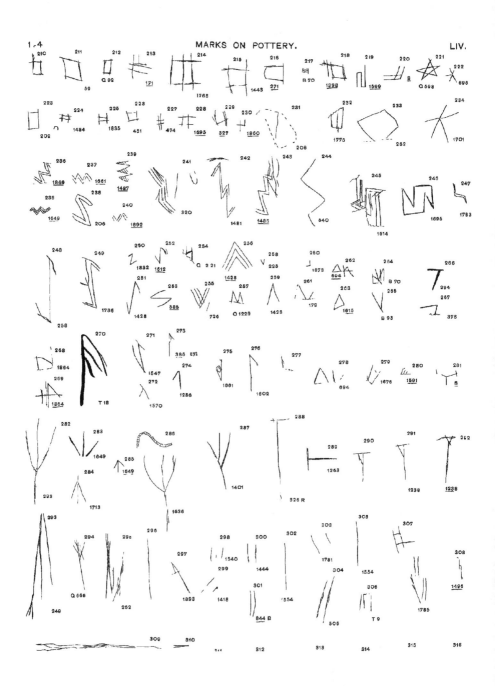

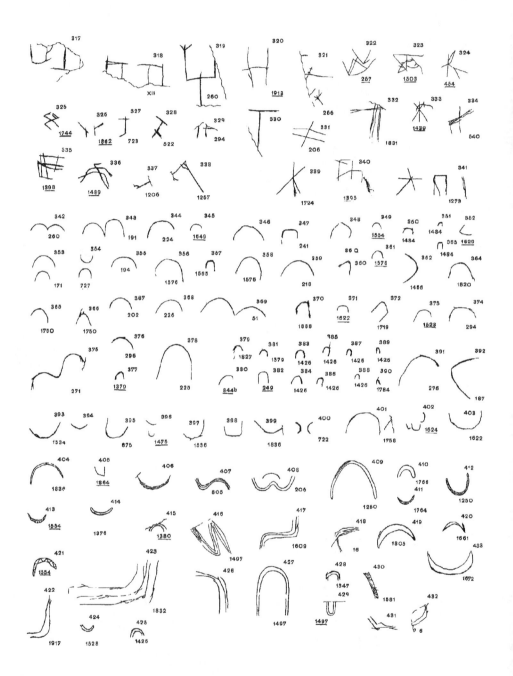

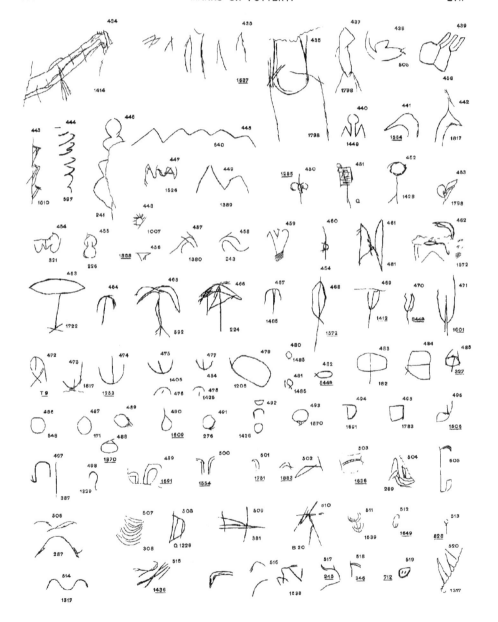

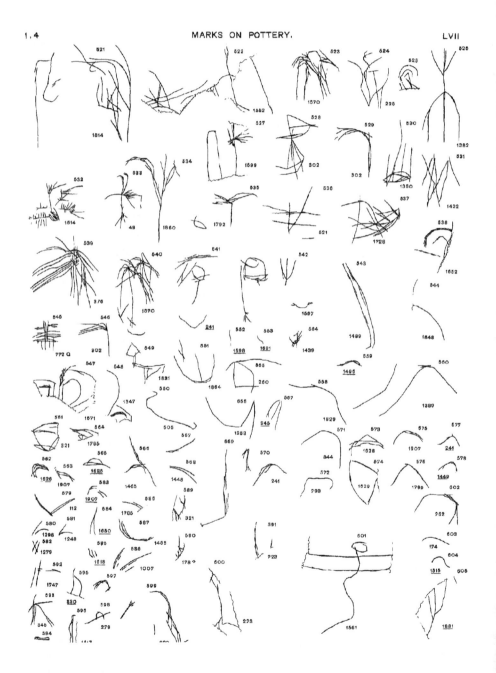

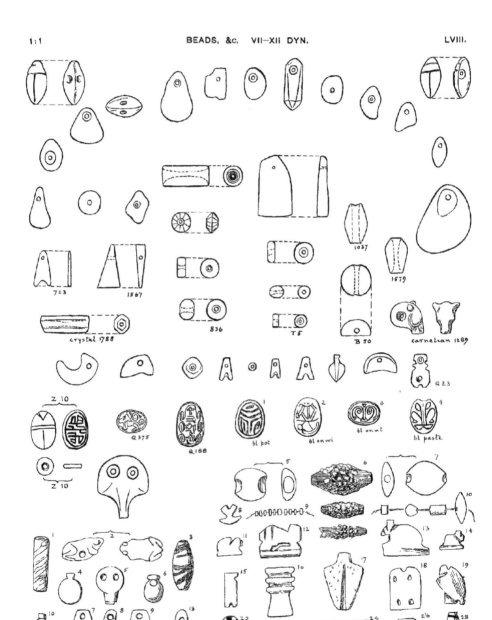

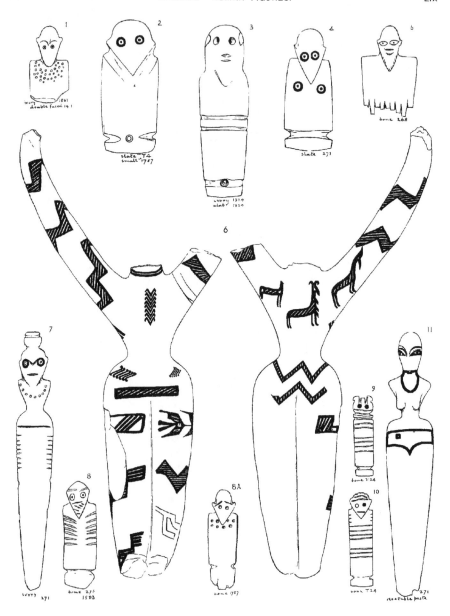

12
limestone 721

13
Limestone 721

16
Limestone & 71:

17
limestone Q 721

14
Lead 721

15
limestone 721

18
glazed quartz

19
1774
green glass
on sand

20
bone
5 town

22
Limestone
gebelen. bought

21
bone bought.

23
Limestone
bought

24
Limestone bought
Gebelen

25
Limestone bought
Gebelen

26
Limestone bought
Gebelen

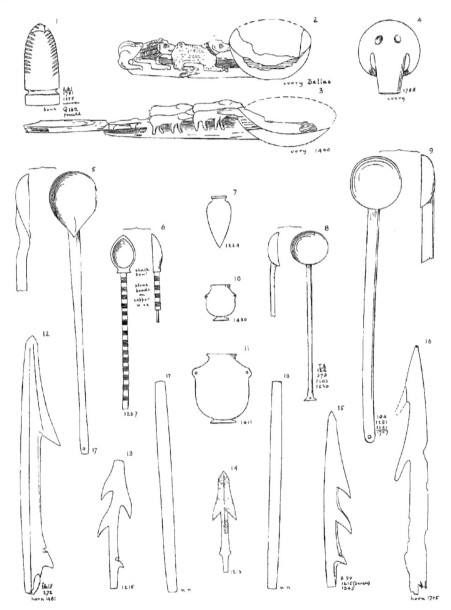

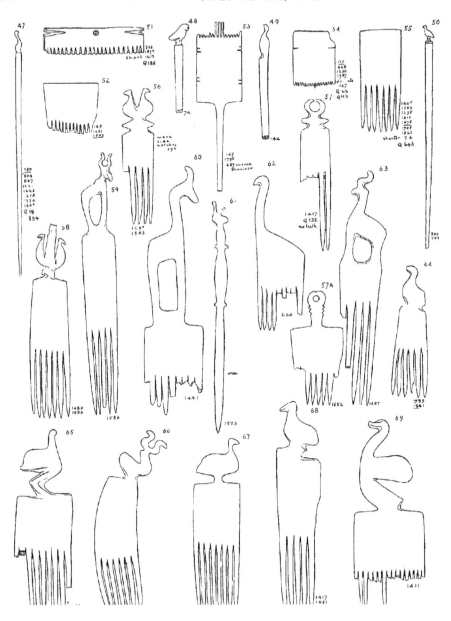

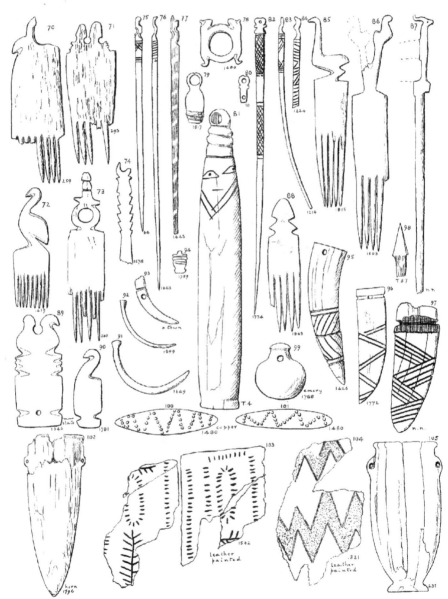

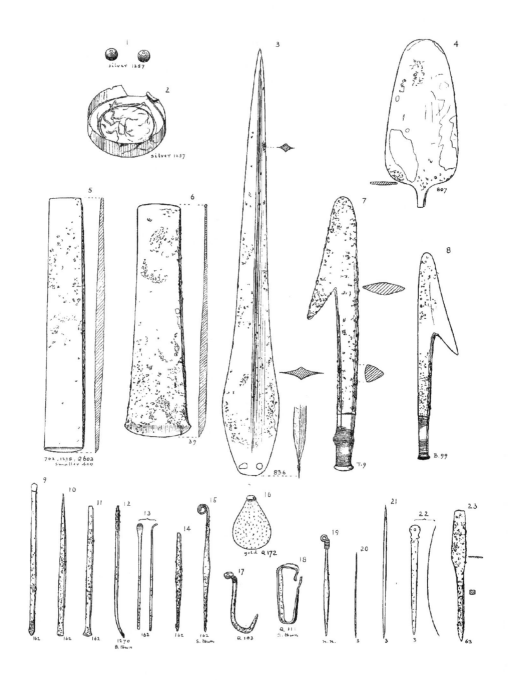

1
silver 1257

2
silver 1257

3

4
807

5

6
39

702.1208, 2608
smaller 400

836

7
T-9

8
B.99

9
162

10
162

11
162

12
1270
B.Town

13
162

14
162

15
162
S.Town

16
gold 2172

17
2103

18
2111
S.Town

19
n.n.

20
3

21
3

22
3

23
63

1

506

2

1220

3

1268

4

5

1048

6

Q414

7

Q576

8

Q100

9

ABYDOS

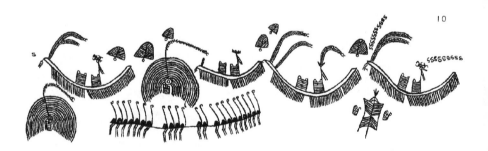

10

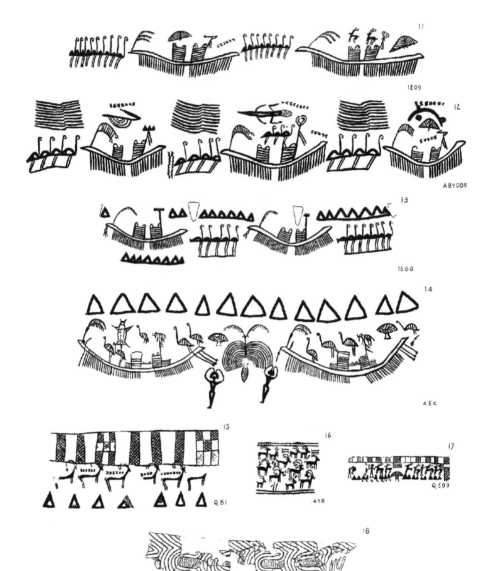

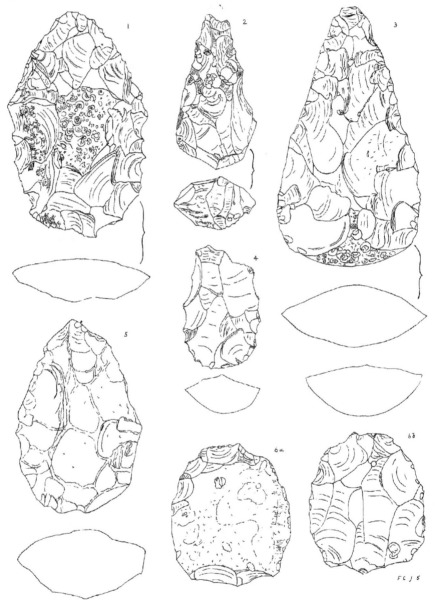

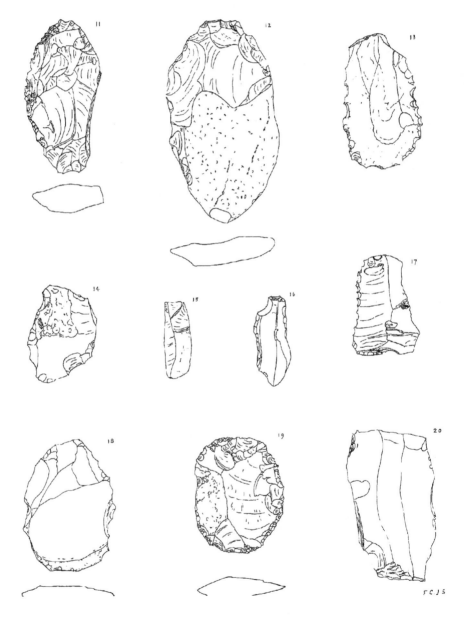

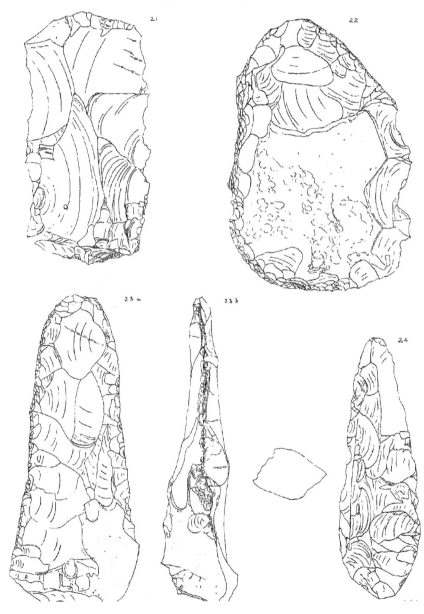

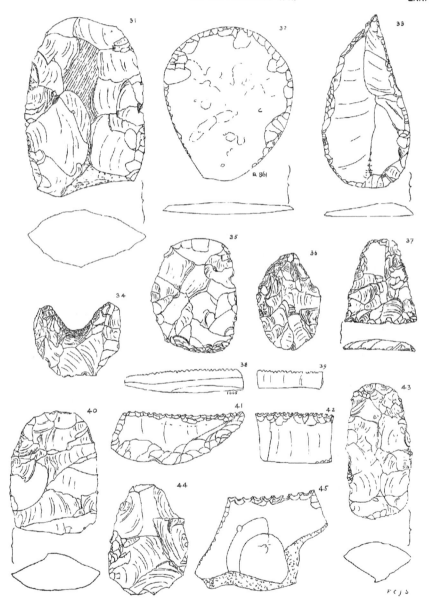

FLINTS FROM GRAVES N.R.

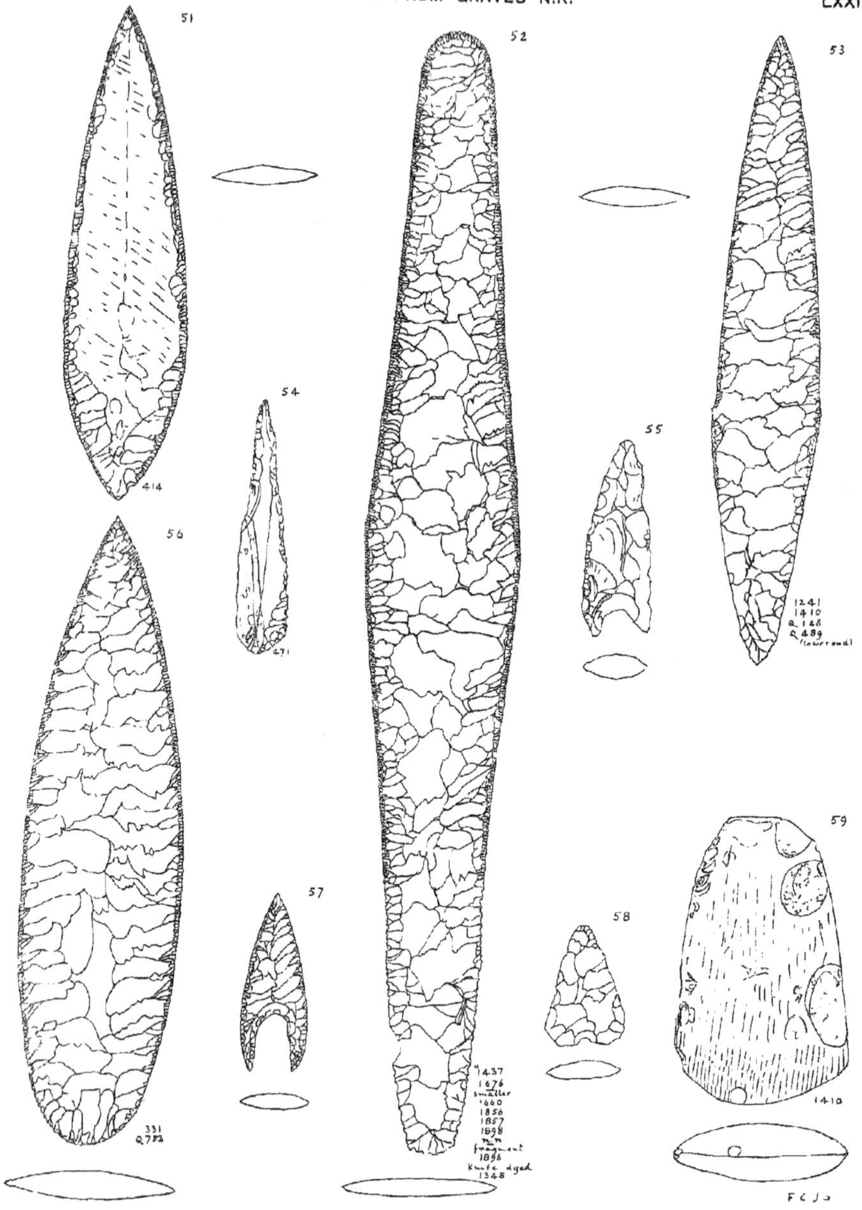
51
414
52
1437
1676
smaller
1660
1856
1857
1898
fragment
1896
Knife dyed
1348
53
1241
1410
Q 148
Q 489
(lower end)
54
471
55
56
331
Q 782
57
58
59
1410
F G J

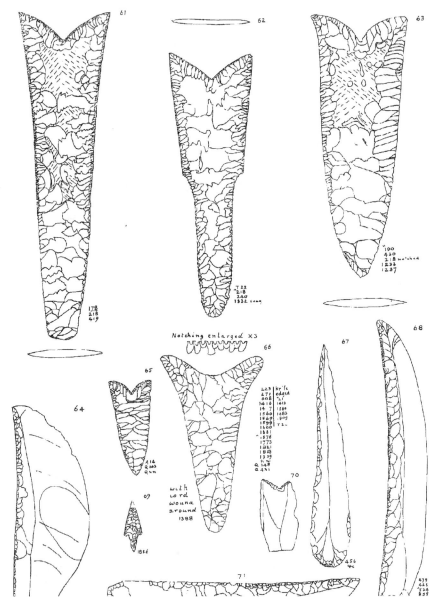

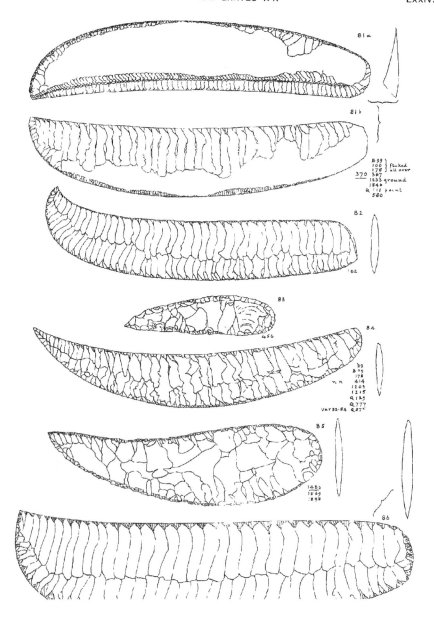

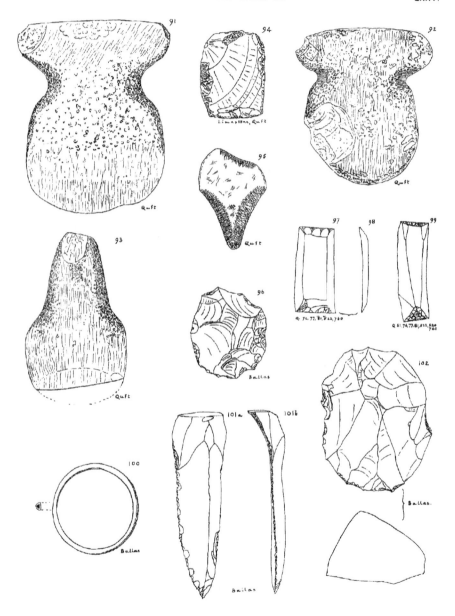

1:5   PALAEOLITHIC FLINTS PLATEAU   GRAVELS NAQADA.

1:2   FLINT KNIFE ABYDOS.

LXXVI

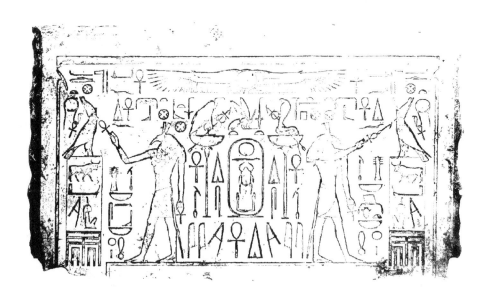

1:1   CARVED IVORY HANDLE OF FLINT KNIFE. SOHAG. PITT-RIVERS COLL.

1 2 STELE OF ANHOTEP, ENGRAVED BY NEZEM

ON R ARM

BLACK GRANITE STATUE OF SENNEFER.
1 2

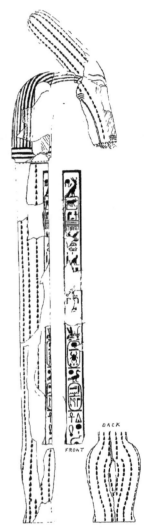

FRONT

BACK

1 10   BLUE GLAZED UAS
OF AMENHOTEP II

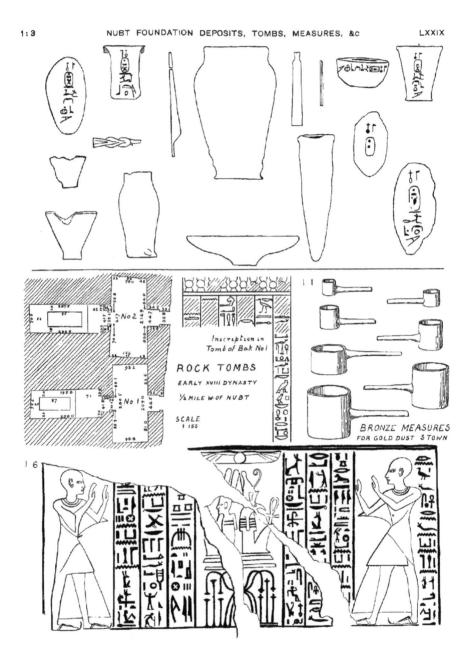

Inscription in
Tomb of Bak No 1

ROCK TOMBS

EARLY XVIII DYNASTY

½ MILE W. OF NUBT

SCALE
1 150

BRONZE MEASURES
FOR GOLD DUST STOWN

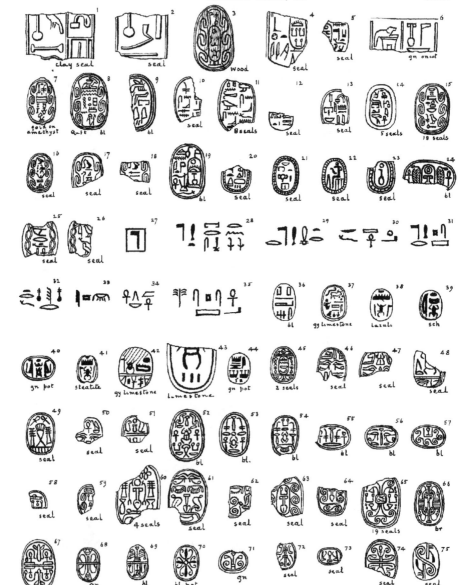

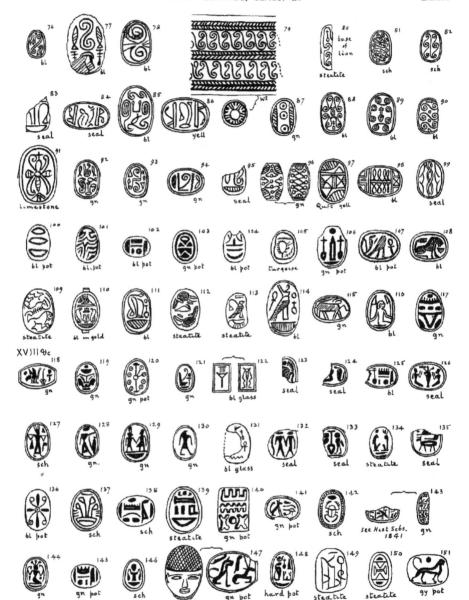

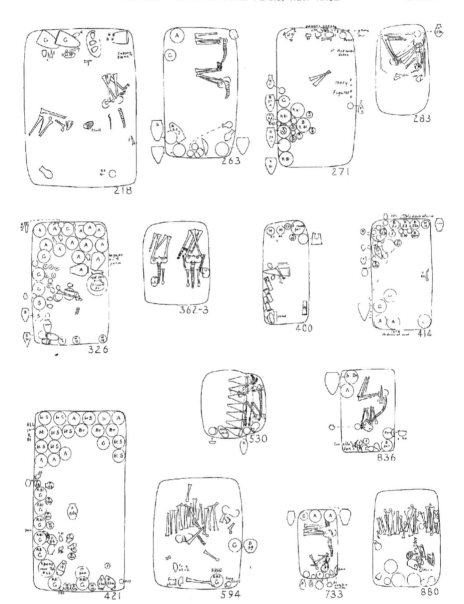

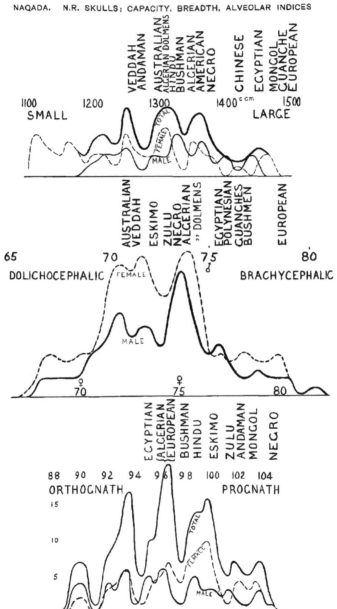

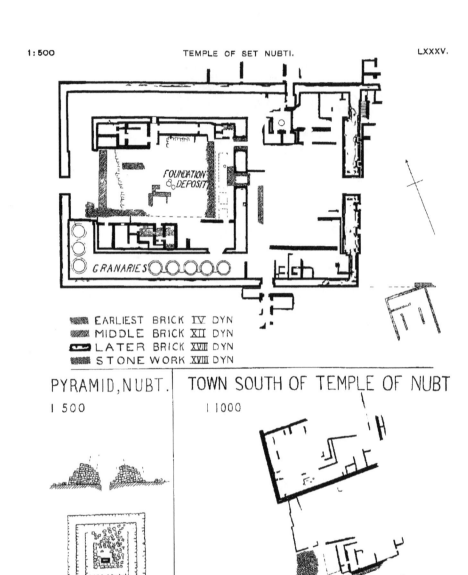

FOUNDATION DEPOSIT

GRANARIES

EARLIEST BRICK IV DYN
MIDDLE BRICK XII DYN
LATER BRICK XVIII DYN
STONE WORK XVIII DYN

PYRAMID, NUBT.
1 500

TOWN SOUTH OF TEMPLE OF NUBT
1 1000

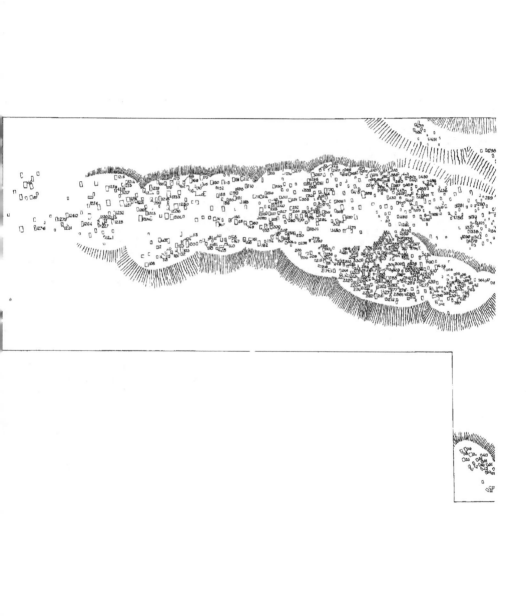

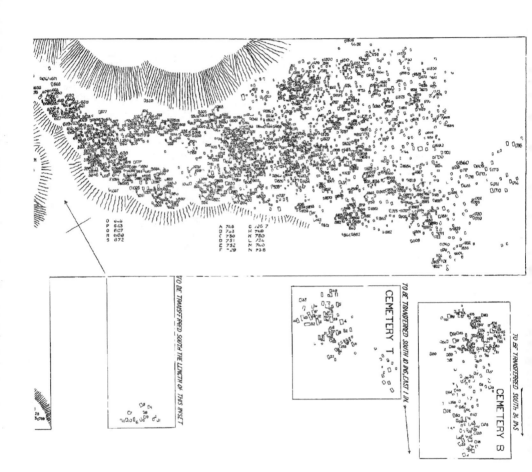

CPSIA information can be obtained
at www.ICGtesting.com
Printed in the USA
LVHW081722020223
738507LV00004B/123